ALSO BY WARREN ZANES

Dusty in Memphis (33⅓ series)

Revolutions in Sound: Warner Bros. Records—The First Fifty Years

Waiting for a Train: Jimmie Rodgers's America (coeditor)

Runnin' Down a Dream: Tom Petty and the Heartbreakers (editor)

PETTY

PETTY

THE BIOGRAPHY **WARREN ZANES**

HENRY HOLT AND COMPANY   NEW YORK

Henry Holt and Company, LLC
Publishers since 1866
175 Fifth Avenue
New York, New York 10010
www.henryholt.com

Henry Holt® and 🅷® are registered trademarks of Henry Holt and Company, LLC.

Library of Congress Cataloging-in-Publication Data

Zanes, Warren.
  Petty : the biography / Warren Zanes. — First edition.
    pages cm
  ISBN 978-0-8050-9968-3 (hardcover) — ISBN 978-0-8050-9969-0 (e-book)
1. Petty, Tom. 2. Rock musicians—United States—Biography. I. Title.
ML410.P3135Z36 2015
782.42166092—dc23
  [B]   2015019677

Henry Holt books are available for special promotions and premiums.
For details contact: Director, Special Markets.

First Edition 2015

Designed by Meryl Sussman Levavi

Printed in the United States of America

1 3 5 7 9 10 8 6 4 2

For Lucian and Piero, always

CONTENTS

PETTY

1976

I wasn't much more than a child, lost in the land of the lost. It was preadolescence. My brother, four years older, had twisted my mother's arm and had her growing pot by the garbage bag full. I thought it was a beanbag chair in his back bedroom, until I caught him smoking it. My sister, two years older, was wearing homemade dresses and collecting volumes of fairy tales from around the world. I would avoid her in the hallways at school. There was no father at home. That was when I heard Tom Petty's music for the first time, on WBCN in Boston. FM radio was in its AOR phase and seemed like it would be there forever. The song was "Breakdown."

The Heartbreakers stepped into a shifting landscape, a moment of category confusion. "New wave" hadn't emerged as the near catchall term that it would become. Singer-songwriters were generally regarded as musicians who played acoustic guitars, didn't dance or otherwise bring any trace of James Brown's influence into the room, and between songs talked lightly of politics to well-behaved audiences. On that first Heartbreakers album, Tom Petty wore a leather jacket—he wasn't going to be thrown in with James Taylor. And the songs were too short, too close to Chuck Berry to land the group in the rock territory where Led Zeppelin still held the cave. The Heartbreakers opened shows for KISS. And then for Al Kooper. They were booked as an opener for Rush, for the Runaways, once even for a Tom Scott and the L.A.

Express show, where an audience member called out, "What is this? The Monkees?" Not sure what else to do, critics regularly dropped Petty and his band into the "punk" category. Soon enough, new wave would give him another place to live. But even that didn't last: before long, people started calling them a "rock-and-roll band."

It was a good moment for music; even if denigrating it was the necessary pose, pissing on Foreigner and Styx as if they were an active threat. Punk, while not a thing of the mainstream, had a kind of cleansing effect that extended upward from below. A lot became possible. Talking Heads, Elvis Costello, Mink Deville, Rockpile, Tom Petty and the Heartbreakers, Television, Graham Parker—all seemed like they belonged to the same family, and punk was somehow their birth mother, though many of them were at work years before Malcolm McLaren started selling clothes on King's Road. For those who did have records out before punk became "official," punk gave them an extended, sometimes dysfunctional family.

In the home I grew up in, we alternated between listening to WROR, an "oldies" station—thanks to a hippie uncle raised in the fifties—and WBCN, which played most of the acts named above. Something in the new music reminded us of what we liked in the old stuff. But Petty seemed to connect those two worlds better than anyone. Not the intellectual gymnast that Elvis Costello was, never as grandly romantic as Springsteen or as simultaneously strange and canny as Talking Heads, Petty nonetheless got in there a little deeper than the others.

"Breakdown" had as much space as "Green Onions." The Heartbreakers often revealed who they were in what they didn't play. It set them apart. If they were born under the sign of the Beatles and the Stones, the band was also a distinctly southern act—though not in the cartoon sense of, say, the Charlie Daniels Band, with the rehashed southern imagery that, for whatever reason, played well in middle America. The Heartbreakers had a different southernness, in some ways more like the Dan Penns and Eddie Hintons, musicians and writers who had been raised on the black sounds around them, players who held back when there was a song in the room, because there was a song in the room.

But there was something more going on, something beyond the groove, the taste, the lean but tough musicality. Petty's voice. He wasn't obvious as a lead singer. But there was a character in there. What would one day be celebrated as his defiance was present from the beginning. But it would have been nothing, would have meant nothing, without his romanticism. The defiance would have been empty. Petty's romanticism wasn't along the lines of Bruce Springsteen's or Tom Waits's, two songwriters who worked with elaborate panoramas of image, character, and place. His narratives were always more skeletal, perhaps less self-conscious. All three writers created songs that could be seen. They were children of the movies, bringing to their songwriting what they learned in darkened theaters. But Petty's scenes were fewer, as though half the storyboards had been thrown in the dumpster out back. Perhaps because of that, Petty made a little more room for the listener. His weren't the meticulously painted landscapes of "Jungleland" or even "Jersey Girl," songs in which people spoke of carrying guns across the river and ran into "corner boys." Not that Petty didn't have the detail—but it was the spare way in which he used it. He wasn't out to do for Florida what the others did for New Jersey and Los Angeles. Maybe because of that, you didn't get tangled up in information that ultimately took you too far from where you lived. "American Girl" seemed to be wide open for listeners to see themselves in the picture. I certainly saw myself. Something happened when that voice delivered those words in that way.

I didn't think it through in this way then, of course, not when I first found Tom Petty and the Heartbreakers. I just knew in the drag of those years he was a good person to have around. It's the time when music means more than it ever will again. But it wasn't just me, and it wasn't just about being young; it seemed like everyone in my house was hanging on one Petty song or another. He grasped our circumstances. My mother eventually stopped growing pot for her kids. But she still listens to *Damn the Torpedoes*.

■

Ten years after hearing my first Heartbreakers records, just out of my teens but by that time in a rock-and-roll band and on the road, I was in my hotel room at the Hyatt on Sunset, the less than spectacular but somehow historically significant hotel Led Zeppelin had christened "the Riot House." We were only there because at some point we had been told to want that, and we were good students of foolishness. My band had just finished a three-night run at the Roxy. Every evening from the stage we informed the audience that we wanted Tom Petty to come down to a show, as if they had some pull. During the days between the gigs, in every interview we did, we said the same thing to journalists. We figured someone out there had to know more than we did about how to get Tom Petty out of the house.

But the last show was over and it was almost 3:00 a.m. I was in the bass player's room, where the party was unfolding, when I heard the phone ring in my adjoining room. I went in and picked it up.

"Is this Warren?"

"Yeah."

"This is Tom Petty."

"Who is this?"

"It's Tom Petty . . . but I just drank a bottle of wine. I'm a little drunk."

"You sound like Tom Petty."

"That happens when I drink."

He apologized for not making the show and invited us to come out to his house the next night. So a couple of us did that, went and met a man who seemed almost as socially awkward as we were. We probably stayed too long. He may not have wanted to tell us it was time to leave. His family slept upstairs while we sat in a room below. It was 5:00 a.m. when the wrought iron gates closed behind us. I figured it was a one-off.

◼

A few years later, twenty-two at the time, I was sitting in Petty's home office. My then girlfriend, Alison, was friends with his family, and I had come to know Petty a bit more on a three-month summer tour during which my band opened for his. Just prior to that tour, a fire burned down his family's Encino home, so the Pettys were renting Charo's Beverly Hills villa. I remembered Charo from Hollywood Squares. I had just quit my rock-and-roll band. I was too young to know just how scared I was and why, so I did the obvious thing: I told the person with me about my next band, what I wanted it to be like, how I'd stay out in LA and put it together there. But the person with me wasn't buying it.

"This isn't where bands come from," he said.

I was immediately disappointed, too disappointed to really hear his point. I'd wanted a cheerleader, someone to validate the story I was telling myself. But instead I was getting a truth, one of the unmovable truths in Tom Petty's worldview. He laid into me a little. "If that's what you want to do . . . I mean, if you want a band," he told me, "you should go back home. Go back home and get one."

However long it had been since he'd run away from Gainesville, Florida, from the rednecks and the college boys calling out for "Satisfaction," however long it had been since that town had both loved him and kicked him down its main streets, he knew it was the place that made him. He didn't find rock and roll in Malibu. He'd brought it with him.

INTRODUCTION

The author Karen Blixen once said, "All sorrows can be borne
if you put them into a story or tell a story about them." But
what if a person can't tell a story about his sorrows? What if
his story tells him?

—Stephen Grosz

The house was different from any Tom Petty had ever lived in. It was in Pacific
Palisades, just off Sunset, nothing a man without money could consider;
but neither was it a home typical of those the rich and famous are looking
for out there in the land of trophies. There were chickens in the yard. It
was like a thing ripped from an Adirondacks postcard and dropped into
a redwood grove by the Pacific. There were no pastels, no Corinthian col-
umns signifying wealth and, however inexactly, taste. It was dark, all
knotty pine, with cracks of light visible through some of the logs.

Not too long after he moved in, an itinerant cleaning lady walked up
the driveway—anything is possible in LA—and he hired her. She stole
what she could before he caught on, more than a month in. Things like
that happened in this place. But, finally, what made it most unlike any
other home he'd lived in was this: he was alone in it.

■

Petty found himself in the "Chicken Shack" right on the heels of a remarkable string of successes. There wasn't much glory left to dream up that he
hadn't already experienced. It had been years since he'd passed through
the various phases that begin when kids sign record contracts: the excitement, the expectations wide and high, the astonishment that, yes, it was

really happening, the seemingly endless waiting, opening slots on tours with the wrong headliners, the hotels blending one into the next, some fun with loose cash, cars, women, houses, a song on the charts, adventures in Winnebagos and buses, some disappointment, monotony, interactions with both the wise men and the clowns of the record industry, and—for the privileged few who actually begin to taste stardom—the unexpected isolation. This had gone on for long enough to normalize into something he could expect to find waiting for him each day when he awoke.

Tom Petty had taken up residence in a situation that even the most hopeful musician has to set aside as fantasy. And he'd honored what he'd been given by doing what he could to make the best possible records, one after another. He held himself to that. Every song had to count. When he wasn't on the road, he was in the studio. His family knew the deal, and suffered for it. By the time he really entered manhood, he was locked into the album cycle and knew little about life outside of it. On the music side, the results were pretty straightforward: in a culture of argument and friendships lost because you couldn't see eye to eye on what acts meant the most, Petty was the guy most everybody agreed on.

His story has a whiff of Horatio Alger and at least a little Elvis to it: a shitkicker from some two-bedroom ranch down in North Florida *got out*. And once he *was* out, he walked, without a lot of fanfare, into the room where the big dreams are kept, where he was given a place to hang his hat and coat. It had happened. Yet there he was, so many years into it, alone in a strange house in Pacific Palisades, staying in bed most days. Getting high was the last thing that seemed to be working. The songs had all but stopped coming.

None of *us* knew this. We saw the guy with well-worn and hard-earned rock-and-roll success, the nod of approval from his heroes, a wry, slightly twisted smile on his face—a musician who, apparently, wouldn't know how to fuck up a hot streak if he had to. And he'd been on one for a long time. Even his inner circle, small by most standards, had not adjusted its view of the man. No one was fully aware of what was going on out there in that house, how low Petty had gone. Or how much lower he would go. He was falling from a high place, and no one caught on when he lost his footing.

A little more than a decade before, after touring with and behind Bob Dylan for almost two years, a formative if sometimes strange, sometimes euphoric, sometimes maddening collaboration arranged by Dylan himself, a chain of creative high points raised Tom Petty, already a platinum-selling artist, to the status of rock-and-roll elder statesman. He was young for the job but few filled the position better.

At the outset of that run, Petty stood alongside George Harrison, Dylan, Roy Orbison, and Jeff Lynne as a Traveling Wilbury. And he was there at a Beatle's request. Then, despite the lukewarm, even *harsh* initial response of MCA, his label at the time, he released his first solo recording and found himself with the biggest record of his career. "Free Fallin'," "I Won't Back Down," and "Runnin' Down a Dream" were playing everywhere. He followed that with another major release, this time done with his longtime band, the Heartbreakers, which generated two hits, including "Learning to Fly." Then, as if by that time the whole thing had a momentum that couldn't be slowed, a greatest hits package came out that yielded another hit in the form of a bonus track, "Mary Jane's Last Dance." *Greatest Hits* ended up going past the ten times platinum mark. In its wake, Petty looped back to solo territory and created *Wildflowers*, the recording he still considers his best. From that album, another hit, "You Don't Know How It Feels," won the Grammy, somewhat casually. A deeper collection, *six CDs* deep, entitled *Playback* was then released. Intended only for the listeners fanatical in their devotion to Petty, it caught everyone off guard and went platinum itself. The timeline was like a pileup of good fortune.

But it was with all of that accumulated success and stature lending a golden sheen to his name that Petty came back down through the clouds. He had acted on what some considered an overdue decision and ended a long marriage that had started where many do, in possibility and promise, before growing complicated, and then going dark. True to the nature of divorce, no one in his family was quite prepared for what would happen on the upper floors when the foundation was ripped out. Petty included. All that had fueled his mind and spirit since he was a young man dreaming his way out of Florida, the grand ambitions, the visions of glory, the self-made character of his success, the drive to write songs—it all seemed like cartoons screened on a monkey's back.

When making a follow-up to *Wildflowers*, Rick Rubin noticed that when Tom Petty did make it into the studio to work, he was often hiding behind a pair of sunglasses, sometimes even walking with a cane. Entertainment wasn't a world in which you asked a lot of questions. So Rubin didn't.

Petty closed himself off from the world he'd built. Visitors came to see him: Stevie Nicks, his manager Tony Dimitriades, a few bandmates. But even that traffic slowed. And when it *was* still coming, most guests didn't get too far past the front door. Some speculated that he'd given himself over to drug addiction. Others felt sure that he was having a midlife breakdown of some kind. For a while there, he was behaving more like an animal that had gone off to die than a man at the peak of his career.

Back among the redwoods, Tom Petty felt like he was at the end of something. And though he wasn't, he would have to pull himself up to see the vague outline of a future worth sticking around for.

1

FAMILY SECRETS

Whenever I smell chicken shit, it reminds me of the house my
father grew up in.

—Tom Petty

Florida was a good enough place to run away to. You at least had a chance there if
you needed to hide from some black mark on your record, some misad-
venture better left in another town. It was more uncharted and more
unchecked than many other places, in the way that parts of the American
West had been at one time. Of course, Florida had no prairie, plains, or
deserts of the kind that gave western life its grand character, its John Ford
vistas. If one writer described Florida as a "lone and distant place," it was a
vain effort to mask the brute facts with romantic but ultimately vague language. Florida was a swamp.

The strange history of the Black Seminoles is one reminder of that
swamp's role as a place one layer beneath the law. Escaped slaves, coming
from the states just north of Florida, didn't always head up the eastern sea-
board in their often hopeless bids for freedom. Florida was the southern
option. Down there, the Seminole Indians took them in by the hundreds.
But this was no underground railroad, no temporary refuge. The escaped
slaves became the Black Seminoles, many of them transported to Oklahoma
reservations as tribe members when the deals were cut years later. In their
case, Florida served its purpose.

It was around 1910 when William Petty needed a place to run to. He
gave no thought as to what his decision to move to Florida might mean for

the next generations—he was just getting out of a bind. Petty, called "Pulp-wood" by some, had been working in the Georgia lumber trade, turning timber into pulp. Without significant forethought, he'd married a Chero-kee woman who worked as a cook in one of the mill camps. He wouldn't be the last in the family line to find himself marrying in haste. Maybe he was in love, but there aren't records for that kind of thing. What he came up against very quickly was this: for a Native American at that time, there weren't options. A Cherokee female wasn't going to have an easy time mov-ing through American life, certainly not at the side of her white husband. Soon enough, the lumberman felt the disdain of the men who worked with him. On a few occasions, it got rough. More than once he and his bride had to move on. At some point, however, the other millworkers found Petty's limit. He got some blood on his hands. That's when Florida started to seem like a good idea. They got away fast and never again saw the state they had once called home.

Even at that time there were a few different Floridas. Wealthy specula-tors like Henry Flagler, "the man who built Florida," belonged to one of them. Flagler, alongside John D. Rockefeller, had made a fortune with Stan-dard Oil. Different from Rockefeller, Flagler blew his fortune developing Florida. His first hotel, the Ponce de Leon, helped establish fantasy as one among Florida's native languages. Flagler was what friends and admirers and some history books call a "visionary." He had witnessed Palm Beach in its natural state, seen a city of luxury in his mind's eye, and then built it. His mansion, Whitehall, was drooled over by the *New York Herald*, wherein it was described as North America's Taj Mahal. His railroad, which he brought down the east coast of the state and out over the waters to the Florida Keys, not without massive expenditure, was a symbol of the kind of ambitions that would make the Florida of today. But in the shadows of such ambitions, there were the laborers on whose backs such dreams were carried. Those laborers lived in the other Florida. And *that* was the one that became home to Petty and his Cherokee bride, whom he called Sally.

When the couple got down there, they moved around, sometimes as migrant laborers in the produce machine. Mixed together with other south-ern poor, blacks, and Caribbeans, all of whom got work and lost work contingent on nature's whims, they may have been free of some discrimi-nations but only by hiding in the midst of others. Those landowners who made money growing citrus products and winter vegetables minimized their gamble with nature by paying the lowest wages they could get away with. A bad turn in the weather—and there were some legendary freezes, including those of the winter of 1894–95—could send waves of misery through the industry. The hardship was always hardest among the laborers.

By the time Farm Security Administration photographers were criss-crossing the nation during the Depression era, capturing in pictures the conditions among the country's very poor, Florida provided plenty of human imagery. Among the migrant workers were faces that told a sorry story of American working life.

Petty and his wife eventually got out of the unforgiving lifestyle of the migrant farmer. Perhaps because some time and miles had passed since that "incident" in Georgia, Petty was able to get back into the pulpwood business and even buy a plot of land. At last, the soil beneath their feet was their own, and nothing meant more if you were coming from the shit-hole of migrant labor.

It was a few acres near a place called Reddick, in Marion County, back in the woods and away from town. There were shady oaks and a few mag-nolias. The soil allowed for farming, and they grew corn and whatever else they needed. With a few chickens to supply eggs and the occasional meat for the table, they had a degree of self-sufficiency, if living at a near sub-sistence level. Inside their home, small by any standards, the walls were patched with varnished newspaper. The trouble in their lives, whenever trouble came, started when Sally's dark skin got unwanted attention. If staying home was one solution to that, it seemed just fine to her. She was a family secret in human form.

"I'd never seen an outhouse until I saw theirs," says Tom Petty of his grandparents' place. "They had a little cornfield next to a tar paper kind of house, up on blocks. I remember newspaper patches on the walls, which struck me as funny, you know? There was a big iron pump that brought water into the kitchen. I don't have any memory of a conversation with my grandfather, just that he wore a hat and sat out on the porch with other men. But he wasn't inviting. Nice enough, I guess, but you didn't walk over to him or anything." At least three children were raised in the Reddick house, including twins named Earl and Pearl. Their skin a little dark, they all did like their mother and got where they needed to be going when color became an issue. "It makes you learn to shut up," says the grandson. "They knew that there was no point in trying to be anything other than a white family." The further one got from being a white family, the harder life became. And theirs was hard enough. A number of Cherokees changed their names to Macintosh.

Fishing, hunting, doing what they could to avoid their father's guiding hand, which often came down hard and without a word passing from his lips, Sally's children lived almost as if they were in the century that had passed rather than the one that was under way. They learned the woods. They knew how to hunt the wild pigs and turkeys in the thicket, to deal with alligators and snakes in or near the water, including those that were better left alone. Some of Florida's best fishermen came out of worlds like that. "I think that's where my father felt most at home," says Petty of his father, Earl. "Being in a small boat on one of those lakes, that's where he came alive. What he loved more than anything was to be in a fucking swamp. And there were so many in central North Florida. There, he was a master at existing. Wasn't afraid of anything. I once saw him push an alligator, from right behind his head, just push him down in the water. Laughing." The presence of the Ocala-Gainesville line, with a whistle heard for miles, was the only sign that there was something going on somewhere else that might prove another option. Knowing a little something about elsewhere, it wasn't a draw to Earl's parents. But the sound eventually got to their children. Earl, in particular, started looking down the tracks.

It's difficult today to understand what a train whistle meant to a young man at that time. It was a symbol as loaded as any Earl would ever know. It was the sound of the end of the worst parts of growing up in Reddick. Like having an Indian for a mother. And that's how he thought of her on bad days. He didn't want to be branded an outsider. "We're not really sure if our grandmother's name was Sally or Fannie," Petty says. "My brother thinks it was Sally, but we just don't know. We weren't told a lot, and I guess we asked even less." When Earl eventually did get on that train and head north, he was old enough to know that part of the plan was to find a woman. And he'd be damned sure, he told himself, that she'd be fair-skinned and from another side of life.

■

Earl Petty met Katherine Avery when he returned from the Second World War, during which he served as an air force groundsman in Egypt. He hadn't just gotten out of Reddick; he'd seen the world. In fact, he'd seen enough of the world to know that Gainesville was about the right distance from Reddick. Any farther was too far. He'd overshot the mark first time around. He didn't need a pyramid in his backyard. And Gainesville was where he found his fair-skinned girl, working at Eli Witt's Candy and Tobacco. He was a driver, and she worked in the office.

Katherine was born in Sycamore, Georgia, to John and Troas Avery. Her family, in search of more, or, at least, better, had moved to Gainesville when she was still young. Sycamore was a small town, not on the path of what was to come. "My mother aspired to be better than that, not to be *country*," Petty says. "But in that respect, she certainly made an interesting choice when she picked a husband." The Florida for which the Averys would set out wasn't one they needed to go to in the night and undercover, like the Pettys. They made their way in broad daylight, fueled by a dream. America had forced its way out of the Depression, and no one wanted to go back where they'd just been. For Katherine and her sisters, Gainesville was the big city. By the time the war ended, she had let herself get caught up in the midcentury hope for something better.

In 1945, the University of Florida in Gainesville had 587 students enrolled. By 1946 it had more than 8,000. That rate of growth meant a few things. One, business was good in the halls of learning. Two, if you lived in town and weren't a part of the world of young people, you were going to be outnumbered. It was a buoyant time. If the state of Florida wasn't growing quite as quickly as the University of Florida, it was boom times nonetheless. Florida was well on its way to becoming *Florida*. Land of Sunshine.

To reimagine the fifties, whether in Gainesville or anywhere else in America, means setting aside some images and ideas about the era that have all but hardened into place. Too often the period is remembered as a time of ruthless conformity, with Little Richard providing counterpoint along the way. In significant ways, the push for conformity was real. But the convenience offered by the "decade" as an organizing tool for history, and the widespread tendency to establish the "straight" fifties in order to celebrate the sixties and its breakthroughs, has distorted the picture of midcentury life. The duck-and-cover fifties, with its blacklists and anxieties played out in Senate subcommittees on juvenile delinquency has become *the* fifties. But was the conformity of the era simply an effort, imposed from above, to control difference? Or was that conformity a choice made by many and for good reason?

In Earl Petty's case, conformity had its benefits. It was bound up with an interest in leaving the Depression and the war behind and a desire to be a part of a situation that was, finally, about the "good life." Fitting in also meant putting distance between himself and the small house back in Reddick. So long as he was a Cherokee, he was an outsider, and far less likely to get a share of the rewards. In the part of the world he'd chosen for himself, even by the late fifties, 99 percent of the population favored laws banning interracial marriage. His parents were on the wrong side of that popular position. No, conformity wasn't a weakness, it was a place to get to as soon as he could. "As a Cherokee," says his son, "Earl would be on the underside of the American dream. But if you were a white male in the fifties, it could be an incredible time.

"In so many ways," he continues, "my father was like a man hiding out in plain view, afraid of being found out. I think there was a lot of theater in his life, a lot of masks, a lot of acting. But I sure didn't know this then. I just thought he was an asshole. It would take me years to get past what he did to me in order to understand his situation. I only saw the outer stuff, the bravado, the machismo, the anger. We knew so little about the world he came from, because he kept it behind a wall he'd built himself. I think he felt he had to. And, you know, he was probably right. I didn't think about what it meant to be a Native American, what it meant to be a kid who grew up in a shack with his Indian mother and his white father, suddenly in a college town, just as America was moving full speed ahead into the glorious fifties. That's quite a scene, really."

There are books that throw light on the era's lost men. *The Organization Man* of 1956 tells a compelling, sometimes chilling story of postwar life. The author, William Whyte, seizes on a shift from an America founded on ideals of individualism and the "Protestant work ethic" to a country wherein a corporate sensibility begins to choke off that spirit. It is, in some respects, the sociological companion piece to *The Man in the Gray Flannel Suit*. Whyte also puts a finger on an aspect of fifties aspiration that speaks to Earl Petty's situation. The suburbs, he argues, were a "new melting pot."

There were those who had been pushed to the margins as ethnic outsiders who, now ensconced in the middle-class suburban environment, could transition into being "white." This obviously had limits, harsh for those, such as African Americans, who had no chance of "passing." But for a mixed-race Earl Petty, it meant having a shot. *If* he did it right.

The same year he married Kitty, 1947, they found a small house where they lived for a few years before moving to the two-bedroom ranch that would be their home for the rest of their lives. As far as being half-Cherokee was concerned, it was not discussed. Within three years of their marriage, their first child, Thomas Earl Petty, was born. It was 1950 when Tom came home from the hospital. With him, Earl and Kitty would move to that second house, a small place off the park, surrounded by live oaks draped with Spanish moss. Just one year after Tom's birth, *Time* magazine would declare the generation to which his parents belonged the "silent generation." Born around the Depression and living through the war, they had things they wanted to leave behind, as if there were a collective memory bank they agreed to seal off. The optimism of midcentury American life was real. Earl felt it as he drove the truck for Eli Witt's tobacco and candy company. But, still, a darkness tugged at him.

Troas Avery, Kitty's mother, didn't simply have issues with her son-in-law Earl Petty; she had issues with all Earls. She'd married two of them. Her eldest daughter, Evelyn, married one. By the time her daughter Kitty did the same, Troas was refusing to speak the name "Earl." She called Kitty's Earl "Petty." She called Evelyn's Earl "Jernigan." The name brought her bad luck. And, in Earl Petty's case, it wasn't just the name—she didn't like *him*. He drank and gambled, without good results in either department. He made it to church on time, yes, but the results weren't so good there either. And now he was going to try his hand at parenting.

2

STRANGER IN THE HOUSE

Many fathers are gone. Some leave, some are left. Some
return, unknown and hungry. Only the dog remembers.
—NICK FLYNN, *ANOTHER BULLSHIT NIGHT IN SUCK CITY*

**Their stories interweave: Tom Petty, Bernie and Tom Leadon, Rodney and Ricky
Rucker,** Jim Lenahan, Don Felder, Marty and Jeff Jourard, David Mason.
These are just a few names. There were others. They liked B movies, read
Mad, stole copies of *Playboy* from their fathers, snuck booze, put dents in
cars. As teenagers, many of them hung out at the same Gainesville music
store, Lipham Music. They saw one another's early performances, loved the
same records, played in each other's bands. Among them, talent and ambition weren't equally dispersed, though a love for the music was. Sometimes
they got into it with each other, over girls or over bands, and stopped
talking. But they were kids bound to one another through a shared experience that preceded the music's arrival: they all came out of the same quiet
that haunted a lot of American homes in the fifties. Rock and roll was the
thing God delivered to break up the silence.

Tom Petty recalls being five years old when he began to get a better
sense of his father's working world. "He was a salesman," says Petty. "He
just didn't always have something to sell. And when he *did* have something
to sell, it didn't always go so well." Earl, no longer a truck driver, had first
entered business as the owner of a grocery store in the black section of
Gainesville, where his son would sometimes play out back with the neighborhood children. On the heels of that, Earl started his own wholesale

operation, Petty's Dry Goods. His eldest son's lasting memory is of his father lifting him into a green panel van with the business's name written on the side. They went store to store, selling the little things that sat on racks by the checkout, the stuff that tended to get dusty. Cheap sunglasses, tie clips, items that might sell when a customer wasn't on his guard.

"It was the strangest collection of things," Petty says. "I remember there being a lot of toys, really crappy plastic toys. There was this mannequin that had six sets of breasts on it. I used to go, 'What the . . . does he sell bras?' He took me with him that one day. And I realized that he would just pull up to these little grocery stores and try to go sell something. But it didn't look to me like he was selling much, just went in and talked like crazy. I watched him do this for a whole day. By the time we got home, I knew I was never, ever going in that truck again." Not long after, Earl went back to selling insurance door to door, mostly in the black part of town.

Even by that time, Earl had shown his son the side of him that would color the boy's entire life. "I'm not the best authority on the relationships fathers have with their sons," explains Petty. Listening to him, one gets the sense that the past has remained uncomfortably close. More than once when the topic of his father arises, Petty gets up, opens the door to his recording studio lounge, and throws what's left in his coffee cup onto the bushes outside his door. He'll talk about his father, doesn't refuse the topic. He just pours more coffee before he starts talking. "I didn't understand there could *be* a relationship," he explains. "I thought a father just put shit on the table, made a living, and we owed him the respect because he put a roof over our head, because for some reason our mother married him or because we just *owe* him respect. I didn't realize that there were kids who had really genuine relationships with their fathers. I remember when I was young that I didn't want to spend time around *any* parents. If I was visiting a friend and his parents showed up, I was gone."

When Petty was a boy, the popular media were rich in sentimental snapshots of happy times in the American household. Walt Disney, who would become something of a latter-day version of Henry Flagler, planning his Floridian dream within a decade of Tom Petty's birth, certainly had ideas of what a family should look like. Disney's visions proliferated in the entertainments his studios sent forth. Norman Rockwell promoted his own tidy pictures of the American family life through his *Saturday Evening Post* covers. Television did its part, with *Leave It to Beaver*, *Father Knows Best*, and *The Adventures of Ozzie and Harriet* all beginning long runs in the midfifties. Amid all that, what father was going to start talking about his Cherokee roots, his life during wartime? The Depression, poverty, the various tastes that clung to the back of his mouth? No one wanted to bring that into the living room. So most kept it to themselves. Certainly Earl did. Until he couldn't. And then it came out as something else.

Images contrary to the tidy scrapbook of American family life did begin circulating, coming from a few different, incongruous sources. It was the *Kinsey Reports*, *The Catcher in the Rye*, *Playboy*, *Death of a Salesman*. It was sociological work like *The Lonely Crowd*. It was Marlon Brando's face. All of it challenged the sanitized images of a harmonious American life: it was information, sometimes shocking, that suggested there was something else going on, another America, kept out of view like panties at the back of a desk drawer. With the exception of *Playboy* and, possibly, Brando, however, this stuff wasn't coming Earl Petty's way. But he was a part of the world it belonged to, a conflicted place of failed repressions.

If *Time* called them the "silent generation," this obviously didn't mean that everyone kept their voices down. They just didn't talk about what they didn't want to talk about. Earl had a temper and a fondness for the bottle. He was no Ozzie Nelson. But still, he preferred to think that he and Ozzie were part of the same general history. Earl's firstborn, however, didn't exactly fit any idealized picture either. Tom may have been a boy, but he was a boy who wasn't interested in sports, wasn't interested in school, wasn't even interested in fishing and hunting. The only thing about the kid that matched the image Earl had in mind was the blond hair. A towheaded boy was playing in Earl's yard.

■

Earl and Kitty's second child, Bruce, was born in 1958. The Petty boys shared the bedroom across the hall from their parents. When Bruce was old enough, Earl installed a bunk bed. More dark-skinned than his brother, Bruce was too young to be a rival of any kind. "We never really competed for things," Bruce explains. "It was a real big brother thing. He was always looking out for me, trying to help me in any way he could." The struggle between Earl and Tom unfolded before Bruce Petty's eyes. The younger brother may not have been a peer, but he was a witness. "It's good, still feels good," Tom says, "just to know there's somebody out there who knows what happened, what it was like."

But what the younger brother didn't see was the beginning of the trouble, the point at which Earl Petty starting letting himself do it. "I remember it first happening when I was probably four," Tom Petty recalls. "Four, maybe five, because it was a '55 Cadillac. I had this crappy slingshot my father had given me, a plastic thing, the first one I ever had. I was in the yard shooting this slingshot. And cars are driving by. I'm just like, 'I wonder if I can get a car.' And whack! This big Cadillac. It was going by pretty slowly, and I just nailed the fin on that thing. The car came to an immediate stop. The driver got out, and he was so fucking mad. I couldn't quite compute why this had made him so mad. He went up to the door and knocked. There was some discussion with my mother, and she looked really distressed, took the slingshot away, and said, 'This is bad. Your dad's not going to like this.'

"I felt kind of weird, not knowing what was coming next. But when my father got home later, he came in, took a belt, and beat the living shit out of me. He beat me so bad that I was covered in raised welts, from my head to my toes. I mean, you can't imagine someone hitting a child like that. Five years old. I remember it so well. My mother and my grandmother laid me in my bed, stripped me, and they took cotton and alcohol, cleaning these big welts all over my body. My mother's rap was, 'You gotta be a better boy. You just can't do that. You can't make him that mad.' But I was fucking *five*. She learned, for her part, that you'd better not mention it to Earl. That was one of the first ones. But there were many, many more." By contrast, Kitty was the gentle one. The angel.

"My father had this kid," Bruce Petty explains, "that was going a hundred and eighty degrees opposite of everybody else and *their* kids. And Earl was trying to stop that with everything he could." Whether it was because Tom was a living cautionary tale with whom he shared a bunk bed or not, Bruce got into sports. And, with his brother and the rest of America, television.

■

The television was always on. For Bruce, it was entertainment. But for his brother, Tom, it had already become something more. "Very early on I realized," Petty says, "that I had to teach myself everything just to exist at the level I wanted to live my life. I felt there was more to be known, more to be understood than I was going to get from the household I was in. I kind of knew that much from very early on. Exactly why, I'm not sure, but I got that maybe what my parents pictured for me wasn't at all what I was going to go with. I knew I didn't want to grow up and be an insurance salesman. That looked really dull to me. And I think it was television that saved my life, that raised and educated me.

"It was an escape, of course, but it was more. And I watched a lot. What I noticed on television was that families were nothing like ours. Everything I saw looked like a much better way of doing things. *Ozzie and Harriet* was a good one, where everybody seemed to be cruising along just fine, Dad had a relationship with the kids, and the family would all come together to work on Ricky's problem. It wasn't like that in my house. Mom and Dad both worked, were dog tired at the end of the day, and my brother and I were pretty much on our own as far as passing the time."

Petty and his father used the image of the perfect American family against each other. Neither measured up. Earl drank too much too often. He beat his son. He fought with his wife. And, for his part, Tom was a disappointment in most every category. Well before rock and roll arrived on the scene to make matters simultaneously better and worse, a cord of anger and resentment connected father and son. The difference between them may have been that Tom sometimes blamed himself for the failures of his family—a common enough response among the young people who kept their parents up at night. Historian David Halberstam has suggested that there was a perverse effect to shows like *Father Knows Best*: young people had to watch those perfect families, only to show up at the dining room table and be greeted by lunatics. "Kids growing up in homes filled with anger and tension often felt the failure was theirs," he writes. Of course, what kid had the presence of mind, or the information, to see it for what it was? Who knew that Ozzie Nelson was in truth a workaholic with little off camera time for his children, another absent father among the many? That wasn't how it looked on television.

"What I did come to notice," recalls Petty, "was that everything really great seemed to be coming from California. The television announcers would say, 'From television city, in Hollywood, it's the *Red Skelton Show!*' And I thought, 'Television city? Man, that's where I need to be.' This is when I was really still a little kid. Television turned me on to a whole different idea of living, and I was a sponge. But pretty soon you start wondering if there isn't something between what you see on television and the shit you're dealing with at home."

In school it was no different: the world of Dick and Jane, through which Petty and almost every other American kid would learn to read, was a forced feeding. So antiseptic as to be a fantasy literature, the Dick and Jane volumes had no trace of outsiders, of grief, of fear, of trouble—it was a world without an *Other*. "I remember them well," Petty says. "That was how we all learned to read: 'See Dick run. See Jane run. See Dick jump. See Jane jump.'" It would take a movement, and many years, to remove those books from American schools. The year 1957 saw a little advance with the publication of *The Cat in the Hat*. Of the many fragmented clues that give some sense of the conflicted nature of American life at midcentury, *The Cat in the Hat*, in its own strange way, is as revealing as anything. There's as much truth in the book as you'll find among any images drawn from the era, certainly more than one finds in the idealized pictures of American life generated by Rockwell or Disney. *The Cat in the Hat* exposes the in-betweenness of it all, the midcentury breakdown in meaning, out of which Tom Petty's generation emerged, a little starved for something to call their own. It's the rock and roll of children's literature.

As Louis Menand explains, the story of *The Cat in the Hat* belongs to the *mater abscondita* tradition. Like so many fairy tales, so much Western fiction, really, *The Cat in the Hat* begins with loss, particularly the loss of the mother. And it's that maternal absence into which the cat arrives. All hell breaks loose, the domestic scene thrown out of control for most of the book. The fish, a kind of stand-in for parental rule, if all but powerless in his bowl, insists to the children that they do the right thing. But the fact is, it's not clear if anyone, whether the kids or the cat, actually knows what the right thing is. No one knew just when mother would be back or in what way that even mattered. The *only* given, the only thing that everyone knew for sure, is that the father is, quite simply, gone. Not worth a mention.

At a moment when it was needed, and to whomever was paying attention, Dr. Seuss gave away some of middle America's secrets. It wasn't as if kids like Tom Petty had any interest in telling their peers what was going on at home. They all kept it from one another. Of course, when a family is in trouble, its members are often hard pressed to believe that other homes might be as fucked up as their own. So why let on, and suffer for that, too? Then, as now, life inside the front door was like its own dark planet. So the feeling was, *keep it there*. No young person in Gainesville was thinking their own world of shit might be like the next family's.

Don Felder was older than Tom Petty but grew up in the same part of town. At Christmas, Don and his brother would load their .22 rifle with rat shot purchased with money they got from returning Coke bottles, and they'd shoot clumps of mistletoe out of the oak trees. They'd tie up in ribbon what they shot down, selling it on the streets of Gainesville for fifty cents a bunch. "That's the South when you're poor," Felder says.

His brother went on to law school and passed the bar. His parents were proud of that. Don, however, played guitar. "I think we were the last family in our town to get a black-and-white television," Felder explains. "It was the size of a washing machine, with a screen in it that was about twelve by twelve inches. When I got my first guitar, I would plug it into a jack in the back of that TV. I'd be watching *Mighty Mouse* and the other cartoons on Saturday, playing the guitar, trying to learn." His father, interested in electronics, may have helped him set up his "amp," but his father didn't see it going anywhere. Why would he? If it came out wrong when the father confronted his son, it was only because Mr. Felder wanted something better for his youngest. "At the time," Felder explains, "I didn't understand what was going on. We parted under very bitter terms." Later, when he was on the road with the Eagles, his father did come to see the band. But there's a point at which the damage is done, and hit singles and backstage hugs can't really undo that.

Down in the Tampa area, Charlie Souza was seven when his father split. He saw the man a few years later, driving by with his girlfriend. Souza's father stopped the car when he recognized his son and gave the nine-year-old

Charlie some loose change to share with his sister. He was gone after that, not reappearing until more than fifteen years later, when he stayed at his son's house for one night before disappearing without a trace the next morning. Never seen again.

Around the time Souza's father first left the family, the boy's mother went into a deep depression, got sick, and remained bedridden much of the time. One day when Souza was almost thirteen, cleaning his room and playing records, a neighborhood boy came by to see if Charlie could come out and play baseball. "No," Souza told him. "Gotta clean my room." The neighbor persisted, asking if he could, on Charlie's behalf, go and check with Charlie's mother. "Sure," Charlie told him. The boy went to Mrs. Souza's bedroom. The music was loud in Charlie's room, loud enough that he didn't hear anything. But when he did go to his mother's room, Charlie found her stabbed to death. The bloody sneaker tracks of his young friend made it easy for the police to find the boy. With the exception of that one night years later, when his father slept on his couch, Charlie Souza was really an orphan. In the midsixties, a few years after his mother's murder, Souza's group, the Tropics, would be the hottest rock-and-roll band in Florida.

■

There was a violence that could, suddenly and unexpectedly, rip the fabric of suburban life. It was as though some rougher, rural past was moving just below, closer than anyone wanted to believe. Petty was witness to it and would eventually do all he could to leave it behind.

"It wasn't very often at all," Petty says, "but sometimes there would be a friends-over-for-dinner kind of night at our house. My mom would invite this other family, the Jenkinses, if I remember their name right. Bob and Liz. They'd come over with their kids. Everyone would wear nice clothes. You know, the crushed velvet skirts and all that. Bob Jenkins was a slicked-back-hair kind of guy but nice enough." At one of those gatherings, on a night when the cold was coming into North Florida, Petty, around nine at the time, went to turn up the heat in the hallway. Bob Jenkins stopped him, told him not to do it, with enough insistence that the young Petty responded in kind. Only after the Jenkinses were gone did Kitty Petty explain to her son that Bob Jenkins didn't like what he called "artificial heat." Petty's mother explained that it upset him. "I was thinking, 'Artificial heat? Heat's not artificial. There's heat, and there's no heat.' I thought it was strange," says Petty. "I thought Bob was just a little weird. My mother told me that they wore a lot of jackets over at the Jenkinses'."

The families had a few more dinners together before the afternoon when Petty heard the adults talking in hushed tones, and he could pick up the Jenkinses' name being mentioned. When his parents left and he was alone with his grandmother, Petty asked her what this was about. "I said, 'What's going on?' And she tells me they've taken Bob Jenkins away. He held a shotgun on his family for twenty-four hours, put them all on the sofa and held the gun on them. The police had come and arrested him. I was like, 'Wow.' But, you know, every now and then you saw a crack in the veneer."

3

COWBOYS AND INDIANS

We got a gun and holster every Christmas. That was our thing.

—BRUCE PETTY

Earl Petty liked seeing his sons playing in the backyard. It was exactly what American boys that age were supposed to be doing. When they weren't out back playing, armed and ready to shoot, they were watching every western they could on television: *The Rifleman*, *Bonanza*, *Have Gun—Will Travel*, *Gunsmoke*, *Wanted: Dead or Alive*. It was as if the boys were either watching the Indians die or taking care of the situation themselves, helping Earl kill off his people. When Elvis came into Tom's world, however, Bruce Petty would have to handle the Indians on his own. Like so many young people in America, his brother was ready to replace the heroes of comic books and westerns with the rock-and-roll stars of the day. Or the day before, as was the case with Petty's interest in midfifties rock and roll. He got his first taste of the music, of Elvis, Jerry Lee Lewis, and Little Richard, a few years after they'd hit.

They say Tom Petty's uncle Earl Jernigan had one of the rubber costumes from *The Creature from the Black Lagoon* hanging in his office. Jernigan worked with film crews that came to Florida for location work, so it's a possibility. He was from the North, a little different from the other men in Petty's world. The others were crackers, rednecks—there were a few different words for them. Jernigan was different and didn't always suffer the others with grace. "He married into a crazy fucking family, and he knew it, and he stayed away from it," says Petty. "So I didn't even know until years later that he was in show business, doing television, doing movies, 110 episodes of *Sea Hunt*. I had no idea. I'm bitter about that, that I wasn't better informed. But he didn't want to have anything to do with anybody in my family. And I can't really blame him." Jernigan's wife, Evelyn, Kitty Petty's older sister, broke form the day she came to ask if Petty, ten at the time, wanted to join a few of his cousins and meet Elvis Presley. The star was in Ocala filming *Follow That Dream*.

Petty remembers a line of Cadillacs, every one of them white, pulling up on Ocala's Main Street. Men with pompadours and mohair suits stepped from the cars, as if the whole thing was choreographed. When Elvis emerged, he was otherworldly in his beauty. You could dress up the star's entourage to look just like him, but it would only underscore the contrast between Elvis and anyone around him. Presley's was a freak beauty. Jernigan made introductions, and Elvis shook Tom Petty's hand. The boy stared up at the star, unable to do more than that. Fans were everywhere in the streets of Ocala, making it difficult for the filmmakers. Within days, Petty says, he traded his slingshot for a box of 45s, many of them Presley classics. Elvis became a symbol of a place Tom Petty wanted to go. In time, the Beatles would be the map to get there. When it came, the British Invasion was, of course, a Copernican revolution. Ed Sullivan was the mechanism through which the core message was delivered: *you* can do this. A generation heard it. In fucked-up homes across America, an alternative was presented. For Tom Petty, from that point on it was going to be a battle about many things, the length of his hair and the state of his report cards among them, the opponents being father and school. But life would begin to display its offerings. He had only a few years to wait. Lying awake through those nights, waiting, he could see Elvis's face, hear the songs in his head.

■

Petty got his first guitar, an almost unplayable Stella, in 1962, just two years before that Ed Sullivan performance. It wasn't much more than a shape to hold, an idea with a strap. But it was enough. That was the same year that the Cuban missile crisis arrived to give Cold War anxieties a basis in reality. If you were living in America at the time, it was a scary moment. If you were living in Florida, it was some terrifying shit going down in your backyard. Earl Petty responded by building a bomb shelter. He arranged cinder blocks around a leveled area. The shelter would have to be above-ground. You wouldn't dig too deep in that part of Florida because of sink-holes. They could pull your house down into another world.

Earl had in his mind an image of carefully stacked cans of beans and soup and peaches in heavy syrup, a small two-burner cook stove, bunks, board games, his wife and two boys in the lamplight. Security for his family in the face of uncertainty. His eldest son's friends, over after school, looked on with interest. Later on they'd see pictures in *Life*, like the ones of the couple who honeymooned for two weeks in an eight-by-eleven-foot bomb shelter, and they'd think of Earl. He wasn't the only man building such a box down that way—there was another just down the block—but he was the only one most of those kids knew personally.

The bomb shelter was never finished. But Earl was among those who did something—or almost did something—about the abstract fear that hung over the nation. Even as the work slowed, Earl remained attracted to the idea of showing his boys what it meant to be a man. Not that they picked up on it in the way he hoped. They never did. Particularly his eldest. "I remember thinking, 'I don't want to be stuck in this bomb shelter with Earl,'" Petty says. "I asked him where the bathroom was going to be, and he points at a bucket. I'm thinking, 'We're all gonna shit in that bucket?' We were aware that the Russians might drop a bomb on us. If you went through town, you'd see signs that said, 'Public Fallout Shelter.' And I knew we weren't far from Cuba. But what could I do? Nothing. But my father's solution didn't have a lot of appeal." The crisis passed. "The floor and the walls were done," Bruce Petty recalls. "It was all concrete blocks, but he never even got a door on it. It just sat out there in the backyard. Still there, I guess."

David Mason was friends with Tom Petty from second grade through junior high. Briefly a part of Petty's first band, the Sundowners, later a founding member of Todd Rundgren's Utopia and in Jackson Browne's touring band, Mason recalls playing around in the unfinished bomb shelter. "The holes in the cinder blocks were filled with dirt," says Mason. "I think there might have been an inner wall and an outer wall. No door, though. No roof. But I guess Mr. Petty wanted to protect his family." Finished or unfinished, the bomb shelter served a purpose. Life at home was easier for the Petty boys when the enemy was *out there*. It distracted their father. Life was more complicated when the battle came inside. There wasn't a bomb shelter for that.

"My father was nice enough to me in his old age," Tom Petty says. "In his way, he tried to apologize. But I think he always felt that he wasn't supposed to get too close to children. As a parent, you just made sure the kids didn't die. You fed them and then you sent them out into the world. But you shouldn't necessarily get to know them. And after he started beating me, I thought, 'I'm not going near that motherfucker.' Strange as it might sound, I think both my mother and my father were probably scared that I was gay. They were always trying to push me into playing baseball or whatever. And I just didn't want to. I liked art, and I liked clothes, and, after the Beatles, I liked having my hair long. I'm sure Earl translated that into, 'Whoa—he's going the wrong way. He's not doing what other boys are doing.' And they didn't know how much I loved girls, because I sure as hell wasn't going to bring a girl home to *that*. I didn't ever discuss a girl with them. I didn't want my parents involved in that, in any fucking way."

"I remember Tom saying, 'My dad's gonna kill me,'" recalls Tom Leadon, a neighbor first but finally one of Petty's closest early musical collaborators. "He'd just gotten his report card. I was like, 'What did you get?' He tells me, two Ds and three Fs. I remember thinking, 'Wow, this could be the dumbest guy I've ever met.' I was fascinated. Of course, I soon found out he wasn't dumb at all. But he sure didn't do much to connect at school."

"Actually, that one was straight Fs, with a D minus in art," Petty says. "Someone gave me some special ink so I could turn an F into a B, but it ended up eating the paper. Made it even worse. But I thought it was all kind of funny. I probably gave it a shot at school for about a minute. There was a point where I realized—especially in high school—that the men and women teaching me may not be as bright as me, and I couldn't suffer that. I looked at them and thought, 'I'm not really sure you know what you're doing.' I could excel at anything I had an interest in. Even a vague interest. Like in English. I got good marks, because I didn't mind reading something. I liked stories. That hooked me. I could get into how words came together, how sentences were built, stories put together. All of that interested me. It was effortless. I used to get these horrible report cards, but there'd be an A in English. My mother would go, 'Why do you only study for this class?' But the truth was, I wasn't studying for any of the classes . . . that just happened.

"With math and other subjects that didn't interest me, I couldn't bluff. I mean, once I had learned basic arithmetic, I didn't see why I needed to learn more. I thought, 'Nobody's ever going to ask me to do an algebra problem, and I don't give a fuck about this.' I ended up skipping a lot of school. I remember taking chorus with my friend Mike Nixon later on. We skipped class all year long. Then Mike shows up one day and says, 'The chorus recital is tonight. We gotta be there.' I thought he was out of his mind. But he says we'll fail if we don't show. So we go, walk out into the auditorium with the entire chorus, kind of move our mouths along. The chorus teacher is just looking daggers at us down front. The school sent letters to our parents, and all this shit went down." Petty shrugs. "I recognize that education is a good thing, but I just wasn't made for school."

The only draw for Petty was the girls. There was a string of obsessions that filled his mind with light. He could see a beautiful face and build something with it. For a kid dealing with trouble at home, those early crushes had the power to transport. It was the first promise of another life within the one he'd been given. "I remember all these girls. But I can't remember a single teacher," Petty says, smiling. "I had remarkable taste in women. I remember going to school for the first time and seeing this girl that was just drop-dead gorgeous. And, I mean, this was kindergarten. I made my way over to her and pretty much sealed the deal. This was *my* gal. If only it had lasted. She turned into the best-looking girl Gainesville ever had. So good-looking that in high school one of the teachers ran off with her."

When Petty was at Howard Bishop Junior High, he discovered that the field had gotten crowded. "It was a small school," Petty says. "And I found this one beautiful girl, Cindy, the prettiest girl there, and she showed some interest in me. I probably made more of it than she did, probably thought it was more real than she did. I imagine every guy she met wanted to take her out. But I still remember the day that it hit me that we weren't an item like I thought we were. It was traumatic for me. I remember the walk home, just feeling . . . I got my heart broken." If the initial feelings of love were outsized for a boy his age, so, too, was the crash. It changed him. After that it would be a matter of protecting himself, of being sure it didn't happen again. He pulled back. There would be girlfriends, but the relationships he pursued would be safe, nothing, Petty made sure, that could hurt him.

"I'll tell you something I've been thinking about lately," Petty says. "That phrase, 'getting your feelings hurt.' I realized that what I equated it to in childhood was something almost paralyzing. When I 'got my feelings hurt,' I really couldn't have felt worse. It was physical. My throat clamped up, and I just wanted to die. I would radiate pain. It took quite a while for this to change. It only dawned on me later in life that getting your feelings hurt can be *lighter* than that. You can get your feelings hurt without it crippling you. But as a young man, and as a child, there was something unusual going on. It wasn't right. I was very sensitive, too delicate. I could be tough as hell in other areas, but when it came to, you know, emotional stuff, I could break like a twig. I felt like I had to protect myself, almost had to close part of myself down. I remember thinking, 'Enough chasing these beautiful girls around junior high. I'm not cut out for this.'"

The trouble with his father, however, wasn't something he could handle by shutting a part of himself down. A deeper distrust of adults spread in him. "There was something about him," Tom Leadon insists, "something that would always set off the adults. Even when we were kids, Tom Petty was the guy that rubbed them the wrong way. They just picked up on it, even if he didn't say anything. It was just his body language or something." The abuse at home continued into junior high school, even escalated, and it was like a scent Petty gave off.

"My father got me out in the woods and on the water more than a few times," he says. "And it was always like he had some point to make, something to teach me about who he was and, I guess, who I was or who he thought I was." Earl Petty felt he needed to show his son that he could knock an alligator out, that he could swing a snake over his head and snap its neck. So he did. Tom remembered it, of course. It worked in that sense. But the son didn't remember it the way his father intended. For a while, with too much friction between them, Tom went to live with his grandmother. But that didn't last. In part because Earl felt that his authority was being challenged. "It lasted until he figured out I had gone," says Petty. "Then he came over there, took me by the fucking hair, and dragged me home. It lasted until he kicked in her screen door, kicked it right off the hinges, bent the door, and beat the living shit out of me all over the house. I mean, one of the worst beatings I ever took. And then he brought me home." Not long after, Petty found out that his mother, the one person who really knew Earl and might be able to protect her son, was sick.

As much as they could, Earl and Kitty kept her illness from their children. The boys knew enough to grasp that something was wrong, but no one told them exactly what was happening. While Earl had moved in and out of jobs during his sons' childhoods, Kitty worked at the tax collector's office, dealing with car registrations. She took Tom along with her to work one day, and he saw that she was happy there, loved by the people she worked with. Her natural warmth was in strong contrast to her husband's country sensibility. Work, her eldest son realized, was an easier place for her to be. Getting sick would eventually mean she couldn't even have that.

Kitty was the buffer between Tom and his father, a woman who'd gotten in a little too deep but would never consider getting out. It just wasn't done. "She should have left him," Petty says. "I don't know why she wouldn't leave him." The health problems, which would only get worse, merely cemented a bad situation. But she didn't have the heart to tell her sons a whole lot. The word "chemotherapy" was heard around the house well before one of Tom's friends explained to him what it meant. Their mother was spending more and more time in her bedroom, the door shut. And then it was bouts with epilepsy. There were periods when she seemed better, but they didn't last. Childhood in the traditional sense ended early, without anyone really noticing. At a certain point, the town would raise the boy.

■

Gainesville will always figure larger in Tom Petty's story than the Los Angeles to which he relocated almost forty years ago. It's more than a backdrop. Something connects a man to the hometown he pushes against to get going in the first place. And Gainesville was made for rock and roll. The University of Florida's remarkable postwar growth aligned with the music's golden years. Rock and roll was on the radio, played live in a network of clubs and at frat houses, coming out of cars, everywhere. The right equipment could be found at Lipham Music, where the local bands could hang out so long as their gig money found its way to the cash register.

Gainesville was its own story. In so many ways, the town wasn't part of the Florida that would carve its image into the popular fantasies of postwar America: the white sand beaches, acres of amusement parks, the limitless promise of space travel; no, the Florida to which Gainesville belonged was nothing but Georgia with a few miles tacked on and a university thrown in.

You could say that the university made the town. But the town didn't just go away. This was the Deep South with a door punched in its side for strangers to walk through. And those strangers brought ideas and customs and diversions and long-playing records that would transform the lives of the locals. The town and the university cross-fertilized. "If you went a few miles down the road," Petty insists, "you were back in redneck land, where the same rules didn't apply." In Gainesville proper, however, a new young America was beginning to realize itself. Because of that place and its particularities, Petty was, in mind and spirit, out of the family house years before he left the bedroom he shared with his brother. He was ready for a new family even before the Beatles arrived. But through the Beatles' example, he was shown how to start one. The Sundowners would just be the first. From that point on, nothing was ever going to mean more to him than the band he was in. From the Sundowners to the Epics, Mudcrutch to the Heartbreakers, every decision would be made in relation to how he could best keep the band together. If family was bullshit and girls were a beautiful road to a lonely place, the bands might be different. That was the thinking. There was something in the Beatles' faces that looked like freedom.

"When I was a kid, I would have loved to have been a rock-and-roll star," Petty says. "I just didn't understand how you got to be one. How did you suddenly have a mohair suit and an orchestra? But the minute I saw the Beatles on *Ed Sullivan*—and it's true for thousands of us—*there* was a way to do it." The Stella acoustic was replaced with a Kay electric. He found a couple guys in the neighborhood, Richie Henson and Robert Crawford, and they started getting together, identifying one another by the length of their hair. "Wooly Bully" was the first song Petty got on top of. Petty met Dennis Lee at a teen dance, and now they were three guitar players and a drummer. They called themselves the Sundowners. Before they actually made music as a four piece, they were already scheduled to play their first gig, intermission at a dance where a deejay was the main act. They played four instrumentals, including "House of the Rising Sun" and "Walk Don't Run." After they performed, a young man came up to the fourteen-year-old Petty, asked him if his band had ever played a frat gig, then asked if they wanted to. "It never stopped from that moment on," says Petty.

Tom Leadon moved to Gainesville from San Diego in the summer of 1964. His father had landed a teaching job at the University of Florida, an assistant professorship in the university's physics department. With ten kids in the Leadon family, all named after saints, there was a lot of unchecked activity in the home, but they always assembled for dinner. As their mother liked to remind them, they weren't gypsies. But with that many children it was a fine line. While still in San Diego, Mrs. Leadon would pin a name and address onto her son Tom's shirt. When they first arrived in Gainesville, the Leadons rented a place on Twenty-Third Street but moved to 412 Northeast Fifteenth Avenue the following year, where their father bought a plot of land and built a house. Behind them was a park. On the other side of that park was the Petty home.

The Pettys were at 1715 Northeast Sixth Terrace. Gainesville is divided into quadrants, with Main Street the north-south divider and University Avenue bisecting the town east-west. "If you go down Sixth Terrace along the park," explains Tom Leadon, "past Sixteenth Avenue, the Pettys' house is on the right. It's a single story with what they call a 'Florida room,' which was really a porch that was a part of the house, tiled and all. Go up a step and there's a living room with a dining area in it and a little kitchen to the right. Go straight back and there's a hallway, with the parents' bedroom to the left and Tom and Bruce's to the right, a bathroom in between. That's pretty much it."

The neighborhood was largely working class. But, being a college town, there was a mix, even there in the northeast section of town. If Dr. Leadon was a professor at the university, that didn't make them rich, but they were safely in the middle class. The northwest part of town was wealthier. Benmont Tench, his father a judge, lived over there. The southeast was black. The university was the southwest quadrant.

Tom Leadon was already a part of the Gainesville music scene before he met Tom Petty. One of his older brothers, Bernie, could play a good flat-top guitar. Bernie knew and loved country music. But that didn't mean he knew a lot about country *people* or about where that music came from. And neither did his younger brother. That would soon change. Just a few years later, Tom Leadon, with or without his mother's permission, would start making his way across the park to the Pettys' home. He'd even be invited in for dinner, where he would sit quietly, politely, mostly unable to follow the conversation because the accents were too thick. Except for his friend Tom's. "Probably because he watched so much television," Leadon figures. "He just didn't sound like them. I could understand him."

Before the two Toms met, however, the Sundowners got fully under way, with the band members' mothers driving them to gigs. In the room that had once housed the inventory of Petty's Dry Goods, there was now a rehearsal space, with just enough room for a drum kit, a few amps, and a few boys. Kitty and Earl Petty couldn't fail to recognize that their son was up to something. They even checked the band out at the Moose Lodge. They might have been impressed, but not so impressed that they didn't draw the line when the next bad report card came in. "My mother said, 'That's it. You're out of the band,'" Petty remembers. "It killed me, so much so that she couldn't keep it up for more than a week."

The hot group in town at the time was the Continentals, which featured Don Felder and Stephen Stills. When Stills left the group, Bernie Leadon came in. Felder and Leadon had already been playing together, bluegrass stuff. With Stephen Stills gone, Bernie got an electric guitar, and the Continentals were over. The Maundy Quintet was born from the ashes. The group would hit the frat circuit hard and become a celebrated local band, competing against Duane and Gregg Allman's early outfits in a few different battles of the bands. Bernie Leadon would eventually head west and, after playing in the Flying Burrito Brothers with Gram Parsons, join the Eagles, bringing Don Felder in not long after.

Tom Leadon was picking up plenty hanging around the Maundy Quintet whenever he could, going to gigs by age twelve. When a friend brought him by the Petty house so that they could listen to a Sundowners' rehearsal from outside a window, Tom Leadon made indirect but significant contact with the neighbor who would eventually become his bandmate. But their paths remained separate for the time being.

David Mason, Petty's childhood friend, returned to Petty's life as a

Sundowner, but only after playing with Felder in the Continentals—while still in middle school. "It blew our minds that he was in the Continentals," recalls Petty. "But David Mason was that good." When Petty called him to come play in the Sundowners, Mason went ahead and checked it out. "I was a little bit underwhelmed. In the Continentals I was around a lot of older guys," says Mason, "learning a lot real quickly. This was different. Pretty soon I left the Sundowners and joined one of the college bands."

They were kids. But the ones who could play would often mix with an older crowd. There was no distinction between varsity and junior varsity—strict divisions that applied elsewhere often didn't in the world of local bands. For all of them, there was a perceived fluidity between what they saw on television, the Stones, Beatles, Animals, Dave Clark Five, what they heard on WGGG, and what they themselves played in venues like the Place and the Moose Club. They were a part of something much larger, even if their heroes seemed as distant as myth. Sixties rock and roll grew up furiously, without a whole lot of adult oversight or involvement. It was a true teenage movement. "There was a lot of stuff aimed at young kids," explains Charles Ramirez, who was one of those teenagers and would later promote shows for Petty's bands. "It really started to hit me when I was in eighth grade and saw Duane and Gregg Allman in the Allman Joys at the local American Legion hall."

With matching suits, ruffled shirts, and Petty singing lead, the Sundowners played every weekend. Initially, Kitty Petty didn't believe her son when he claimed that the money on his bureau was from playing shows. He was only fourteen and fifteen while in the Sundowners. Before that, she'd sneak him some money when he needed it, behind Earl's back. Now he was making his own cash, and soon enough would be working at Lipham Music. From the parental perspective, it was a question of "How could it last?" From the teenager's perspective, it was simply a matter of making sure it did.

"The first time you count four and, suddenly, rock and roll is playing—it's bigger than life itself," says Petty describing his first shows. "It was the greatest moment in my experience, really. I couldn't believe it was happening, that we were making music. No one can understand what a blast to the moon that is unless they've done it. Once we got going, we covered

James Brown's *Live at the Apollo*, Animals hits, Paul Revere and the Raiders. It was a great period." Playing the songs meant getting inside them. Even that early, Petty could find clues about what made a song work, what made one better than the next. He was quietly taking it all in, no aspirations beyond the next gig, learning to play bass, learning to sing. The fragility of what he'd found, however, its fleeting nature, hadn't yet dawned on him.

"We did these gigs called 'socials,' which were these little gatherings hosted by fraternities," says Petty. "You could do one of those around six p.m., then go play a dance somewhere. So we had a social and a dance one Friday night, and Dennis Lee, the drummer, is yelling at me as we load gear out of my house. He was a bossy guy, ordering me around. Earl leans out the window, says to me, 'Don't take that shit from him. You don't have to be talked to like that.' I was like, 'Yeah, I know.' We got to the gig, and it keeps going. Dennis is just on my ass, laying down the law. And he hit my rage button. I said, 'Give me any more shit, and I'm going to leave.' He says, 'I'd like to see that happen. I'd kick your ass.' So I just turned to one of my buddies who was with me, told him to help me load my gear out. This is the way you are when you're fifteen. I get my amp and stuff loaded out, turn around, there's a fist in my face. My own drummer beat the living shit out of me. Beat me bad. The frat guys just stood around in a circle, cheering it on. I remember my mother crying all night because I was so fucked up. That was kind of the end of me working with Dennis Lee." As fast as he was in a band, Petty was out of one. But knowing there was conflict with Lee, he was out ahead of this one. Maybe he was learning to take care of himself.

It was 1966 when the Epics asked Petty to join their group. Ricky Rucker, Rodney Rucker, and Dickie Underwood liked enough of what they saw in Petty and wanted him to come in as their singer. Not that the audition went particularly well. But they'd just canned their first singer, Herbie Bohannon, so the timing was good. "I remember sitting in their living room, having to sing a couple songs for them," Petty says. "I did 'Little Black Egg' by the Nightcrawlers. Rodney responded by saying, 'That's the worst singing I've ever heard.'" Ricky Rucker convinced his brother to give the singer another chance, however, and by the audition's end Petty was asked to do a gig with the band. The trouble between Petty and Dennis Lee eventually made the Epics look like a solution, if initially it was little more than what Petty calls "a busman's holiday." By the end of Petty's first show as an Epic, he'd found himself setting his bass aside and fronting a band. "It was at Graham Hall, one of the university's dormitories," recalls Dickie Underwood. "Petty was like a wild man, all over the stage. That was probably the first time he got to be the front guy. And he loved it. And so did the people watching us. We all said, 'This guy is good.' So we told him that he'd have a lot more fun with us than he would with the Sundowners. That was our argument."

The bass player the Epics had been working with, an "older guy" in his twenties, was let go. Though Petty remembers the trial gig being not at Graham Hall but one of the rougher places the Epics favored, after that first show he was out of the Sundowners and into the Epics, the new bass player, sharing lead vocals with Rodney Rucker. What really interested Petty, however, was the fact that the Ruckers had gigs booked. But he was made to realize that not all gigs are equal. "The Sundowners played more posh places than the Epics," Petty explains. "Nice teen clubs and moose halls. The Epics would just play down and dirty fucking places, a whole circuit of hick towns."

"Dickie and I would ride around and find these little places to rent, little halls," says Ricky Rucker. "We found this one hole in the wall, the Orange Lake Civic Center, that we could get for like five dollars. We'd make posters and put them up. We'd sell Cokes at the show. We were good at getting gigs. When Petty joined, he was hanging around Tommy Leadon—I guess they met through Lipham's Music—and I saw that Tommy Leadon was better on guitar than I was. I thought, 'We could use this guy.'" The lineup solidified. Tom Petty and Tom Leadon were now in a band together. Rodney Rucker, not happily, was moved off guitar, becoming the Epics' primary lead singer. They covered songs by the Rascals, the Stones. Leadon would slow down 45s to figure out the chord changes and solos. They had what Ricky Rucker calls a "primitive" sound.

■

By that time, Earl Petty had started to make it his business to try talking his son out of doing the music thing. But he couldn't help himself: he did like the Ruckers and Dickie Underwood. Earl would appear out back when they were around. And they liked him too. "He approved of it when Petty started hanging around us," Dickie Underwood insists, "because we liked to hunt and fish, and he was an old redneck from Marion County, out in the woods." Ricky Rucker agrees: "He was like all the older men we ever knew, my brother and I and Dickie, so we got a kick out of him." Tom Leadon puts it somewhat differently: "Dickie said to me several times, 'Well, Mr. Petty likes us because we're normal.'"

The Ruckers didn't just like hunting and fishing; they liked drinking and chasing girls. A lot. "We always thought, 'This is the ultimate party,'" Ricky Rucker explains. "It was all about meeting girls and going crazy, doing crazy things. Not jail-type things, but crazy. Tommy was all for having fun, but he had a whole thing about the music. He really wanted to play music." The Ruckers and Underwood approved of that focus, as long as the music didn't get in the way of being in a band.

Leadon and Petty began to distinguish themselves, shape their own views of how much time and energy a group should put into getting their show right. When Tampa's Tropics, the band with whom Charlie Souza played, got a strobe light and raised their performances a notch with its effect, the Ruckers wanted one for the Epics. But that wasn't all the Tropics did: they also spent time perfecting their dance steps, learning new covers, writing and arranging a few originals. Their show even had a James Brown portion that didn't just feature Brown's hits. It included the "cape routine" for which Brown was known. They had their theater down. The Tropics made it onto *American Bandstand* and were buying houses and cars with gig money. As teenagers. The Ruckers and Dickie Underwood didn't put that whole picture together in the way Petty and Leadon did. "The biggest problem we had with Tom Leadon," Dickie Underwood insists, "was that he took things way too seriously sometimes."

The age difference between Petty, the even younger Leadon, and the rest of the band was defining. The two younger members sometimes felt like foot soldiers to the Ruckers. "A means to an end" is how Petty describes their role. At a 1967 gig at the Live Oak Civic Center, the Ruckers brought Don Felder along. "Felder had been hanging around the Ruckers for a while," explains Petty. "I remember there were poker games and drinking and girls and all that. A moving party. Tommy [Leadon] and I were second-class citizens. I mean, even in Felder's book—how many years later?—he calls the Epics the Rucker Brothers Band. The Rucker Brothers Band?"

At the Live Oak Civic Center, Felder started dancing, slow, with a local girl. If Gainesville was something of a safe haven for long-haired musicians, outside of the town you were back in Florida. Felder was forgetting this. While the Epics were playing, Felder made a move and went outside with the girl. Before long, her boyfriend, drunk, became aware of the situation and set out to fix things in the old way. Felder describes himself at the time as being "one hundred and twenty-five pounds soaking wet," the girl's boyfriend as "a linebacker." The fight was only just beginning when Felder got his arm wrenched out of its socket. In a lot of pain, he signaled the Ruckers, who were in the middle of a song.

"I saw it from the stage," Petty explains. "This guy starts mixing it up with Felder. And a circle forms around the fight. Rodney Rucker, our lead singer, leaps off the stage and straight into the middle of it. Then, of course, the fight grows. So Rick Rucker puts his guitar down, gets off the stage and into the middle of it, leaving three of us up there playing music. The last straw, to me, was when our drummer got up and left the stage to get in it. That pretty much stopped the music. And when you stop the music, you've really got problems.

"Almost my whole band was in this fight, and the odds didn't look good. Leadon and I, as fast as we could, had to start getting our gear packed up. And somehow we got it—and the rest of the band—into the car, with guys throwing shit at us as we pull away. It was scary. A couple cars followed us out of town. For me and for Tommy, it was kind of a turning point, I guess. We realized that these guys are just not with the same program we are." Felder went away with a shoulder that still dislocates today. Where was he when the fight really got going? "I was cowering in the corner."

Adventures of that kind brought Petty and Leadon closer. They often met in the park between their houses to work out harmonies. If any one thing seemed to separate the decent bands from the really good ones, it was harmony singing. The two teenagers found they had a good vocal blend and worked to make it better still. By their last years at Gainesville High, Petty and his friend Mike Nixon would be smoking dope before the start of school and leaving together not long after homeroom, sometimes bringing Leadon along, going off to play music or listen to it or to hang out with other musicians. Leadon's and Petty's shared goal was in place early: to be in with a group of guys who all wanted it as much as they did. When Petty left the Epics for the first time, it was the only time he gave up, frustrated, on that ambition to find a band that shared their view of the world and their ideas for what could be done with it.

4

SALESMEN

What really happened was this: we allowed the salesman into the sanctity of the home.

—Russell Banks

"The doorbell rang, and my father opened it," Petty explains. **"Letting this guy in** who had something to sell him. This kind of shit actually went on in our home." The man who stood there, smiling and extending his hand to Earl, was dressed in a black suit, white shirt, and tie. He could have been selling anything, from religion to toilet seats. In this case, he was peddling education, art school. And for whatever reason, the whole family was home to watch Earl welcome the man into the small living room.

Tom wasn't usually around when the others were. Especially since he'd finished high school. He came in late, woke up late, left the house when everyone else was into their own things. But that day they were all there, and it was obvious that Earl didn't see the salesman as a bother so much as a kindred spirit, as if they knew each other on the basis of a shared vocation. "He brought this guy in like they were old friends or something," Petty remembers. "My dad points to a chair, welcomes his guest to sit, and takes a place opposite him." As Earl settled in for the pitch, Kitty offered the man something to drink.

The salesman handed Earl, not his son, a brochure. The school was in Tampa. Making some reasonable assumptions about his audience, the visitor insisted that this kind of art school wasn't the territory of the modern artists Earl might have seen featured in the *Saturday Evening Post*, the paint-splattering clowns up in New York City. This was a practical education, geared toward young people who wanted to get into the advertising field. There was a lot of money there, the salesman explained. "If there was one thing my dad thought I could do—and it was *one* thing—it was draw," says Petty. "He thought I was good with a pencil." Earl had seen a horse his son had sketched. He was surprised that it looked like a horse.

Likely the salesman had a good feeling. The head of the household, as he several times referred to Earl, had invited him in. The head of the household's wife had offered him something to drink. If he could get that far, he was quite possibly in the game. Those were good days in the salesman's line of work. The Vietnam War was fantastic for business. You could get school records, in this case Gainesville High's, find out which families had a recent graduate who might be affected by the draft. Then it was a matter of knocking on some doors and doing your thing. You wouldn't even have to mention the war, conscription, or any of that. You'd be selling deferment as much as higher education, but no one needed to talk about it that way.

"I wasn't putting up any resistance, and we were talking about school," Petty laughs. "So I think everyone was a bit confused by that." The Pettys didn't know a lot about their son's girlfriend at the time, a young woman named Jan Mathews whom Tom had met at an Epics gig in Dunnellon. "She was really my first real girlfriend," Petty says. "I wouldn't say we were in love. We hung around a lot. She was a friend. My parents didn't know much about her. I kept the two sides of life separate, even then." The Pettys certainly didn't get that Jan lived in the vicinity of the Tampa art school. They also didn't know that, for the last time in his life, Tom was ready to see how it would go *not* being in a band. The Epics had worn him out. Sitting in the living room that day in Gainesville, listening as his father talked with the salesman, Petty thought that Tampa sounded like a solution to a host of problems.

"I took the Greyhound down to Tampa," recalls Petty. "And when I got there, they put me up in this hotel the school was using as a dorm. The whole thing was just a little off. I got a roommate, this overweight kid, and we went record shopping together. I don't remember what I got, but he picked up a Ventures record, which I thought was a little strange. I think it was 1969, you know? Not exactly a Ventures moment." Once situated, what his teachers at Gainesville High said about him remained true: Thomas Petty didn't "apply himself." He failed to show up for a single class, wouldn't know what the classrooms looked like or where exactly they were. He got by for a time, spending his days at the area's beaches, hanging out in his room, or, occasionally, going to the library to read. But as far as school attendance records went, he didn't exist.

The situation would quickly catch up with him. But not before he used the school's job placement team to find work as a dishwasher at a barbecue restaurant in town. It was only open for lunch. On Petty's first day, the owner watched from across the kitchen as his new employee stood, facing his first stack of greasy barbecue trays, unsure how to proceed. "I was clueless," Petty says. "I'd gotten that far without picking up on some of the basics." After an hour, the owner put the new guy on the meat-scraping detail. It didn't require a lot of expertise. After long hours of smoking the meat, it came off the bone easily. Likely the owner would have admitted that it wasn't a job for anyone with a weak stomach, but he was surprised when Petty threw up on the floor in the back. "The owner watched this," Petty recalls. "And he says, 'Okay, he's not in the meat department.'" It was down to sweeping and mopping the place out after closing. That lasted for almost two weeks. Then Petty just stopped going. The school was onto him by that time, anyway.

The administrators couldn't grasp why someone would pay for school but never go to a class. Petty had no answer for them. But Jan Mathews was the kind of girl rock and rollers know how to find. She bailed him out, got him a job at her father's funeral home in St. Petersburg. She had to beg her father to make the hire. With a little additional pressure from his wife, the reluctant funeral director gave in. He didn't like his daughter's boyfriend, but he knew what he had to do to keep peace in his home. Petty lived out back, away from the main part of the funeral home, over the garage where the limos were kept. A few other men bunked there with him. Older guys. One of them was a junior manager by the name of Kermit, who had ambitions to become a funeral director. The other employees didn't share Kermit's sense for the sacred nature of their work. They would hide bodies on Kermit, do things with them that would have made loved ones uneasy. In his first few days, Petty watched as a couple of men put a monster mask on one of the bodies, pulled the sheet back over the corpse, and told Kermit to take a look, that this was the worst case of skin cancer they'd ever seen.

Petty cleaned the cars, kept track of the flowers that arrived for the more lavish funeral services—he took pictures of each bouquet, compiling photo albums of floral arrangements for the families of the deceased—and once went on a ride to get a body. He had his guitar but little luck finding places where no one would catch him playing. He had his girlfriend, but he couldn't get to her very easily, since she was a few miles up the road at her family's home.

"Then I was caught sneaking into their house for a little midnight love," he says. "I'd walked all the way there, not that it was unusual for a guy my age looking for that kind of thing. But I was busted there in her bed. And it scared me so bad, I ran out the front door, jumped in the old man's Lincoln Continental, and drove off. Her father's car, for Christ's sake. It had the keys in it, for whatever reason." Petty drove far enough down St. Petersburg's suburban streets, back toward the funeral home, to realize he had no place to go. When he returned, he went into the house. "This guy couldn't even look at me," Petty remembers. "I don't know what went down while I was gone, but he was obviously afraid to fire me because of his daughter. I just thought, 'This is a bad situation for everyone, and I don't feel good about being somewhere I shouldn't be.'"

The Epics weren't happy when Petty left for Tampa. But no one in the band planned on stopping what they were doing simply because they'd lost a bass player. All the local groups had seen members come and go. Keeping a band intact was nothing anyone in town was particularly good at. Musicians dropped out along the way and always would. You'd lose one, put up an ad at Lipham's, and hope to get another.

Tom Leadon brought Buzzy Mayhew in as Petty's replacement on bass. Buzzy was a few years older than Leadon, a friend of his older brother Bernie's from the Army Reserves and an employee at Lipham Music, alongside Rodney Rucker. The group put Mayhew on a crash course, teaching him the Epics set list. The rehearsals took place at the church downtown to which the band had relocated. It was an old stone building with some unused space that came their way through a member of the Jaycees who had seen the band and liked them.

Leadon remembers the band doing almost ten rehearsals with Mayhew.

It was a lot in a short time. They were getting ready for a gig in Sebring that Rodney Rucker had lined up. By all accounts, Rodney Rucker made every effort to answer the phones at Lipham's, because when someone called asking about a local band to hire, the Epics would have another gig booked. Old Mr. Lipham and his son Buster never seemed to catch on to Rodney's gifts as an agent. Or didn't care.

The Epics had played in Sebring before and gone over very well. They were favorites and planned to maintain that status. Ricky and Tom Leadon were singing harmonies behind Rodney. Mayhew had done well enough in the rehearsals. The feeling was good as they took to the stage, ready to carry the Epics into their next chapter. And then Mayhew seemed to forget everything he learned in rehearsal. He went cold.

Petty didn't look up Leadon or the Ruckers straight away when he returned from Tampa. Instead, he found his old friend Mike Nixon and, for the first time, dropped acid. In the early hours of their trip, Nixon and Petty were in a friend's apartment when they heard people at the door. Among the arrivals was the young woman who had broken Petty's heart in junior high school, Cindy, whom he'd never stopped thinking about. Seeing his hair, which he'd grown out since high school, she told him how much she liked it. It went from there. "It was greater than great," Petty remembers. "A huge night for me." It was as though he was realizing the very connection that he'd most longed for. This wasn't like what he had with his girlfriends. The small group stayed around the apartment, smoking cigarettes on the roof outside the kitchen window, before going out to where the interstate was being constructed, laughing and trying to skip stones on the water below the overpass where they stood.

Though LSD can't promise certain results, it does sometimes deliver epiphanies, most of them too fragile to make it to morning. Petty had one. As their small group made their way around town, one apartment to another, in the kitchen of another friend they'd met up with, Petty saw it clearly: he was nothing and would be nothing if he wasn't in a rock-and-roll band. It all seemed to come together in his head. It was as good a feeling as he'd ever known. But by morning, the Cindy part of it was gone. "She let me know it was just for that night," Petty says. "And it scarred my brain all over again. In a matter of hours, I'd let myself believe another story, the one I'd wanted to believe for a long time. I only saw her a few times after that. But finally, she took me into a room at someone's place and said, 'You keep trying, but you-and-me isn't going to happen.' When I wrote 'Even the Losers' years later, that night came back. I obsessed over her so much. She's probably in a lot of songs." The band part of the epiphany, however, lasted beyond morning.

When Rodney Rucker called a few days later, asking Petty if he'd reconsider joining the Epics—"I think Rodney basically begged him to come back," says Leadon—Petty knew exactly what he needed to say. He was back in the band, and he'd do everything he could to never be without one again.

As early as fourteen, Petty understood that people treated you differently when you showed up with a guitar and three other guys. It gave a kid an identity. It was even better if you rehearsed. Fresh from Tampa, still feeling the weight of insight after the drugs had worn off, Petty was in a better place, though without any more to show for it than he had prior to leaving.

By that time, Gainesville had continued to evolve as one of the country's little recognized but important rock-and-roll towns. There as elsewhere, a collision of elements made the last years of the sixties something unplanned, unrepeatable, and almost perfect. Radios played R&B and soul music mixed with pop mixed with rock and roll, beautiful stuff that was coming on too fast to be categorized by color or sound. By virtue of the fact that no one yet knew exactly what they were doing, music was at its freshest and most inventive. In Gainesville, new bands were coming into being all the time, even if some of them, like mayflies, lived for little more than a day.

Petty might not yet have been bold enough to imagine it for himself, but he knew that because of rock and roll, some locals—otherwise shiftless southern kids, and more than occasionally Gainesville's problem—were going to put together lives that weren't based on catching catfish, trapping squirrels, working in the town's turpentine factory, or gutting pigs in the local slaughterhouses. The feeling that universities were supposed to give, that feeling of possibility and promise, these kids got from playing in bands.

By the time he returned from Tampa, there were groups that were actually making records. A few locals left town, headed west to Los Angeles. Bernie Leadon quit the Maundy Quintet, arguably the best of Gainesville's local bands, so that he could go after more. Not much later, he appeared on *The Glen Campbell Show*. Then he joined the Flying Burrito Brothers, with a couple guys from the Byrds. The Allman Brothers, the former Allman Joys from down the road in Daytona Beach, would show up to a Gainesville battle of the bands hosted by Lipham Music, just before they blew up as a national act. Things were happening. And in Petty, too, there was a shift. Another foreign substance entered his system. Ambition.

5

MUD

Hippies? Why, I'm the original.
—Jerry Lee Lewis

The twin smells of dirty barbecue platters and embalming fluids had done their work on Tom Petty, proof enough that rock and roll was better than the alternatives. Ricky and Rodney Rucker had rented a duplex apartment in North Gainesville, attaching themselves to some neighbors, younger, college-age women who helped keep the party going. Soon enough, Petty moved in, too. He was, again, out of the house for the moment.

By the summer of 1969, the Epics had a residency at Trader Tom's, considered the best club in town after Dub's Steer Room. In Tom Leadon's view, it was the most productive time for that version of the band. They were either playing or rehearsing. Their show was at its tightest. But they were also no longer the Epics. The band had decided on a new name: Mudcrutch. "What happened to the Epics?" Ricky Rucker says. "That name had stopped working."

The Beatles had changed American life, but it wasn't simply the legendary "sixties" from there on out. For rock-and-roll bands, another leap, almost as significant if less obsessively celebrated, came in the form of Jimi Hendrix and Cream. No longer would Florida groups like the Epics look to the Tropics and the Nation Rockin' Shadows for inspiration. No more would bands wear suit and tie. No more would they be practicing dance steps. Even the hipper shirts with puffy white sleeves that Dickie

Underwood's grandmother had sewn for the members of the Epics, worn with matching white pants, even those wouldn't survive the shift. Matching suits, no matter how many beads you draped over them, were still uniforms. And it wasn't the moment for uniforms.

A lot of the major Florida groups didn't manage the transition well. Some disbanded entirely. The Tropics got to New York but found themselves to be relics of another time. They heard "Purple Haze" on a jukebox at the Greasy Spoon coffee shop in Greenwich Village, crossed paths with the Doors, had an opening act named Tiny Tim, and saw Frank Zappa and the Mothers of Invention perform. In the midst of all that, they came onstage in their band outfits and did their choreography. "I couldn't wait to get back home," Charlie Souza says. "Where I still had a chance at being cool."

Clothes, performance styles, language, sex—all contributed to the cultural leap that would come to be called the "sixties." But to live through it was to experience a series of departures, each one defining itself against whatever came before. As a category, "cool" was redefining itself so regularly that some people, like Souza, felt they weren't quite keeping up. Some got so high it wasn't an issue. Jeff Beck saw Jimi Hendrix and figured it was time to become a licensed plumber. For a while there, the American teenager could still settle into the parents' world at the end of the day, if smirking all the while. Now teen culture was going to rip off its clothes and walk naked through the center of town. No longer were young people the children of Dick Clark, with a little Alfred E. Neuman thrown in. Abbie Hoffman and Timothy Leary were the chaperones. By the decade's end, those bands in matching suits were as much a thing *not to be* as any Ozzie Nelson sitting in his upholstered chair, nodding out over the evening paper. But there were still starts and stops. Hendrix had to open for the Monkees before he could get on with things. In Gainesville, where local bands grappled with the unchanging reality of having to land the next gig, things played out with a degree of subtlety. But in retrospect, this was the moment in which Tom Petty could at last start becoming Tom Petty.

Before they took on the name Mudcrutch, the Epics had always lifted their material from records. That's what bands did. Not just the songs, the recordings. The closer you could get to the record, the better. Same arrangement, same key, same guitar solos. When Rodney Rucker was singing out of his vocal range, no one even thought to transpose the music. If the record was in G, so was the Epics' version. Rucker would have to meet them there. When they played the frat houses, they were, in Petty's words, "just a big jukebox for a drunken crowd." The teen clubs might have had better listeners, but the audiences were still looking to hear the records they knew. When the Epics got their first opportunity to record at a studio, that was the spirit they captured. They covered Buffalo Springfield's "On the Way Home" and, less likely, Cat Mother and the All Night Newsboys medley of fifties rock and roll, including "Sweet Little Sixteen," "Party Doll," "Chantilly Lace," and far too many more. Everybody in the band sang. Petty remembers being on amphetamines, "prescribed" to him by one of the Ruckers' neighbors because Petty was short on sleep. He also remembers that they wouldn't have gotten into a studio at all if they hadn't, for a short time, found a manager, a kid who got it into his head that handling a rock-and-roll band might be fun, and if the Ruckers hadn't leaned on that kid to buy them some studio time.

The new manager was watching the clock for the whole two hours, not so happy with the reality of the job. But the Epics were thrilled. Petty had never heard his bass played direct through a mixing board to tape. It was like hearing for the first time what a bass should sound like. "I loved it. I'm sure the drugs helped, but it sounded so good." The recording captured a fleeting moment. No one would listen to it and think that there was some special talent in there. No one saw the band that way. No one saw Petty that way, either. As Jeff Jourard put it, "I wouldn't have put my money on him. Not then."

■

Jim Lenahan had known Petty for several years, first through school, where they were in homeroom together and regularly kicked out for having long hair. Lenahan had joined the Sundowners one summer in 1965, when the band was playing Fridays and Saturdays at the Keystone Heights Pier and Lenahan's group, the Certain Amount, had lost a few members to summer activities. When Rodney Rucker finally left the Epics, and the group needed a lead singer, it was Lenahan who came in. He would be a part of Tom Petty's world for the next forty-five years.

Jim Lenahan's mother was a single parent, earning a living as a teacher.

"A widowed schoolteacher, that's right," Lenahan laughs, "and we still had more money than the Petty family. As blue collar as you can get." At five years old, he was singing on the radio. His aunt hosted the *Youth Variety Hour*, and he'd join her every Saturday until he finally couldn't tear himself away from the cartoons. His material included "Freight Train" and "Cry Me a River," but Elvis Presley covers like "Hound Dog" and "Heartbreak Hotel" were also a regular part of the show. Along with the other performers from the variety hour, he traveled around doing performances at Moose Lodges. From there it was the marching band in junior high school, drums in a surf band, and, finally, the Beatles hitting, and all of that coming together. Within a short time, he was deep in the same local scene that produced Petty and Leadon.

Lenahan knew the Ruckers, ran into them regularly and had once admonished Rodney, suggesting he make the choice between hunting and playing in the Epics. "Hunting, no problem," Lenahan says. "He didn't have to think twice about that one." The truth was, after Rodney Rucker had been moved off the guitar into the front man position, he'd never felt quite right. "I don't think he liked that he was just the singer," explains Dickie Underwood. "His guitar was like his baby blanket. He could hide behind it. We'd taken that away." And it was dove-hunting season.

By Lenahan's arrival, the Epics had become Mudcrutch. The only person who thinks maybe Tom Petty *didn't* come up with the new name is Tom Petty. No one is fighting for credit. But Mudcrutch was selected, and it stuck. As with so many names, its strangeness would lift soon enough, becoming more like something imposed by nature. One of the Ruckers painted "Mudcrutch" on the side of his van, "in the shape of a large cock," as Petty recalls. If only for a few weeks, with the band still a four piece, Petty sang lead. But that was temporary.

Lenahan was at a party soon after Rodney Rucker left the Epics and ran into Rodney's brother, Ricky. "Ricky was a huge guy, and he was real drunk that night," says Lenahan. "He needed a singer. He cornered me and said, 'Hey, you just joined our band. You don't like it, I'll kick your ass.' I was like, 'Okay.' That's how I got into that band." With Lenahan on vocals, Ricky Rucker and Tom Leadon on guitars, Petty on bass, and Underwood on drums, a new chapter had begun. A very short new chapter. Underwood got called up and would be heading to Vietnam. With his best friend leaving for the war, Ricky Rucker got as philosophical about it all as he had been about anything up to that point in his life. "I figured I'd better find something to do to make a living." The newly christened Mudcrutch was a three piece. They didn't even get the van with the cock on the side.

Mudcrutch could play coffeehouses as a trio. And they did some of that. But it wasn't going to make them enough money to get by. The other major concern was the draft, which they hoped to avoid. The Ruckers had faked the hearing test and were ready to teach others how to accomplish that. Not everyone took the lessons. Petty enrolled in Santa Fe Junior College there in town, which gave him shelter from being drafted. But this school experience was no different than any other. It didn't last more than a matter of weeks. He certainly wasn't inspiring anyone to invest further in his education. That would be it. Petty was back in the family home but not in school and ripe for conscription. Earl was starting to ask for some food money. At the least, Petty needed to find work.

Word was out among the locals that you could go get a job at the university's grounds department. Petty and Tom Leadon went down to apply. "It was a dollar twenty-five an hour, a really bad wage, but it was an okay job," Petty explains. "I just changed the screens on a water purification system they'd set up in Lake Alice. They were dredging the lake, trying to get all of the water hyacinths out so there would be more oxygen in the water, which was filled with alligators, all kinds of wildlife. I had a few adventures with snakes out there." Left by himself, he didn't have much to do once the screens were replaced. He'd find a nice spot to sit and wait for the truck to pick him up. All of that went on for a while, until the supervisor saw Petty resting in the sun, collecting a wage.

"Basically all I did was sit around," he says. "But one day I'm there on the grass, waiting for the truck, and they pull up and this guy goes ape shit on me, gets really mad. He starts yelling. It just hadn't occurred to me that I should make a show of it. I'd done the work. But after that, they didn't want me around anymore. The problem was, you couldn't just fire someone. You had to have good reason. The university had its policies. So, from then on, the idea was that they'd *make* me quit." When Petty came back the next day, he was thrown in with another group, what one of the other workers called "a truck full of retards." He was the only one among his new team who hadn't come in from the nearby mental health facility. But if they thought that would break Petty, they had the wrong guy. You could argue that he'd been in rock-and-roll bands long enough already to withstand most any company.

"I didn't mind," Petty insists. "It could have been worse. I could have been on a truck full of rednecks that wanted to kill me for having long hair. But, then, after they saw that the strategy wasn't working, they had me picking up rocks, gave me a canvas bag and told me to get to work. I was dragging this bag of rocks, without any point to it. The foreman was a hellacious redneck who couldn't read—had to ask what it said on cans of paint—and he just hated me. When I asked why I was dragging these rocks around, he just said, 'Shut up and do what I tell you.' I finally went, 'Okay, you win. I quit.'"

The next job Petty got through the city employment office. Like some strange extension of his time in the funeral business, he was on the grounds crew of a local graveyard. Some among his circle started calling him "walking death." On a few occasions, he helped to dig a grave, but mostly it was heavy labor in high heat, mowing lawns, keeping the trees and bushes trimmed and neat. He couldn't avoid breaking into a sweat, which might have been fine onstage but wasn't anything he wanted to do with a rake in his hand. There was no way it was going to last. That was the last straight job he held. Fired, again.

■

Despite how long Petty, Leadon, and Lenahan had been playing in bands and how well they were known on the scene, Mudcrutch couldn't find the players to complete its lineup. "We were asking everybody, and no one was interested," Tom Leadon says.

"There wasn't an endless supply of people, of musicians that wanted to dedicate their lives to being in a band," Petty explains. "If you found somebody willing to do that, that was interesting. And the really good players always had something going on. Like the Maundy Quintet guys, Don Felder and Bernie Leadon. Then Bernie was gone, out in California and in the Flying Burrito Brothers, making records. And Felder had Flow, and they got a record deal. The only way to get there was to find guys who were ready to give one hundred percent. And we just weren't finding them."

But it wasn't just a matter of identifying players who could make the commitment. Mudcrutch also needed musicians who were ready to play in a band that performed some of its own material. They'd have to come up with parts rather than copy records. Petty had started to write in earnest. Several years later, when the Heartbreakers had their first song on the charts, Petty would recall in interviews how he took note of what Don Felder had started doing with his group Flow. Flow's lead singer was John Winter, from an Ocala band called the Incidentals and someone Petty already admired. "They did a lot of Zombies, which I loved, but could do the R&B thing, too, handle Otis Redding covers," recalls Petty. "I remember Felix Cavaliere embraced John Winter at one point. But I saw Winter play with Felder at some hippie house party, and it blew my mind how good they were. And no more covers. Everything was original. I talked to Don after, and he said, 'We're not going to get anywhere if we don't get record deals, and we're not going to get record deals playing other people's hits all the time.' It stuck with me. I'd started to write songs early on, but the bands I was in played covers. It just didn't occur to us to do otherwise." Petty's writing was intermittent, done for no one but himself. As a practice, it was not yet the personal sanctuary it would become. What Felder was pointing to, however, was the practical value of having original material.

Jim Lenahan proved a good audience for Petty's early songs. "There were great bands, like Ron and the Starfires, great bands with great singers," Lenahan says. "But they just didn't see the point in writing their own songs. And they never went anywhere. Part of the reason I wanted to be in Mudcrutch was because I knew Petty was writing songs. And I thought they were good songs." Lenahan also had a car, and Petty didn't. It put them in a lot of contact. Petty didn't so much know it, but he needed someone to listen. On your own, it was never easy to gauge what you had. Lenahan listened and didn't tell Petty to stop.

With no job and without the Ruckers' apartment as a place to go since the brothers had left the band, Petty was back to sleeping in the bunk bed at his parents' house. Years earlier, he and Bruce Petty took turns sitting on the hallway kerosene heater before school. It got cold in the North Florida winters. That's where they'd eat their breakfast. Now, with Tom out of school and out of work, Bruce Petty had his brother back again. But they didn't see each other in the hallway. Tom slept late, came in late. It wasn't much more than a bed that he needed. But, depending on what kind of place his girlfriends had and how things were going with those girlfriends, it was important backup.

The members of Mudcrutch wouldn't find out until years later that Buster Lipham, Petty's former boss at Lipham Music, had discouraged more than a few musicians from answering the ad Mudcrutch had posted at the store. Randall Marsh was one of them. When he saw "drummer wanted," he ran it past the store manager. Buster told Randall that he shouldn't get involved, that those guys weren't going anywhere. For whatever reason, Randall didn't listen. When Randall Marsh walked into the Mudcrutch world, he came with a rehearsal spot, a rented farmhouse where he lived with a few other guys. That farmhouse gave Petty a place to work with the band but also a place to hide out.

No time was wasted—Mudcrutch was setting up the gear at Marsh's farm a mile outside of town the night after his audition, ready to rehearse, when they heard one of Marsh's roommates running scales in the next room. "We looked at Randall," says Lenahan, "and said, 'Tell him to come out. Let's hear him.' So Mike Campbell comes out with the worst guitar I have ever seen in my life. It looked like it had been cut out of a door. He was super skinny, just looked unhealthy. He plugged into Leadon's amp. We asked if he could play 'Johnny B. Goode.' He ripped into that opening, and our jaws dropped. By the end of the song, we said, 'You're in our band now.' He said, 'No, I'm in school.' But Petty had a powerful gift when it came to fixing problems like that." It was, in Petty's words, "an amazing stroke of good luck and fate." They were a five piece again.

The new Mudcrutch started playing gigs right away. After one of those early shows, the band was packing up their gear when Amy Gunderson, a girl Petty dated on and off, rushed in to tell Petty about a car accident in which his family had been involved. "Someone went to Amy, and she found me, told me, 'You gotta go home,'" remembers Petty. "I think we were playing at the American Legion Hall." He let the others finish with the gear and got Amy to drive him to the house.

Bruce Petty had been sleeping in the backseat of the car when it happened. Earl was driving. It was afternoon, but Earl had already been drinking—though his family says not a lot. Families have a way of tidying up the place before guests arrive. Kitty Petty was in the front seat beside her husband, not happy about him getting into the booze that early in the day. They were driving over the crest of a hill when they rear-ended a car that had stopped in the middle of the road. You could argue that—no matter the drink—this wasn't Earl's fault. And they did.

Bruce's body hit the seat in front of him so hard that the frame beneath the vinyl buckled into a U-shape. Everyone was knocked out cold by the impact. After the crash and the moment of stillness that followed, Bruce Petty was the first to come to. He looked around, at first thinking his parents, unconscious, their heads bloodied, were dead. A couple of bottles had rolled out from under the front seat, and he instinctively threw them into the woods. The police came, and an ambulance was there not long after.

The rescue team got Earl and Kitty into the ambulance, which quickly pulled away. After that, the few people who had stopped at the scene of the accident also left. Then the police. Their report said nothing about the driver's condition. Neither did it mention that, with everyone else gone from the scene of the accident, Bruce Petty was still there, apparently forgotten. He stood there for a few minutes before a stranger pulled up. Seeing a kid standing around a wrecked car, the driver asked Bruce if he was okay. That was how he got home.

By the time the eldest Petty boy got to the house, Bruce was home, and his parents had already been released from the hospital. "I went in, and I don't know how much information I picked up walking across the front room," Petty recalls, "but I said I wanted to see my mother right away. My grandmother was there, and she said, 'This is really bad. I don't know if you should go in to see her.' But I said, 'Look, I'm going in.' And I did, and it was devastating. I came out and said, 'Why isn't she in the hospital? This doesn't look right to me.' My grandmother said that the hospital had sent her home, that the doctor would see her tomorrow. My dad had been in the crash, of course. They were coming back from a fishing trip. He had a cut on his forehead, was just kind of zoned out, not saying anything. My grandmother, who hated him, was like, 'Look at him. He's acting like something happened to *him*.' I just thought, 'This is fucked.'"

After the accident, Kitty Petty's health further declined. Between the cancer and the epilepsy, she had already lived too much time behind a closed door. But the accident took her deeper into her bedroom. "My mother was never herself again," Petty says. "I was losing her, and it was awful. I was internalizing it, trying to deal, at least the best way I could. I knew

I had to just keep pushing ahead, get more and more independent. It was like I really realized then that, you know, 'I'm going to have to look after myself, because there's nobody here that's going to do it.'" The other band members knew almost nothing about what was going on at Petty's home.

6

FARMING

Every culture has its southerners.
—Susan Sontag

Mike Campbell only seemed like he appeared out of nowhere. It was an effect of just how shy he was. He'd worked so hard on being invisible that he was actually making some headway. Campbell came down to Gainesville from Jacksonville, a military kid. He was there for school. His father was career air force, divorced from his mother when Mike was fifteen, the same week the Beatles played Jacksonville. Not that Mike could have afforded a ticket. But he certainly knew they were there. He was no different than the other Mudcrutch guys: the *Ed Sullivan Show* appearance was where he started his calendar.

There were early signs of a gift. It wasn't Mozart territory, but Campbell's parents got a call from the school after his class had done some flute-o-phone lessons. The teacher thought maybe this kid had something. That resulted in accordion instruction, admittedly not the instrument that was going to propel the British Invasion. But Campbell got a musical foundation, even if he soon found out that every kid's parents received that same call after the flute-o-phone lessons.

Perhaps, if one is looking for an origin story that might explain who Mike Campbell was relative to what he became, one might turn to a childhood scene that stayed in Campbell's mind: as a boy, he would watch his father come home from work, before his parents split and his father got stationed in Okinawa. He'd see him putting on albums with the Sun Records logo. "He'd go to the record player, put on either Johnny Cash or an Elvis record," recalls Campbell, "and he would just lie on the couch, playing the whole thing. When it was done, he'd get up, turn it over, just lay there all quiet and listen through again." Staring at his father from the living room doorway, Campbell wondered what the man was doing, what he was hearing, what he was listening for. It was Cash who seemed to do the deepest work on him. "When I finally asked him," Campbell says, "why he liked Johnny Cash so much, he goes, 'Because he sings about the truth.' I'm not sure just what I took that to mean, not then. But I do know that that idea stuck with me, the idea that you could listen for that. And no doubt those guitars worked their way into my subconscious." But it wasn't until his father was out of the house that music became an obsession. "I didn't focus on it a whole lot until the Beatles came along. I saw them and I wanted a guitar. The Beatles showed up when people were ready for some medicine, soul medicine. After that, I played guitar from the time I came home from school until I went to bed."

Campbell got to Chuck Berry through the Beatles and the Beach Boys. But at the same time, he figured out Dylan's "Baby, Let Me Follow You Down" and the fingerpicking for "Don't Think Twice, It's All Right." Up in his room, slowing down the turntable, forcing the records to go at a pace that would allow him to catch up, Campbell got better than he realized. If he later caught Mudcrutch's attention with "Johnny B. Goode," it wasn't the first time Chuck Berry helped him get a little respect. "A friend of mine, kind of a bohemian type," Campbell remembers, "knew this jug band, guys in their twenties and thirties who lived in downtown Jacksonville in a kind of commune—hippies, sex and drugs, stuff I had no idea about. But they were professional musicians, if on a low scale, making their living playing music. My friend brought me there, and they had kazoos and jugs and guitars and stuff. I was just sitting there, and my friend says, 'Mike, show them the Chuck Berry song you showed me.' It might have been 'Roll Over Beethoven,' maybe 'Johnny B. Goode.' But I saw the older guys go like, 'Wow!' and then look at each other surprised. I thought, 'These guys think I'm good. Maybe I *am* good.'" The guitar his father had sent him from Okinawa, unrecognizable as a guitar to those who limited their worldviews to Fenders and Gibsons, hadn't come with a self-esteem switch.

Gainesville wasn't in Campbell's plans until a guidance counselor talked him out of attending junior college in the Jacksonville area. She sat him down, listened to Campbell explain that he needed to stick around to help his mother, who was working in a soda shop to make the rent. She let him tell her that he was the oldest sibling, and the family counted on him. She heard the story, but when he was done, she let him know that she didn't buy it. Campbell had the grades for the University of Florida and the possibility of getting an air force loan through his father. "She looked at me and said, 'Are you crazy? You've got an opportunity here. If you go to junior college, you'll never make it out of here. You'd be giving up what might be the biggest opportunity of your life.' She got through to me."

On one of his first nights in Gainesville, Campbell walked into the Plaza of the Americas, there in the middle of campus, and saw a band set up, getting ready to play. For a moment, he thought this must be what San Francisco was like. The University of Florida music school had rejected him, on the basis of a lack of formal training, so he was in general education, thinking about architecture as a major. But he could see that out there on the plaza no formal training was required. Once he'd been in his dorm for a while, he found some like-minded students. "We'd do blues-based jamming. Free-form stuff," Campbell says. "At that time, you could sometimes just show up and get a shot at playing in the middle of campus. Then I found a bass player, a guy named Hal, who turned me on to acid for the first time, and not long after, we saw an ad for a drummer looking to join a band. It was Randall Marsh. We called our three piece 'Dead or Alive.'"

Campbell was crossing the campus one day when he saw another band playing and headed over. He didn't know the band's name, but they struck him as interesting. "Most of the groups on campus were doing blues, long jams—poorly," he says. "This band was playing short songs, singing harmonies, kind of boppy and country rock. I thought, 'Wow, that's cool.' Then I found out they were called Mudcrutch. And I don't know how much after that it was, but next thing I knew, I saw an ad on a bulletin board that Mudcrutch was looking for a drummer. By that time, our trio was done, and I was living with Randall at the farm. So I told him about the posting, said they were really pretty interesting. And I thought it would be great to get him out of the house. I was kind of sick of him."

When Marsh brought the three members of Mudcrutch out to the farm,

Campbell was listening from his room. "I was just sitting back there reading a book, but I was thinking, 'God, that sounds like fun.' And Randall tells them that there's a guy in back who plays guitar. He comes in and asks me if I want to play. 'Yeah, sure,' I tell him. I got my little Japanese guitar, went out there, the only one with short hair, cutoff jeans, and this stupid little guitar. You could just see their disappointment, like, 'Oh, great. The drummer's good, but does he have to bring this guy along?' They ask what songs I know, and I say, 'Johnny B. Goode.'"

■

The farm where Marsh and Campbell lived came to be called Mudcrutch Farm. Once the band was working, it was where the after-gig parties would take place. "If we met someone who seemed like a person we'd like to get to know better," Petty says, "we'd give them the address. When we were finally playing Dubs [Steer Room], which was a mile from the farm, we were really turning into night people, at it until the sun came up." At the farm, Tom Leadon and Mike Campbell would often drift off by themselves, forming a connection through their shared obsession with guitar.

"Leadon and I would get together at a party or whatever and pick up our guitars, and we wouldn't stop for six or eight hours," explains Campbell. "He had the bluegrass stuff that was all new to me. He knew a lot of songs, Doc Watson, Hank Williams, all kinds of things. The music I'd been playing was heavy blues, jammy stuff, psychedelic. Here was something that was kind of like happy, uplifting. We developed quite a guitar bond. I picked up on a whole world from him." Campbell had been attracted to the economy of what Mudcrutch was doing, the short songs with a punch to them, but the band made a home in the valley between the two styles.

"He would work out these harmonies with Tommy Leadon, you know, they'd do these twin guitar things, all worked out, really elaborate," Marty Jourard remembers. "Always super precise. It's his personality. Very controlled. And, yeah, fucking amazing. It was there from the beginning." You couldn't escape the influence of the Allmans in that part of the world. Campbell admits to pushing the band to let the solos go longer. Using a small sound-on-sound recorder, he crafted an instrumental that he describes as both rock and roll and a "mini-symphony." It was called "Turd," and it clocked in at over ten minutes. Down there in Gainesville, on the edge of a new decade, they could get away with a Turd. The band soon put on its first Farm Festival, and the turnout surprised everyone. The hippies came from miles around. No one was dropping acid just to hear songs that were under three minutes—and they were eating acid like it was candy.

Lenahan, as lead singer, was suffering. "The band got into this whole jamming kind of thing," he says. "Long instrumental sections. I loved singing harmonies, but I hated standing there shaking a fucking tambourine for twenty minutes while they did these dual-harmony guitar things. It was great, yes, but if you're butting heads over how long the instrumental sections should go, and you're the only guy who isn't playing an instrument, you've kind of lost that argument before it even starts."

A band meeting was called. "They were all out on the porch," explains Lenahan, "sitting in rocking chairs, and I was like, 'Uh-oh, this is not going to be good.'" Tom Leadon was the one who did the firing. Mudcrutch was now a four piece, with Tom Petty on lead vocals.

■

Jerry Wexler and Tom Dowd liked fishing in Miami. Both men had watched their lives change as the success of Atlantic Records exceeded their most fanciful projections, and sport fishing was among the welcome effects of all that good fortune. Wexler was the son of a window washer from the Bronx. He liked fishing in Miami so much that he suggested to Dowd that they buy a house down there, which they did. The problem with that was the work was beginning to interfere with the fishing. They kept having to get back to New York or Memphis. Wexler suggested they find a studio down in Miami. Dowd found Criteria Studios. Within a few years, Criteria had become one of the legendary rooms of its time. People thought of it as Atlantic Records South. Eric Clapton cut the *Layla* album there. Other clients included Bob Dylan, Bob Marley, Fleetwood Mac, Aretha Franklin, the Bee Gees. And Gainesville's Mudcrutch.

"Randall's friend Gerald Maddox came into a little money. His family owned a pepper farm," explains Tom Leadon, "and they had a bumper crop that year. He said he'd help us get some studio time. We called Criteria and found that we couldn't afford the sixteen track. But we'd heard that *Sgt. Pepper* was done on a four track. So we asked if we could do four-track recording. But Ron Albert, the same guy who worked on *Layla*, said he wouldn't work with less than eight tracks."

Tom Leadon's brother Bernie had been in Los Angeles for some time, playing in the Flying Burrito Brothers and doing session work, and by then had started the conversations that would lead to the formation of his new group, the Eagles. He advised his brother on how to prepare for the studio, suggesting that the band get used to playing the songs without vocals so that they would be ready for tracking. He talked to his brother about microphone placement and using acoustic guitars in the studio. No one really put it together that Ron Albert, who would be engineering the Mudcrutch session, was the same guy who had done Aretha Franklin records, Clapton, the Allman Brothers, Delaney and Bonnie. Bernie Leadon's tips were generous but unnecessary.

The band stayed in a motel the night before. There wasn't money enough to get more than one room. Petty hardly slept. Over the next several years, they'd learn how to get less efficient in the studio. They'd learn how to second-guess themselves and lose confidence in their direction, particularly when they needed it the most. They'd learn how to spend a lot of money that didn't belong to them. But that next day at Criteria they didn't know better than to work quickly and put a couple songs on tape. "Up in Mississippi Tonight" and "Cause Is Understood" were both Petty originals. The day started with "Up in Mississippi Tonight," and they did a second take only because they felt funny about stopping after one. It couldn't be that easy, they thought. But Ron Albert said the first take was indeed the keeper. Leadon overdubbed some acoustic. They cut the second song. To Mudcrutch, the day was a dream. The only problem was that it went too fast. It almost seemed like minutes later that they were holding boxes of singles in their hands. They had a record.

Their excitement got almost as far as Ron Albert. But not quite. To him, they were just another regional band. Albert saw a lot of them come and go, filler between the big clients. The very idea that the A-side referred to Mississippi as something you went *up* to suggested that these boys had a local sense of the world.

In tribute to their benefactor, Gerald Maddox, Mudcrutch named their label Pepper Records. They wrote "BMI" next to the songs because that's what they'd seen on other 45s and LPs. Boomer Hough, formerly the drum-

mer for the Maundy Quintet, was a deejay at WGGG. Because Tom Leadon
had been as close to being the Maundy Quintet's mascot as anyone, he was
eager to bring the single over to Boomer to get some local airplay. WGGG
was the biggest station in town. Making a record was a thrill, but getting
it on the radio was the one thing they all knew would feel even better. That
was why you made records, to be in a car and hear your song on the radio.
The whole band knew that much. Going in to see Boomer Hough, Leadon
didn't dial back his excitement. Why would he? He rushed past the secretary at the station and went straight to where he knew he'd find his friend.
He was sure Hough would be happy for him. The Maundy Quintet had
cut a single, so Boomer knew the feeling firsthand. And that Maundy single
had gone to number one on WGGG, played alongside the biggest hits of
the day.

But as it turned out, Hough listened, a little distant even before the
needle dropped, and then passed on the opportunity to play the single.
Leadon, in his late teens, had learned a few things along the way but not
how to hide his feelings. The secretary was embarrassed for them both.

It was a time when Gainesville bands could rally their friends and find
themselves at the top of the charts. Locally, at least. WGGG wasn't the only
station in town. The Mudcrutch members went after others. They hit the
phones, forcing WGGG to respond. Tom Leadon guesses that Boomer
Hough went out and bought WGGG a copy of the single, not ready to have
to ask Leadon for one. Mudcrutch went to number one on WGGG. They'd
pressed five hundred singles. Number one or not, they didn't sell many.
But it helped them for the moment, kept the gigs coming. Most of the singles ended up in Leadon's closet, where they'd remain when he moved
west, the next member of Mudcrutch to pull out of that dream. No one
ever got the records from that closet. Likely the next tenant dumped them.
No one gets to know ahead of time what that crap in the closet is going to
be worth.

■

Two years younger may as well be ten when you're in high school. But by
the time Tom Leadon came up on twenty years old, he and Petty had become
a little more like peers, though the shadow of that two-year difference
would always linger. It's something that could never be completely undone.

But neither could the bond between the two young men. Since his early teens, Leadon had been what he describes as "part of the deal" in Petty's life. When Petty went on a movie date, it was expected that Leadon would come along. And he often did. On the occasions when he couldn't make it, Petty would re-create the movie for him the next day.

"He'd sit there and spend an hour, tell me the whole movie," Leadon says. "The dialogue, the scenes in detail. He did it several times. I was amazed that he could remember all of it. I think it was real to him in a way. Like he was experiencing it. It'd be like, 'They came over the hill. The credits were rolling . . .' And he had a way of looking you right in the eye, like he wanted to make sure you were getting it. Even if he was driving. I learned that I just couldn't sit in the backseat if he was describing a movie, or he'd never see the road. I'd get into the front seat with him and Jan [Mathews], or Jane [Benyo], whoever it was at the time. It was less danger-ous that way. But it couldn't have been easy on the girlfriends, with the three of us sitting in the front seat."

From the days when the Epics were rehearsing in the storage space left empty by Petty's Dry Goods, amplifier tubes heating up a room that was often in the high nineties to begin with, Petty and Leadon were of one mind. They didn't just suffer the heat together. They sang together, figured out arrangements, wondered if the Ruckers were going to show. They both watched Bernie Leadon get out of town and find something more. And they both planned to do the same thing. But as Mudcrutch was beginning to crystallize, Tom Leadon was getting restless. He'd been Petty's right hand for a long time, but he certainly wasn't sentimental about it. That's not what happens with kids who want to make records. Instead, he started making a little trouble for himself, and for Mudcrutch. More than forty years later, he still wonders how he might have done it differently.

The Eagles' first record came out in 1972. With three top-forty singles, they were as close to omnipresent as a young band could get. When the group came to Atlanta, the whole Leadon family drove up to see the show. There was Bernie, a rock-and-roll star. It made his younger brother more eager than ever. What Tom Leadon saw was that the Eagles were polished, their harmonies locked in, the songs punchy and sweet. That night, he stayed in the hotel with the band. It was a different world, and the kind you wanted to stay in, because when you left it, all else appeared to have been drained of color. Driving back to Gainesville, Tom Leadon held on to a fragment he'd been given: his brother had invited him to move to Los Angeles, told him he could help him make some connections.

No one in Mudcrutch, with the exception of Leadon, had been west of the Mississippi. Mudcrutch had risen to the top of the local scene. They'd even created new scenes and risen to the top of those, with the Mudcrutch Farm Festivals becoming mini-Woodstocks until the cops shut them down for good. In Leadon's view, the band wasn't going to grow until they had more room to grow. They were pushing up against the walls of their pen. And though no one in Mudcrutch was opposed to making a move, they weren't quite sure how to do it. Or when. They had a steady booking at Dub's Steer Room, the best club in Gainesville, and walking away from that wouldn't be easy.

Leadon had other frustrations. He was drifting away from Petty. He'd gotten himself a girlfriend he wanted to spend more and more time with. Petty had always been strict about rehearsing, so when Leadon said he wanted to go camping with her, it wasn't well received. But that wasn't the problem that would break them apart.

In 1969 *Playboy* named Gainesville the "most promiscuous" college town in America. There's no question that Gainesville and its university had a steady party going on. In 1964, James "Dub" Thomas opened his club six miles from the heart of campus. There are those who say it was Florida's best room for rock and roll, including a writer for the *Orlando Sentinel*, who later described the club: "A trend setter, Dub's introduced the forerunner to the wet T-shirt contest when [Dub] started his mini-skirt contests on Thursday nights. Hundreds of unenlightened college students would hoot and howl, the volume of which determined the winners. Dub, of course, served as the master of ceremonies."

It was Jim Lenahan who brought Dub out to Mudcrutch Farm and got the band an audience with the club owner. When Dub agreed to bring the band in, it was Lenahan who dealt with him. With Lenahan gone, however, Leadon was handling the booking. Leadon's status as the kid in the band didn't make that easy for him. He got frustrated when Dub wouldn't return his calls. And the miniskirt contests, for which bands would provide the music, began to wear on Leadon. It felt cheap. "When you do this week after week," Leadon says, "it's horrible." He didn't say anything, however—that opinion was *his* business, not band business.

On Leadon's second to last night in the band, Dub was on the stage playing emcee. The miniskirt contest was about to start. The room was full. Dub was talking to the crowd about renovations he planned to do. He was hyping his own club, and the crowd was cheering him on. The room, he told them, would get larger. In addition, he'd be getting bigger and better acts to play the club. Leadon, standing behind him, waiting for the contest to begin, felt the blood rush to his head. Somewhere the Eagles were playing a sold-out show, and here he was, feeling like he was being publicly insulted by the owner of a small-town strip club. *Bigger and better acts?* Was that a comment on Mudcrutch? "I couldn't let it go. That's how I was in those days. I had a really bad temper."

When the band went on break, Leadon made his way to the room out back where the pool tables were. Petty found him and asked what was going on. No one wanted this tension onstage. Petty's advice was unambiguous: let it go. They had one week left in their booking. Don't burn this bridge. Small town. Leadon heard him out. But the next week, they were back, and Leadon hadn't let it go. He approached Dub and asked that he please not say anything about "bigger and better bands," that he not slight them in front of the university audience that kept them working. Dub replied by telling Leadon, "I'll say whatever the hell I want to say."

It would have been better if Leadon stopped there, but he didn't. "I had no business saying anything to this guy about how he runs his club. He was king there. But I'd been stewing too long, and I said, 'If you do say something like that, I'll turn the P.A. off when you're talking.'" Without Tom Leadon knowing it, his brother Bernie had come out that night, back home on a break from touring with the Eagles. When Bernie walked in, Dub saw him and, knowing him well from Maundy Quintet days, greeted him, saying, "Congratulations on your success with the Eagles. Tonight I really want to hit your brother." Bernie was quick with a response: "Don't do that. Why don't you just fire them?"

When Dub got on the stage to emcee, there was no joviality, no show. The miniskirt contest, not usually an event that demanded a lot of careful production, fell flat. The owner was not in a happy mood. The other members of Mudcrutch didn't know exactly what had happened, but they knew something had and who was behind it. When they finished their set, Dub went up to Tom Leadon and said, "Pack up your equipment. You're done here."

The band got out quickly. Leadon went home, deflated, quieter. It wasn't the outcome he'd been looking for. Alone in his dark apartment, he considered leaving Mudcrutch. He'd obviously grown discontented. But it wouldn't be easy. "They were my best friends. We shared so much," he says, reflecting as though it just happened. "All those dreams." But it would be made easy for him. The next day Mike Campbell and Keith McAllister, the band's roadie and friend, came by to get the P.A. from Leadon's house, where the band had been rehearsing. It was Campbell who delivered the message: Leadon was out of the band. No one even wanted to hear his side of things. Petty was too angry to go to Leadon himself. "It was very hard for me to talk, at least at that time," Leadon says. "I couldn't express myself. But it was the beginning of a very lonely time."

7

CHEMISTRY LESSONS

There's nothing more rewarding than a fresh set of problems.
—DONALD BARTHELME

It was 2007, and Danny Roberts was mad as hell. And he didn't have any interest in keeping a lid on it. For those who wanted to hear, he was ready to tell his side of things. Of course, if the Internet is your megaphone, you can always find *someone* to listen and sign off on your rant. The World Wide Web can even offer the impression that people give a shit. Roberts was ready to storm the castle where Tom Petty and the Heartbreakers were surely living well. It became an obsession for him. Even he had to admit that little could have stopped him, short of a massive car accident a few months later, which left him hospitalized for a number of weeks.

It was the Heartbreakers documentary, *Runnin' Down a Dream*, directed by Peter Bogdanovich, that pissed him off. Not that Roberts was an ambassador of goodwill before that—he'd allowed himself to talk shit about Tom Petty on more than one occasion, well in advance of the film's release. But the documentary provided him with a new platform. For the first time, the Mudcrutch part of the Heartbreakers' history was given a close study. And nowhere in it was there mention of Danny Roberts's contribution or participation. But the more compelling point of friction went beyond that: a band promo shot, originally featuring the five members of Mudcrutch, the five members that comprised the group during Roberts's tenure, had been doctored. Through whatever means, airbrushing or creative "crop-ping," Danny Roberts was removed from the photo. In effect, he'd been erased from a story that was part of *who he was*. It went beyond embarass-ment. It was, in his view, an affront. Why, he asked? And no answers came his way.

■

Tom Leadon's absence from Mudcrutch was conspicuous. Every time some-one left the band, it lost momentum. It was like a string of divorces. Too many of those and marriage itself can seem a folly. The band needed a collective faith in its mission. Leadon's departure meant another "musician wanted" note on the Lipham Music board. Losing a member, whether he was fired or he quit, brought on a low burning anxiety. Only when a new member joined would that anxiety be lifted. The right choice could even throw off an energy that would make a crowded Ford Econoline a better place to be. For a time.

Mudcrutch remained alert, considering possible replacements, looking at other bands and thinking about who they might try to steal. There was a danger of fatigue settling in or of band members considering other ways to burn through their twenties. Not that long before Leadon's departure Mike Campbell had been talked out of going to college—but he could always reverse his thinking.

Whoever joined the band had to be *all in*. From where Mudcrutch stood, it appeared that Don Felder and Bernie Leadon had walked through the golden gates. The Eagles were both a symbol of possibility and an uncom-fortable reminder of where Mudcrutch was: shackled to a schedule of local gigs, with the same faces looking up at them from the same small dance floors. They needed someone in the band who was as interested in chang-ing that as they were. No part-timers. You share the dream and the taxes imposed on those who chase it.

Benmont Tench heard about Mudcrutch losing Jim Lenahan. He was away at boarding school, Phillips Exeter Academy, when he got the news from a friend, Stewart Powers, who kept him updated on the Gainesville scene. Phillips Exeter was considered one of the very best secondary schools in the country, a seat of privilege. Abraham Lincoln sent his son there. Gore Vidal and George Plimpton were Exeter students. Daniel Webster went there in the eighteenth century, Mark Zuckerberg in the twenty-first. Tench, the son of a Gainesville judge, may have shared a town with Petty but not a whole lot more.

While in New Hampshire at school, Tench read the letters Powers sent describing Mudcrutch as a "cool band in town." But a later mention regarding Jim Lenahan's departure was less optimistic. "The drag is that the singer quit," Powers wrote, "and now the bass player, Petty, is singing, and he's not nearly as good." When Tench came home on a break, another of his Gainesville friends, Sandy Stringfellow, coaxed the underage Tench into going out to Lake City to see Mudcrutch play. By that time evicted from Mudcrutch Farm, the band, still a four piece, had relocated to Lake City and were doing a residency at a bar that required them to wear bolo ties and white cowboy shirts. Stringfellow was helping Mudcrutch with their gear and managed to sneak Tench into the club. "They were really, really good," Tench remembers. "These were older guys that we looked up to because there were girls around them like crazy. They were very opinionated and seemed to know what they were talking about when it came to music. One of the guitar players had a brother in the Flying Burrito Brothers. And they played the shit out of 'Dizzy Miss Lizzy.'"

Some weeks later, Stringfellow again called Benmont Tench, this time to see if he wanted to get onstage with Mudcrutch at Dub's. "I knew some of these guys from Lipham's," says Tench, "but I can't tell you when I first met Petty. Maybe when I was twelve or so. He was one of a bunch of older kids hanging around the store. They had their hair combed down in the front like the Beatles. And if you're in Florida, you've got humidity to deal with. Your hair's gonna flip up and curl and do all this stuff. These guys managed to keep that under control. They were intimidating. They were fifteen, sixteen. I assumed they were up to no good."

The question in Tench's mind when Sandy called about the Dub's gig, however, was whether it was worth the hassle of packing his Farfisa organ into his mother's car. He suspected that the band was inviting him because Sandy had intervened on his behalf. Mudcrutch knew David Mason and Trantham Whitley, the two best keyboard players in town. "They were just bored," Tench insists. "I think they were like, 'He can play all right, and he's friends with Sandy, and we're bored out of our fucking skulls. Let's do something different.'" It could have gone either way, but Tench decided to load his instrument into the car, along with a little Fender Princeton Reverb. When he got up there, he played the rest of the night. "It was so damn much fun. After that, they started calling me to sit in with them. A couple nights after I played Dub's, I got up with the band at the University of Florida auditorium. Lynyrd Skynyrd opened up the show." By that time, however, Tench had been accepted to Tulane University and was due to leave Gainesville for New Orleans in the fall. As his parents had conveyed, "That's what you do."

Tench was away at Tulane when he got word that Mudcrutch was a three piece, that Tom Leadon was out. Home on break, he went to see the results of the downsizing, making his own pronouncement: "They were a terrible three piece." Petty disagrees. Regardless, at that moment, Tench wouldn't have guessed he would feel compelled to join the band. And local fans wouldn't have assumed that Petty would emerge as the band's unequivocal leader. Anyone who says they saw the glory coming has probably forgotten that they didn't.

■

The earlier Mudcrutch Farm Festivals were a good moment for the band. With Leadon and Lenahan still in the group, the festivals were the hillbilly cousin of Monterey Pop, of Woodstock. No longer was young Gainesville about AM radio, TV variety shows, and teen dances. It was about smoking dope and hanging out on lawns watching bands play long versions of short songs. Mudcrutch catered to these needs with their self-promoted shows, organic in conception and enormously popular, pulling in thousands at their peak. But the Farm Festivals came and went quickly, after the third occurrence.

The Rose Community Center concerts, however, the brainchild of Bruce Nearon, shared the spirit of the festivals while based at the university and on better terms with the police. Charles Ramirez, who collaborated with Nearon, still feels like there's a little too much of Dub's in the Tom Petty and the Heartbreakers story. "It's always 'Dub's this and Dub's that,'" Ramirez complains. "I understand why the band would remember Dub's. I mean, you don't play a place five or six nights a week without remembering it. And that experience certainly made them tight. It probably doesn't hurt that Dub had naked dancing girls on the stage. I'm sure the band remembered *that*. But there's another thing about Dub's: he'd fire you if you played anything original. He was a businessman, selling drinks. He would do whatever it took to sell drinks. If a band playing top-forty hits and topless dancers sold drinks, then that's what he was gonna provide. When *we* put on shows, we were just the opposite. We wanted bands that did originals. We encouraged that. We were putting on concerts. We weren't a bar. We gave local bands a way of seeing themselves as something more."

The Rose Community Center shows started as a fund-raising mechanism for a student architecture project. Bruce Nearon wanted to turn the old movie theater in Gainesville's black neighborhood, the Rose Theater, into a community center. It was a Quonset hut, owned by a local family. The university approved the project. But it would cost fifty thousand dollars to see it through. With his roomate, Ramirez, Nearon decided to promote some shows to raise the money. The Rose Community Center was never completed. Or started, for that matter. But Nearon and his team became the local promoters who fit the spirit of the moment. Licensed as a student organization, Rose Community Center put on some of that era's best-remembered concerts. The second one they ever promoted was the inaugural Halloween Masquerade Ball, held outdoors at the university's Plaza of the Americas. The university chapter of the Yippies helped organize it. They got the university's approval to start the show at midnight and go until 4:00 a.m. Five thousand people attended.

Danny Roberts was in the group Power, the headliner of that first Halloween Masquerade Ball. Before Power, he'd been in a few other groups in the Lakeland area. He was no different than Petty, Leadon, the Ruckers, Don Felder, and so many more. A different Florida town but the same story.

Power was playing shows with Frank Zappa's Mothers of Invention, the original Fleetwood Mac featuring Peter Green, Delaney and Bonnie, James Gang. They even opened a handful of shows on Black Sabbath's first US tour. It was no surprise that the Rose Community Center wanted Power for its first Halloween Ball. "They were really good, like Cream," says Mike Campbell. "Danny Roberts was playing bass, and they had this guitar player named Donnie 'Dumptruck' Hanna. He was scary, intimidating, he was so good. Great stage presence. He'd do this thing where he'd sit down, play bass pedals from an organ, harmonica, and guitar. All at once. A one-man-band kind of thing. I thought, 'This guy's fucking amazing.'"

Power knew as well as any band that the reason to make it in Florida was to get out of Florida. With regional success confirmed, they chose New York as their next proving ground and went up to play on a bill with NRBQ and Dreams, a jazz fusion act that included Will Lee, the Brecker Brothers, and Billy Cobham. They went over well and were quickly offered more shows. But it may be that band members don't really begin to know one another until they get out of town. Donnie Dumptruck showed the others a little something about himself when he said that, in fact, he couldn't stay in New York for any further performances. He had some students in Winter Haven who had booked guitar lessons with him for the next week. He didn't want to have to reschedule. Two-thirds of Power felt sure a band shouldn't drive from Florida to New York just to turn around again after one show. Power was finished.

Roberts was back in Florida within weeks, quickly joining his brother in a Fort Lauderdale band. "The drummer of that band went on to be in Quiet Riot," Roberts says. "We were called . . . What was the name of that band? I'll think of it." Arriving at a club gig, one of the band members shut the car door on Roberts's finger. And that one ended without a whole lot of glory attached. He was unable to play for six months.

Bruce Nearon knew that Power had split up. He figured he'd call Roberts, see if he wanted to put something together for the second annual Halloween Masquerade Ball. He didn't know about the finger. Mudcrutch was headlining, playing as a three piece. Road Turkey, future Heartbreaker Stan Lynch's and Marty Jourard's band, was also on the bill. Roberts was still healing, but he figured he'd do a solo thing, play some blues numbers, get himself back into the scene. Mudcrutch was coming on after him. In the window between Roberts's set and the Mudcrutch performance, Roberts moved the little bit of gear he'd brought. "I was carrying my stuff from the stage to the stairwell, and they were coming up the stairs. Tom comes up and goes, 'Hey, wanna join our band?'"

8

EVEN THE LOSERS

The humor, the sadness, the EVERYTHING-ness and American-ness of these pictures!

—Jack Kerouac

Charles Ramirez was working that Halloween Ball but didn't pick up on the backstage changes to Mudcrutch personnel. Packs of hippies in costume, tripping on acid, proved a distraction. It only registered later. "We did a show with Mudcrutch once when they had a banjo player, a real hot picker, do the whole set with them," says Ramirez. "They were really a true country-rock band. Then Tommy Leadon was gone, and Danny Roberts was playing guitar. I was like, 'What the fuck is going on here?' Then Benmont joins. By then, they were definitely more rock. I think Roberts probably brought that. Maybe that's a direction everybody in that band wanted to go. But you wouldn't have known it a year earlier." If he didn't say yes right away, Roberts wouldn't take long to join Mudcrutch. Soon after he'd move to Gainesville. But no one, it seems, knew exactly what all the comings and goings meant.

"They told me they were really excited because Danny Roberts was a popular, well-known musician in the area," Benmont Tench says. "He played bass and guitar, and they told me he sang like Gregg Allman. And I'm kind of thinking, 'Well, I like the Allman Brothers. But that's not what I like about Mudcrutch.' But they were really enthusiastic. He certainly brought a lot to it, but, I mean, something wasn't . . . I don't know." The idea was that Petty and Roberts would switch off on bass and guitar, playing guitar on the songs for which they sang lead. If you asked who the lead singer was, it wouldn't have been easy for anyone to answer with confidence. For a minute there, Petty was.

"Danny Roberts was much more extroverted," explains Marty Jourard. "He was essentially the lead singer in Power. And they were a big deal. He played wild guitar, good too, and he and Campbell really worked out a lot of two-guitar stuff." Roberts had the more powerful, more obvious voice. Lenahan describes him as "a much more pro singer than Tom." He covered the white soul and rock thing in ways that his bandmate couldn't. Tapes from live shows at the time capture the situation. Petty's voice is laid-back, a voice with personality that no one was quite ready to see as the unchallenged front-runner. Even Petty wasn't sure—and you can hear that. "When they asked me to join the group," Roberts insists, "they asked me to sing Tom's stuff. I thought it was insane. But they said, 'Tom's got a funny voice.'" Given the transitional moment and the lack of assurance within Mudcrutch as to what should happen next, Roberts's entrance affected the balance of the whole musical operation, without anyone really resisting it. Mudcrutch was only half-sure as to what exactly they were or what they should become. Roberts took them into a period that, eventually, they'd have to find their way out of.

This was the scene Benmont Tench faced when he finally joined Mudcrutch as a full-time member. "Benmont was a kind of nerdy little guy that would come watch us play," recalls Mike Campbell. "He was from a very different world, wore glasses, a turtleneck, went to prep school, came from a rich family. I just thought, 'Oh, he's just a college kid, and we're cool, out in the world with girlfriends, smoking pot and taking drugs and playing music. And then he played the piano. I was like, 'Whoa!' He could play circles around us."

As a boy, Tench's parents made him play with an egg timer on the piano, set for an hour, every day. He hated it, but it wasn't his choice as to whether he did it or not. He made his hours count, however, traveling far and wide in what he played. "Even just the radio in the midsixties was amazing," Tench says. "It could be 'Busted' by Ray Charles, or Sinatra doing 'That's Life' into 'Satisfaction' into the Yardbirds doing 'Over, Under, Sideways, Down.' I suppose I latched onto some of that eclecticism." At boarding school, starting in the fall of 1967, he heard John Mayall's Bluesbreakers and the other British blues acts that made him consider more deeply the South and its music. On trips home, he'd ask the family's housekeeper about the black music he was discovering up north. "Her name was Elizabeth Joe," he recalls. "I'd known her forever. She helped bring me up. I'd say to her, 'This B. B. King record is amazing. Have you ever seen B. B. King?' And she'd say, 'Oh, yeah, he comes through here all the time. But you want to see Joe Tex. Joe Tex is the guy.'" It was a particular historical juncture, when southern children of privilege could have that relationship with the hired help. As Memphis producer and musician Jim Dickinson describes in Robert Gordon's *It Came from Memphis*: "We all learned it from the yardman."

"My parents were very smart, very well read. Intelligent but not effete. Not elitist, not snobs," Tench explains. "Well, I mean, everybody's a little snobbish about something, I suppose. They were a bit Anglophile. But I came out of it all not interested in anything but piano. Piano, reading books, and going to movies. I didn't have any connection to that hunting and fishing culture around me. And I didn't yet think that piano would help me connect with all these girls that didn't even know I existed. It worked for other people but not for me. I remember a girl writing in my yearbook something like, 'You play so great it makes me sick.' And I'm thinking, 'Well, that's certainly a mixed message.'"

At Tulane University, Tench was an art major, because, in his words, "all rock musicians went to art school." He would play with Mudcrutch when he could, but that wasn't often. He was finishing his first year there when Petty called him at 2:00 a.m., after a gig in Naples, Florida. "I was cramming for an economics final," Benmont explains. "The phone rings, and it's Tom. He says, 'We just played such and such a place.' I'm like, 'Cool.' Then he says, 'What are you doing?' And I say, 'I'm cramming for an economics final.' He says, 'No, *what* are you *doing*?' And I go, 'You're right.' I went home after that final and played with them all summer."

When the bill arrived in the mail for the next year's tuition, Tench's parents wrote the check, unaware that their son had another plan. Tench's sister headed back to college. She was at Newcomb College in New Orleans, the sister college to Tulane. It was conspicuous that her brother was still in Gainesville, sleeping late and coming in long after his parents had gone to bed, while she was starting her semester. "At first they wanted to know why my sister was starting and I wasn't," Tench recalls. "So I said, 'Yeah, well, the guys register a week or two later than the women.' That bought me maybe a day. Then all hell broke loose." The judge told his son that if he wasn't in college, he would need to find another place to live. No free room and board. "That's when Tom came over to talk with my father," laughs Tench. "I think he went into my father's study. My dad had a study with his desk in it and a bunch of law books. I have no idea what Tom said. It was just the two of them. But my dad was a formidable character."

"He was a judge," Petty says. "So this wasn't the crowd I usually hung with. But he heard me out, back there in his office, surrounded by books. Looking back, I'm not sure where I got the balls to do that kind of thing. But I just told him that this was all going to work out. There was a plan, I assured him." But there wasn't much of a plan, only a goal: to make records and sell them, to play shows in places other than Florida. Whatever happened in the judge's study, however, worked. Tench still had a place to live at the end of that day. "I wasn't there," Tench says, "but I think Tom kind of said, 'Look, this thing is going to work out. It's gonna be really good. You don't need to throw him out of the house.' Mainly, I believe Tom didn't want me to end up crashing on his couch."

"Tom Petty," Jim Lenahan insists, "is really good at getting people to quit school and join his band. He got Benmont to do it. He got me to do it. He got Mike to do it. He got a lot of people to quit college so they could be in his band." With Benmont severing his ties with Tulane and the art student's life, Petty needed to actualize the vision he'd shared with Judge Tench. A University of Florida student by the name of Mike Lembo wanted to help Mudcrutch do this. Self-described as "the kid who drove the van," Lembo didn't just drive the van; he owned it. The Mudcrutch family went through a growth spurt. No one was entirely sure what a manager was supposed to do, which gave Lembo a certain advantage. "We had no clue," Petty says. "We assumed that a manager was there just to make sure we had gigs coming in. Long-range planning was beyond us at that point. The thing I really remember about Mike Lembo was shoes. He said, 'You guys gotta get decent shoes. A decent pair of shoes can make your jeans look good.' I'm thinking, 'Hmmm. That does make sense.' So I said, 'Why don't you buy us all shoes then?' We all got these flashy shoes. He meant well, but he was in over his head."

"Mike Lembo came off as being older than he actually was," says Danny Roberts. "He was a real sharp talker and looked really slick. So he became our manager, helped us get a lot of things organized. He and Tom and I did a run all over Florida in his van, went to every club between Miami and Tallahassee. We booked a string of gigs. Then we played a string of gigs. By the time we were at the end of them, we were really tight. And that was the material we were going to record for the demo. We were hot on it."

■

Most people don't remember 1973 as the year President Richard Nixon was nominated for a Nobel Peace Prize. But it was that, among other things. It was also the year Congress voted to end funding for operations in Indochina, and the White House announced that it would continue bombing despite that congressional vote. It was the year the Watergate scandal got ugly. It was a season of distrust. More than ever before, the music on the radio seemed like one of the more reliable places to get your truths, whether they came from the Staple Singers or Mott the Hoople.

Within Mudcrutch, Petty was coming forward as the leader, not just by virtue of his singing and songwriting. "I think very few people are as ambitious as Tom Petty," Mike Campbell says. "He just has that drive, always did. Thank God somebody in our group had that. Tom Leadon was ambitious, but nobody's like Tom Petty." When Leadon came back through Florida as a member of Linda Ronstadt's band, it increased Petty's concern that somehow he was getting left behind. Spending much of his time at his girlfriend Jane Benyo's apartment, Petty would meet up with Danny Roberts and plan the band's next move. "Tom kind of lived with Jane," says Roberts. "His home was a few streets away, but he was mostly there. It was great. We'd meet every day at Tom and Jane's, sit there and smoke cigarettes and herb, and then start playing songs and talking about what to do, how to do it. We started piecing together how we would make a demo and then do a trip out west and hit on this person, hit on that person. We went to Tom Leadon to see if he could help us out."

Making the demo was the necessary first step. No label was going to want to see the band or hear them without some kind of decent recording in hand. Judge Tench's living room became Mudcrutch's recording studio. Rick Reed worked at Marvin Kay's music store before opening his own stereo shop. Mudcrutch roadie Keith McAllister bought strings from Reed at Marvin Kay's. By 1974, Reed had a 1973 Dodge Maxivan outfitted with a Stevenson mixer and an Ampex two-track recorder he'd roll in. He'd learned a few things about audio recording as a student at Oberlin, making money back home recording high school bands in the area, selling what he made in batches of a couple hundred. After pulling into the Tench driveway, he ran a snake from the van into the living room, working with McAllister to set up microphones. The band had just come off the run that Mike Lembo booked. They didn't do much more than two or three takes of each song. After two days at the house and one day editing together a master, they were done. It was mostly Petty originals, though there was also "On the Street," a Tench original, and "Once Upon a Time Somewhere," a Petty/Tench cowrite, both of which Petty sang. Roberts took the lead on two of the eight tracks, "Mad Dog," his own composition, and "Move Over Rover," the other Tench song on the demo.

"We didn't spend a lot of time working on songs as a band," says Petty. "There was no really deep thinking about the material. No one was going, 'Well, you know, that could be better lyrically.' That just didn't come up. If someone brought something in, we just did it. We weren't aware how to make a great song. I was close but not ready." Throughout the demo are moments where you can hear Mudcrutch being another band, whether in Roberts's and Campbell's Allman Brothers–inspired twin guitar parts, or Roberts's Blood, Sweat, and Tears chord changes in "Mad Dog." Still young and still so close to their apprenticeship as a cover band, they can't be faulted for not knowing fully who they were. The playing is strong throughout. You can hear that Benmont Tench is already a highly evolved player, and the band doesn't shy away from putting him right up front. When Campbell pulls away from Roberts's guitar, his economy and taste show themselves. And Petty sings like he knows he's meant to be there. It's actually hard to believe that the band had any hesitations about making Petty the sole lead singer. And not everyone agrees that they did hesitate. A character comes out when Petty opens his mouth. You knew there was a story there.

The odd man out is Roberts. There's no question that his playing and singing are as good as anyone's in the band. He was their equal, maybe even one step ahead of some of them. But there's little individuality in what he does. His two lead vocals, often difficult to understand, come off like he knows what he should sound like but not who he is. By contrast, Petty, perhaps only because he didn't have the ability to be anyone other than himself, is already interesting. Eccentric, personal, with a certain confidence. The songs are only beginning to suggest where he'd take it, but there's an emerging sense of who he is. The demo proves that Mudcrutch had songs and could play them and that there was someone there who could be a leader. "I don't think it was that good," says Petty. "There was a song called 'She's a Screamer' that was just crap. Ben's 'On the Street' was the best thing. There's another song called 'Making Some Noise' that's kind of a Mexican-sounding song about taking a girl to a rooster fight. None of it was that good." Petty's judgments aside, there was more than enough material to work with. But making a demo was the easy part. Now they had to get people to listen. They started sending tapes out to record companies.

It didn't take long for the rejections to come in. Initially, that was all they got. But then they heard from Playboy Records. Hugh Hefner's label had a hit with Hamilton, Joe Frank & Reynolds's "Don't Pull Your Love." Playboy was also at work on a record by Barbi Benton, Hefner's girlfriend. It was a spotty operation. But its A&R man, Pete Welding, sent along a song-by-song analysis that excited Mudcrutch. No one at any other label had given the music that kind of close listen. If Welding's scrutiny ultimately led to a rejection, it was a rejection so positive it was reason enough to start planning a road trip to meet the man. In Petty's mind, Welding practically asked them to come west.

"The greatest trip of my life" is how Petty describes that trip to Los Angeles. It was Danny Roberts, Keith McAllister, and Petty, together in Roberts's van, a Volkswagen bus outfitted to be a camper. It had an icebox. Roberts made some chili. They brought along a Coleman stove, an ounce of pot, some speed, and a few sandwiches. It was the year of the oil embargo, the beginning of a fuel crisis. They drove straight, with the exception of one longer stop when they were low on gas and had to get in a line, waiting until the pumps opened at seven the next morning. That and one run-in with the police.

"We got to that area where Texas, New Mexico, and Mexico are all really close," says Roberts. "It was about two or three in the morning. We'd just smoked a joint, and all of a sudden there's a 'prepare to stop' sign. So we stop, and this big Texan with a badge leans in the window and says, 'So, which we smokin'?'" Roberts, who had been splitting the driving with McAllister and was at the wheel, was quick to say that it was Marlboros. But as soon as he said that, three other men stepped from the shadows to join the first policeman, and they started stripping the van, looking for whatever could be found. Petty, asleep until the side door opened and a policeman woke him, climbed out with the others. Smoking cigarette after cigarette, the three travelers knew that the pot was in the middle of a toilet paper roll that Roberts had put between two other rolls. And the speed was in his boot. Nothing was found. Toward the end of a long search, they began to think that they might indeed see Hollywood. They got back on the road, and smoked another joint to celebrate.

■

"The thing about LA was that it was exactly what I hoped it would be," says Petty. "We drove down the streets and everywhere you looked were signs for record companies. MGM, RCA, Capitol, A&M. It was obvious that we had come to the right place." They went by Playboy Records, but they were told that Pete Welding had left the company. Someone else in A&R listened but turned the tape machine off within thirty seconds. "I thought, 'Shit, this isn't going to be easy,'" Petty recalls. "But the fact is, we could just walk into these places, and a lot of the time, someone would listen. It certainly doesn't happen like that anymore. A van from Florida rolls into town, and the guys driving it get meetings? That was another time." In a telephone booth, looking through a phone book for record company addresses, Petty saw a piece of paper on the ground. For whatever reason, he picked it up. It was a list of twenty-five record labels and their numbers and addresses. Obviously, he wasn't the first one to be out there doing this. His heart went in two directions, glad for the list but discouraged that he didn't have an exclusive on this dream.

By the end of three days, they had interest from three labels. London Records was the most promising. It was a label everyone knew from Stones records. Capitol wanted them to record a demo. Why? They had one. MGM wanted them to do a single. Why? They wanted to make albums. London told them to go home and get their band. That made the most sense. "But, really, we just thought that if a label put out records," Petty explains, "that was all we needed to know. We didn't get that there was a difference between record companies." Petty called home to tell the rest of the band. No one knew quite what to think. How could it have been that easy?

"Hollywood was . . . I mean, how does one describe that?" asks Danny Roberts. "We were kids from Florida. This was another world. We went to the Whisky because we'd always heard about the club. We go in, get a little booth. Holy shit! And it's rocking. Then I hear a voice near us that sounds familiar. I listen for a few minutes, and then, finally, I have to get up and look over this little divider between the booths. It was Ringo Starr, Harry Nilsson, and Jesse Ed Davis. It was the only night we went out in Hollywood. And if that happens, I mean, do you think we wanted to go back to Gainesville to do anything more than pack our stuff?"

9

CORDELL

Through the freak we derive an image of the normal; to know an age's typical freaks is, in fact, to know its points of standardization.

—Susan Stewart

A little more than a year after being kicked out of Mudcrutch, Jim Lenahan left Gainesville for Orlando and a job at Disney World. He'd gone to college, learned a few things about the theater, and from there it was a matter of considering where and how he might apply his accumulated knowledge. Disney World was still show business, right? He could come back to Gainesville on weekends, see his girlfriend, Alice, and do lights for whatever band was playing the University of Florida Rathskeller. It had been long enough since he had been fired from Mudcrutch that he had outlasted any lingering ill will and worked with the group when he could, including the second Halloween Ball on the Plaza of the Americas. Then the fuel shortages came.

"The Arab oil embargo hit, the first one, and nobody was coming to Florida," Lenahan says. "Disney World makes all their money from people driving down from the North. And no one was driving because they didn't know if they could get gas. Ticket sales plummeted, and they laid off twenty thousand employees in one fell swoop. And they did it by seniority. I'd been there for, what, three months? Which isn't a whole lot of seniority." Lenahan took a job on the night shift at the Magic Market and moved back in with his mother. The wee hours at the Magic Market adjusted his view of the future. His American dream was looking soiled.

Working his shift one night, no customers in the store, Gainesville quiet, his mind not so much restless as turned off, Lenahan saw someone coming into the store. "Tom Petty walks into the Magic Market," he recalls. "He's with maybe Danny or Randall, and says something like, 'We got six offers. You're the stage manager. We leave next week.' Drops it like a bomb. Of course, I'm working at Magic Market. I wasn't thinking, 'Stage manager? For a band with no shows booked?' I was like everyone else. If Petty had room in that dream for me, I wasn't going to let reality stand in the way."

Keith McAllister and his girlfriend, Ramie, Benmont Tench, Mike Campbell, Randall Marsh, Danny Roberts, Jim Lenahan, Tom Petty, and Jane Benyo. With cash to get them so far from Gainesville that turning back would make less sense than pushing on, they planned the journey. They had one small truck, Danny's van, and a station wagon that Benmont's mother gave him. Oil embargo be damned. Then, in the midst of all the packing, Petty married Jane Benyo.

"I married Jane right before we came out to California," says Petty. "I think it was a week before we left. We'd been going out for a while, didn't officially live together, but I spent a lot of time at her apartment. She shared a place with Jim Lenahan's girlfriend, Alice, who would later become his wife. And we got along good, but she was adamant that we get married before we leave." Jane Benyo was tall, blond, with pronounced cheekbones like her boyfriend. They'd been together on and off for more than a year. In Gainesville, to some eyes, they seemed like a matched set. "She was a good rock-and-roll girlfriend to him," says Mike Campbell, "really behind what he wanted to do. For a long time." Benyo had picked the right time to insist that they marry. Petty's view of the future was oriented around a single point on the horizon. A record deal was almost in his hands. It was all he saw. And if that deal could happen, after the long years of working toward it, surely everything else could fall in behind it. He could barely sleep. If there was any moment in which marriage might have seemed like not such a big deal, it was this one. He could roll the concept of marriage into the whole glorious picture. That's all he was being asked to do. But it wasn't love that was keeping him up at night.

"I've given it a lot of thought," says Petty, "and I think it was a bit of a conspiracy between Jane, my mother, and my grandmother. I think Jane wanted to find a way to make sure I didn't elbow her out of the picture. And my mother was a Christian woman. Jane was going over there a lot, hanging out, talking to them. Jane's rap to me was, 'What's the difference? We're going to be together anyway. This way everyone will be happy.' And in her mind, we were already married. But I didn't want to do it. I was very vocal about it, too. On the first trip to the church, I jumped out of the car and tried to run away. Then my mother called me and said she wanted me to come over to the house. I did, and she said, 'Listen, for my sake, please get married before you go out there. It's the right thing to do.'" Petty honored his mother's request. Then he got back to what he'd been doing. It was done in haste, under pressure, without a lot of thought.

■

They were outside of Keith McAllister's, loading the truck, when the phone rang and Petty went inside to get it. "I thought it was someone calling about a car we had for sale," Petty says. "But it's Denny Cordell. He'd heard the demo we dropped off at Shelter Records in LA. He tells me he wants to sign the group, that we're like the next Rolling Stones. Well, I knew who Denny Cordell was, that he'd done the Joe Cocker records and "A Whiter Shade of Pale" for Procol Harum. But I had to tell him that we already promised London Records that we'd sign with them. Of course, Denny was the real thing, a man of the record business, and he wasn't going to let that become an issue."

Cordell convinced Petty to bring his caravan through Tulsa, where Shelter had its Church Studio and Cordell could meet the group. Tulsa may not have had the glamour of Hollywood, but Petty knew that Cordell's partner, Leon Russell, was the king of Tulsa. And that they made records out there. And that some of those records became hits. When he went back outside where they were packing things into the vehicles, everyone liked the idea. A lot.

Denny Cordell and Leon Russell ran a record company much the way Russell put together Joe Cocker's Mad Dogs and Englishmen tour, which was basically a hippie commune on wheels. The Mad Dogs and Englishmen experience would stand as a kind of summit of seventies excess, with three drummers and a choir and endless hangers-on. But Russell's and Cordell's careers started well before that. Leon Russell had been a member of the Wrecking Crew, playing on Phil Spector records, Beach Boys and Byrds records, Monkees and Paul Revere and the Raiders records. He'd been a member of the Shindogs, the house band on television's *Shindig!* He'd had his own hits and seen his songs become hits for other artists, from Gary Lewis and the Playboys to the Carpenters. When George Harrison organized the Bangladesh concert, he called Russell, who helped put the band together. At those shows, Russell stood out like the natural star he was.

Denny Cordell had worked with Chris Blackwell at Island Records when Island was just beginning its ascent. Cordell's production of the Moody Blues' debut led to the number one UK hit "Go Now," after which he left Blackwell's label, though the two would remain good friends. In quick succession, he then worked with Georgie Fame, the Move, Procol Harum, and Joe Cocker.

Cordell and Russell pooled their significant creative and business backgrounds to form Shelter Records. As the seventies got under way, they were hot. It's little surprise that when Cordell got Mudcrutch to Tulsa, he helped them forget London Records. The members of Mudcrutch parked their caravan, found Cordell at the diner where he'd suggested they meet, and liked the man instantly. Whether it was his history as a record maker, his natural charisma, or the three thousand dollars in cash that he pressed into Petty's hand, he convinced Mudcrutch to become a Shelter act. If Denny's interest in them was benevolent in many respects, he did suggest the band get a lawyer.

Cordell brought Mudcrutch straight into one of Shelter's Tulsa recording studios. There were two, one at Leon Russell's sprawling house and another, on Third Street and Trenton Avenue, called the Church Studio. The latter was where Mudcrutch would set up, after spending their first night in a local motel. Built in 1913 for the Church of the United Brethren in Christ, it was a large place, taking up a good part of the block, and had gotten a makeover from Leon Russell the year before. Whatever Cordell was hoping to see once he got in there with Mudcrutch, it must have revealed itself. After only a day in the Church, he gave them Shelter's LA address and told them to go to Los Angeles. "He was sold on us, and we were sold on him," says Petty. "London Records looked cool to us, but the guy over there was an executive. Cordell made records, records that were a big deal. Shelter was this label run by a couple of renegades, artists, guys who were actually out there finding music and cutting records. We didn't need to deliberate."

As with any other young band, they thought that the hardest part was now over. They'd played for years, working toward this. They'd been advanced some money on a handshake basis, would sign a contract once settled in Los Angeles, and had a producer with hits to his credit. They'd cut some tracks in Leon Russell's studio, and now they would drive to Los Angeles and go straight to their record company's office, where, after a few nights in a questionable motel, they would get two houses in the San Fernando Valley part of Los Angeles, with swimming pools. "When we were in that motel in East Los Angeles, the Hollywood Premiere Hotel, Jane told me she was pregnant," says Petty. "We'd just gotten to LA, and she tells me this. She must have known back in Gainesville. My mother probably knew, too. She'd probably stopped taking her pills is what I think. I just kept looking ahead, which was all I could do, really. There was so much happening at once. I couldn't possibly know what it all meant. A lot of musicians I've known have run when that flag went up." Everyone in Mudcrutch, Petty included, figured that all they had to do now was make records. No one understood that getting a record contract was the equivalent of having a lottery ticket in hand—it felt too much like winning the lottery itself.

The Shelter office was in a building down at the end of Hollywood Boulevard, east of Western Avenue. "A big one-story house. That was the record company," Petty explains. "There were a lot of rooms, and one big hallway through it. The publishing division was over on the left. There was a big reception area. Then it was different people's offices as you went down the hall to the back porch that had been turned into Cordell's office. Next door was a huge building, two stories, that was also Shelter's, and where they'd later build a studio. We went to Shelter every day, just hung out. We knew everybody. We hung with them on weekends, fucked all the secretaries. It was that kind of thing, where everybody was friends and pulling for everybody else." Once settled, the band was ready to work. And then everything slowed down.

Cordell was sitting with Petty, playing records for him, making him think about where Mudcrutch fit in the world, making him write. "I remember one time we finished working," says Petty, "and Denny rolled in—this was in the really early days—and he came by and said, 'Come on, we're gonna hit some clubs.' I was like, 'Man, I'm tired.' Denny goes, 'Mick Jagger doesn't do a gig and put on his slippers afterwards. Let's go.' And off we went. I reckon he probably knew it would be a year before I was going to be ready. I think he got that I just wasn't there yet, that he'd have to coax it out of me. We didn't know how far off we were."

But Cordell took to Petty. "We listened to a lot of music," Petty remembers. "It'd be six o'clock, and I would've been hanging around Shelter all day, and I'd go to his office. We'd smoke some dope, and he'd go, 'Hey man, you ever hear Lloyd Price?' And I often didn't know what he was playing me. I'd never had the money to buy that many records. And his collection was huge. He'd play it and be telling me, 'Bass and drums is the foundation of every record you like. You get that right, make a groove, and it's gonna work.' The groove, that was his focus. It's like Duck Dunn told me later, kinda rolling his eyes, watching an engineer try to make something sound perfect: 'Did you ever hear four guys really playing good together sound *bad*?' Denny was working on the fundamentals, the stuff you have to learn before you can really make your way from the stage to the recording studio. But he was also teaching me something about taste. 'Cause if you have good taste, then you at least know what you're chasing, right? But that meant that sometimes there'd be a record I liked, but I'd play it for him, and he'd go, 'That's bullshit.' I'd be like, 'Really?' He'd say, 'No, it's not speaking to me. It's not real.' Then I'd have to go figure out what the hell he meant. And he was always right."

The band's other singer, Danny Roberts, worked the record company from a different angle, quickly finding a girlfriend in the Shelter office. From the time of their arrival, Roberts seemed to be operating at a remove from the rest of the band. The money Mudcrutch got from the record label each month, intended for rent and food, was split equally among the band members. But, in Petty's recollection, Roberts parked his VW in the driveway of one of the two houses and felt this would exempt him from paying rent. He'd sleep in his vehicle. "I guess the idea was that he'd use the bathroom when he needed it," Petty says, smiling, "and we'd offer that as a complimentary service." If accurate, it wasn't exactly the all-for-one-and-one-for-all mentality. But the trouble went beyond questions relating to bathroom rental. Roberts wanted to bring his own songs into the recording studio. As Mudcrutch started the first of their several recording sessions, Roberts wasn't getting the response he hoped for from Cordell. "I just felt like Danny wasn't getting exactly where we wanted to go," Petty says. "There was one song of his we were doing that Cordell went cold on, but Danny kept insisting that this song would make sense when he put the guitar solo on. Cordell just said, kind of flatly, 'Oh, really? I've never seen that happen before.'"

With mattresses on the floors and lawn furniture in the living rooms of their houses, the band was in some in-between world. They weren't playing shows because they didn't have any recordings or any audience. Clubs like the Starwood and the Whisky weren't an option for a band unless it had a record that was getting some attention or a local following. Van Halen passed out flyers at nearby high schools, and that worked for them. They'd be stars in the LA clubs. At one point Mudcrutch cut a demo of other people's hits, because someone at London Records had earlier suggested they could make extra money in LA playing as a cover band. But with material like Bobby Bland's version of "I've Got to Use My Imagination," they were not moving toward the top forty. And their hearts weren't in it—that was too close to where they were coming from, a step back. Cordell took them to the Village Recorders to begin making a record, but Petty describes it as "a complete disaster." What would eventually be the first and only Mudcrutch single on Shelter, "Depot Street," came out of those sessions.

Through his association with Chris Blackwell, Cordell knew his Jamaican music, how good much of it was, and what made the best of it work. He also recognized that reggae was about to explode on the international market. "We didn't know anything about reggae," explains Danny Roberts. "But Denny got us together in the studio, me and Mike, and he shows us these reggae rhythms, Mike a guitar part and me a bass part. He's like, 'Play it like this. And you play it like this.' We'd gone through it probably thirty feaking times. Then we're about a quarter of the way through a take and in walks Joe Cocker and Henry McCullough, his guitar player, the guy who was with him at Woodstock. They're trying to be real quiet. But we see who it is. Holy shit! Couldn't believe it. But we kept playing, and that was the take of 'Depot Street' we used."

Denny set up a meeting to play "Depot Street" for the staff at Shelter. They all gathered in the main meeting room, where Cordell could turn it up, get his staff a little excited. But when the moment arrived, with the song cued up and the staff ready to listen, it wasn't "Depot Street" they heard when someone pressed play. Danny Roberts's in-house girlfriend, Andrea, had switched the tape for another recording, one of Roberts's compositions. The couple awkwardly played it off as a bad prank, but Roberts obviously wanted more for himself and wasn't getting it. Cordell, annoyed, asked that the correct tape be put into the machine, and the meeting carried on.

There was some satisfaction for Petty in having a song that seemed, to most of the staff, like a single ready for release. But it was a muted satisfaction. The record would go out, radio would be serviced, and nothing would happen. "To me 'Depot Street' was a novelty record," says Petty. "I was hearing reggae for the first time, because Denny and Chris Blackwell had gone over and signed everyone in Jamaica and bought all their publishing. And they'd put out *The Harder They Come* and these seminal reggae records. From the time I hit town, reggae was everywhere. And I loved it. I just never thought I'd be *doing* it. But it was the only thing worth listening to from that session at the Village Recorders. Cordell loved it, and it got put out as a single, but, after that, Denny had to kind of sit down with us and say, 'Hey, you gotta work on being a recording band, on figuring that out. And you need more songs. When you get songs, we'll record.'" Around that same time, the Dwight Twilley Band also signed to Shelter. Mudcrutch watched them make a record, release it, and score a hit. Nothing was so easy for Mudcrutch.

For his part, Danny Roberts's recollections are sometimes at odds with Petty's, though not in every way. No one denies that Denny Cordell was less than enchanted with Randall Marsh as a drummer. But producers and drummers are, more often than not, the ones who will feel the friction first when things aren't working in the studio. Roberts, however, makes more of the issue. "I kept hearing from Andrea how displeased Denny was," he says. "And that if he was displeased with Randall, he was just as bothered by us for not doing anything about it. That was why he quit coming to sessions. So at one point, we were recording at Producer's Workshop, going through songs and songs and songs, not getting anything. And I put down my bass and just left. It was right down the street from Shelter, so I went down there, just sat down on a couch, and thought about what the hell was going on here. That was when I got on the phone and called Marty Jourard so that I could get Stan Lynch's number. And Marty says, 'I can do one better—Stan's right here!' And Stan was interested in this idea of joining Mudcrutch."

Roberts insists that no one else in Mudcrutch was taken with his plan to replace Randall Marsh with Stan Lynch. He brought the idea to Keith McAllister first, which might be the most telling sign of where Roberts sat with his bandmates. When he did take the idea to the band, no one agreed, he claims. "Had that one issue been dealt with," Roberts insists, "I would've been very happy to stay in the band and just do the thing, because it was really cool. But no one was with me, and I said, 'Well, then I guess I'm going to go back to Florida for a bit.' And that was it." Roberts insists that not long after he left, the band called him five days in a row, begging him to return. Even Denny Cordell, he says, reached out in a vain effort to bring him back. But no one else can or does confirm that part of the story. "I have no memory of that happening," Petty says. "I remember him leaving and giving a speech about Ringo doing one of his songs, Johnny Cash doing one. We were a little pissed at Andrea for filling Danny with all this bullshit. We were playing the Shelter Christmas party the day he told us. We did the gig. Campbell was fuming. I think Danny would have walked here from Florida if Denny Cordell had called him to come back." When asked about the call Roberts made to ask him about joining Mudcrutch, Stan Lynch says he has no memory of receiving such a call. In the end, the stories of Roberts's final days are confused, tangled in frayed memories.

At Cordell's suggestion, Mudcrutch went back to Tulsa to do some recording in a studio that wouldn't cost the company extra money. "We all flew to Tulsa, but Denny only stayed a day," says Petty. "He told the engineer to take care of us, told us to learn all we could. And he left us there. We cut 'I Can't Fight It,' 'Cry to Me,' the Solomon Burke song, I think. It was a lot of trial and error. But with Danny gone, nobody sang but me. And I wanted another singer in the band. Even then I didn't want to be the only one. And we needed another writer. And harmony singing. I mean, no one was thinking this was a Tom Petty thing. Maybe Cordell. But I wasn't. It was awkward, though, because I wrote songs on the guitar, and now I was stuck on bass all the time. I'd have to teach someone else my guitar part. We needed a solution of some kind. That's when we called Charlie Souza, the bass player who had been in the Tropics."

Souza had been a hero to the teenage Petty. "The Tropics were really good," Petty says. "Great vocals. And Charlie was a really good bass player. When I'd go to see them, I'd think, 'Man, this band is on fire.' They just did the hits of the day, but they did them real good." The call came out of nowhere. Souza was playing in a bar with his band Bacchus, a power trio he'd formed with Tropics guitar player Eric Turner. Petty asked him if he wanted to come out to LA and sent him a copy of "Depot Street."

"It sounded like a pretty good record," Souza recalls. "But I was playing Hendrix stuff with Eric Turner, so it was like a little pop song to me. But I thought it would be adventurous if I went out there to scope it out. They mailed me a plane ticket, and Tom picked me up at LAX in his little blue Opel, took me around to meet the guys. We went into rehearsals at a place on Lankershim Boulevard. Next thing I knew, I was in the band." Souza flew home, met the equipment truck that picked up his furniture, and followed it out to LA, with his wife and cat traveling at his side. Stopping in Tulsa, Souza went into the studio with Mudcrutch, cutting "Don't Do Me Like That" with the band. It had been written quickly, the tag phrase something Petty remembered his father saying. But Petty didn't think there was anything to the track and quickly set it aside, forgetting about it. His focus was on writing more. When a song didn't seem to make sense with the band, he didn't linger unnecessarily. With Petty's permission, Cordell later pitched it to the J. Geils Band when they were out looking for material, but the Boston group passed on the song.

In Tulsa for those few days, Mudcrutch picked up a show opening for Asleep at the Wheel. "It was a country bar," Souza says. "Being in the Tropics, I was taught to do steps and jump around when I play. And I couldn't give that up, no matter what band I was in. But that night, I ripped my pants right down the back. I was standing in front of Benmont's keyboard, and he got the biggest kick out of it. I pulled my shirt down in the back to cover it, but still. Years later, I read something Benmont had written, something about, 'Yeah, and he ripped his pants.' Not that I played bass or sang great harmonies. I was the guy that ripped his pants."

Back in LA, after the Tulsa sessions, the band set up at Leon Russell's house. Without ever meeting Russell, Petty had been asked to house-sit for him, with the agreement that Mudcrutch could use the studio. In Petty's view, the musical results weren't particularly good. But they did get a song called "Hometown Blues." Charlie Souza could get a few notes out of a saxophone, so Petty had him play a part, then put down a harmony. In the middle of the sessions, Souza did his best to convince Petty to cut a Souza original. "I tried," Souza says. "It was one I wrote about a spaceman and a UFO coming down, called 'Brother in the Sky.' Tom thought I was nuts, so there was . . . there was a little edginess between us."

"I was like, 'Oh shit, this isn't working.' And he'd just moved here," Petty says. "And he thinks he's in the band. I mean, I guess he was in the band. But we were all thinking, 'Maybe we just need to give it more time. He's clearly a good player and a good singer, but he's just not on our channel, you know?'" Nobody wanted the job of telling Souza he was out of the band. They deliberated long enough that, in the end, no one had to.

"I walked into Leon Russell's house one day," explains Souza, "and Tom says, 'The band has broken up.' I didn't understand, couldn't figure out why. It took me three or four decades to figure it out." The other band members were almost as thrown. Cordell had timed out. He didn't want to chase something that he wasn't sure he'd get, something that, most likely, would end up costing him more than he felt like spending even if he *did* get it. The gamble wasn't worth it. And the money that seemed like it would just keep coming from Shelter wasn't.

"The band breaks up because Cordell calls me to the office one day and says, 'We're dropping the band. I have to drop the band because it's taking too long and it's too expensive,'" Petty recalls. "Then he tells me that he wants to keep me, that I'm under contract." Not wanting to leave Mike Campbell behind, even though Cordell had promised to set Petty up with the best studio musicians in Los Angeles, Petty convinced Cordell to support them both as they worked on the music. "I asked Mike to please not leave," says Petty. "But then I had to let everyone else know what was happening. And Denny wasn't going to be there—he had me do the dirty work. It was one of the hardest days of my life. But I went over there to Leon's house, where we all met, and I told them the band had just been dropped from Shelter."

10

WAITING FOR LEON

> After the Charlie Souza experiment exploded in my face and
> Denny Cordell dropped the band, it was like an every man
> for himself kind of thing. I'd put so much into Mudcrutch, and
> now it was just dust. I had nothing, absolutely nothing to
> show for years of work. There wasn't one person who knew
> my name at that point who didn't already know it when I
> started the band. I had nothing to show for it all.
>
> —Tom Petty

Petty was living in the Winona Motel, near the Shelter office. In November 1974,
his daughter Adria had been born in a Burbank hospital. One part over-
whelmed, one part enchanted, he made the decision, together with Jane,
that she should take Adria back to Florida. Back there, the two of them
could stay with family. No one was sure where things were going with
Petty's recording career, but it needed all of his attention before it got to the
point at which no one *cared* where things were going. He had no band and
was a solo artist who knew little to nothing about how to be one. Were he
a child of privilege, he might have had parents encouraging him to try
something else, to go back to school or join the family business or attach
himself to some cousin's good fortune. But that wasn't the world he came
from. No one was throwing out life preservers or had better ideas than the
Winona Motel. But fate had something in store for Petty that exceeded
anything he might have concocted for himself. Strange plans, involving
long nights in a Los Angeles owned and operated by the city's generally
wasted and often wayward community of rock-and-roll stars. It would be
up to Petty whether or not he would glean something of value from the
bodies he bumped into in the dark.

Jim Lenahan says that he was working at Leon Russell's house, doing
some kind of repairs, what he calls "that hippie thing where everybody

chips in to get something done very slowly," when Leon Russell asked him who came up with the song "Lost in Your Eyes." "We were knocking out walls and stuff," says Lenahan. "Leon comes walking in and asks me, 'Who is the guy who wrote it?' Tells me I should have that guy call him." Petty had already stopped house-sitting for Leon Russell by that time and hadn't even met Russell. Though Mudcrutch had split up, their demos still circulated within Shelter, and that's where Russell had heard them.

"Lost in Your Eyes" revealed a shade more of what Petty could do in a song. Cut in Tulsa around the same time as "Don't Do Me Like That," it shows him for what he'd become: a singer of emotion. For all the Chuck Berry covers, the love for R&B and the Beatles, the rock side of the later Mudcrutch, it was that emotion which would make his material matter. Regardless of tempo, regardless of style. He would never oversell a song, never push its feelings on you, but he learned, somehow, to bring the truth out of a lyric. "Lost in Your Eyes" had a believability that went beyond the living room demos that got the band signed. It may not be a perfect production, but it has within it all of the raw materials that would bring so much life to Petty's catalogue and certainly conveys just how artfully Benmont Tench could come along behind Petty and punctuate every moment of feeling, never overreaching. As a recording, it's partway there. As a song, it's more than that. If "Depot Street" found Petty drifting off into someone else's interests, "Lost in Your Eyes" was all his. Not that Petty treated it as such. Too much second-guessing went on up in his head. He'd thrown the song off to the side. Leon Russell helped Petty see that there was something going on in that song that was worth considering.

"I'd gone from living in a rock star's mansion to a motel room. Which, for some reason, didn't bother me," Petty says. "I didn't need much. Shelter was across the street, and my whole social world was there. Then the phone rings in that room at the Winona Motel, and it's Leon Russell. He didn't even know I was the guy living in his house when he wasn't there. We'd never been face-to-face. But he's like, 'I've been listening to those tapes of Mudcrutch, the stuff you did in Tulsa. There's some great songs there. That one "Lost in Your Eyes" is fantastic. And I was wondering if you'd be interested in writing some songs with me.' I was like, 'Sure! I don't really have much going on.' He asks me where I am and if I'm doing anything right at that moment. Next thing I know, a white Rolls-Royce pulls up. People must have assumed it was a pimp. My window looked out on the parking lot. I saw this and . . . *hell*, let's go, right?"

They went back to Encino, to Russell's home studio, where they talked and listened to a lot of tracks in the studio. Nervous, Petty weighed in on which ones he felt were strong and which weren't, figuring it was best to play it straight. Russell appeared to care what he thought. But Petty didn't know what it all meant until Russell laid out the plan. "This was 1975. Leon's still a big star," explains Petty. "So I'm just trying to give my opinion. Why he wants it, I have no idea. But suddenly Leon had stepped into Denny's territory. Prior to that, he hadn't taken any notice of Mudcrutch. He just happened to hear something in the publishing office. When I let Denny know, Denny just went, 'No shit? Great, great.' You know, like, let's see what happens. So Leon tells me I need to live closer to him, that I need to be close by because we're going to be working every day. He says, 'I keep really weird hours. Is that okay?' 'Sure,' I tell him. How weird could they be? There are only twenty-four hours to choose from in a day. I figured I'd seen all of them already."

Petty moved himself into the Travelodge near Leon Russell's place and began going over each day to work. Or to begin thinking about work. Or to be ready in case anyone else started thinking about work. There were so many hangers-on that Russell had installed a pay phone in the foyer of the large home. He didn't like people using his private line, but at the same time, it seems he didn't want them to leave. "I'd go over," says Petty, "and nothing would happen until midnight. I'd be there, just hanging out with this cast of characters coming through the house. Like Gary Busey, who I'd sit around and talk with, who I knew as Teddy Jack Eddy. That was the name he went by. *He* was something. Played drums on some of the sessions." Busey had graduated from Nathan Hale High School in Tulsa, drifted between playing in bands and acting. Russell used him on a number of recordings, even took him on the road. Teddy Jack Eddy was bringing something to the party. Enthusiasm? A thirst? Something.

"Eventually, Leon explains a little more of his idea to me: we're going to do an album with a different producer on every track," says Petty. "So we need to write a song for each of these producers. But the first thing we need to do, he tells me, is line up the producers. Leon says to me, 'What do you think of Brian Wilson?' I'm like, "Yeah, that'd be pretty good.' I simply don't know what to make of this. Leon looks at me and says, 'Then let's go see him.' And with that we pile into the Rolls-Royce and head for Brian's Bel Air house. And then there we are, and there he is, and holy shit!" Russell's level of access was commensurate with his star power at the time. Every idea he had for a producer—and they all looked good to Petty—was possible. Russell's calls got answered. As long as there was gas in the Rolls, they could get to anyone.

"With Brian Wilson, it was a time when his situation wasn't in the press to any significant degree," says Petty. "You didn't know what was going on there. So when I saw him, I was shocked. He wasn't in good health, was really heavy. His house was *filled* with a lot of shady-ass people. And he was the mad hatter, you know? Not crazy but very eccentric. But no matter how much we loved his production, it just wasn't going to work for Leon, who had a lot of room to move, frankly, and could have worked with almost anyone. But Brian, at least right then, was too shaky to pursue. So Leon says, 'How about George Harrison?' That's the way it went."

When Harrison showed up, he had his own song, so no work was needed on Petty's part. He came in with Ringo and drummer Jim Keltner. "We went to Sound City, and Ringo, Keltner, and Leon played," remembers Petty. "Then we went back that night to Leon's, just hanging out. They were all cool guys, and I was awestruck. It just wasn't real. How could that be real?"

The arranger H. B. Barnum got the call and came to Russell's house, bringing a group of backup singers with him. Petty watched them sitting around the piano, playing and singing while they waited for something to happen. Terry Melcher got the call, showing up at Russell's door flummoxed because the vehicle he and Sly Stone had just arrived in was going back out the driveway without him. "I answered the door," Petty says, "and he's there, and he says to me, 'I came here with Sly, and he just got into the driver's seat and drove my car out of here. Who are you?' I was like, 'I work with Leon. Do you want to come in?' So he does, we smoke some pot, and he stays all night talking. Leon kind of peeled off and went somewhere, but Terry Melcher stayed, telling me about the Byrds records and the Paul Revere and the Raiders he'd produced. I knew all those records. And he was pleased that someone did. We had a great time. He even went into the Charles Manson story. It was fantastic. It wasn't songwriting. But I was learning more than I probably even realized at the time. I was thinking I was more like a paid conversationalist or something, but I was sitting with the masters, hearing just what they thought about it all. I could ask whatever questions I had. It was cosmic."

Leon Russell, with Petty at his side, ended up going into Gold Star Recording Studios with Melcher, tracking with members of the Wrecking Crew and doing it like Phil Spector would have, cutting live but stacking instruments. "It was multiple bass players," says Petty, "and maybe four guitar players, a bunch of keyboards, drums and percussion. Just crazy shit. I'd never seen that, and I was *fascinated* watching it. They all played from charts, without any singing or guide vocal. But, once again, I didn't need to write anything. Terry had picked a song. It sounded like Phil Spector. And I just watched it all go down, like I always did." It went on for months. Different producers moving in and out.

"It was some kind of rock-and-roll dream," Petty laughs. "My band had just been dropped from its label. Musically, I was feeling kind of like I was without a home. But here I was, meeting some of the Beatles, the Byrds' producer, Brian Wilson. I had to wonder what was going on. Like, what am I doing here? And I started thinking, 'Well, I must have been put here for a reason. This must be what I'm supposed to be doing. Somehow. Through that whole period, I never ended up writing anything with Leon. Nothing. I just watched these legends come in and out of the picture. They talked to me, told me things. I got to watch them in recording studios. I don't think Leon really knew what he wanted to do next, but he was great to me. I learned a lot from him. I saw a lot of things that maybe you shouldn't do, and some things you should. Cautionary tales were in every other room I passed through."

The other members of Mudcrutch remained closer to the earth, to shopping centers and laundromats. Benmont Tench was playing in an R&B cover band to make extra money. Randall Marsh went on to form a three piece with one of the early members of the Motels. Mike Campbell, of course, stayed on the modest payroll, doing the few sessions that Shelter lined up for Petty, including the one that resulted in "Since You Said You Loved Me," which also featured Al Kooper on organ and piano, Jim Gordon on drums, Emory Gordy on bass, and Petty on guitar.

Band or no band, the former members of Mudcrutch were still part of a community of Gainesville expatriates. Petty had drifted but not too far away. When the others asked what he'd been doing, he tried to describe Leon Russell's world but fell short. "Of course I had that you-won't-believe-where-I've-been feeling, but then I'd launch into it and it was just, you know, too much. It kind of ended with me saying, 'Never mind. If I told you, you wouldn't fucking believe it.' And I was ready to be done with that scene. I didn't see a future writing with Leon. I felt ready to do my own kind of music. Denny still had an interest in doing that, and I was still under contract."

No one was waiting for Petty to form a band. Everyone, including Campbell, who figured himself to be a sideman, assumed Petty was bound to be a solo artist. If he hadn't had enough of bands by the time Mudcrutch ended, what would it take? But fresh from Leon Russell's world, Petty was ready to try again. He wanted a band—he wanted to lead a band *and* to be in one. "When I ran into the Heartbreakers," Petty says, "I was happy. I just saw the sense in that. They weren't the Heartbreakers yet, obviously. But to see them was like, *this* is normal; this is good. These are all Gainesville guys. I could've been driving around in a Rolls-Royce visiting mansions at 3:00 a.m., seeing all the hangers-on living off rock stars' leftovers. But I was getting that there were those who could handle their trip, who were able to actually get a track cut, and those who did nothing but talk. When George and Ringo showed up, shit happened. They were friendly, made sure I felt like I was part of the room and the discussion. Some people saw me as additional baggage. I remember Bobby Womack coming in, and that was pretty strange. That was kind of a late-night scene. It made me ready to be back with my people. Not rock stars. Not session players. My band." Except, of course, the band he found wasn't his band. It was Benmont Tench's.

"I knew this guy Tim Kramer from boarding school," Tench explains. "When Mudcrutch went to the Village to record the 'Depot Street' single, Tim was making coffee. After that, he moved up the ladder, far enough that they told him he could use the studio to record when a room wasn't booked. So he called me up, because he liked my songs. I was playing in a band called the Nasti City Soul Revue, out of Altadena, a four-piece band with five soul singers. It wasn't what I wanted to do. I wanted to play with

Mike [Campbell]. Barring that, Stan [Lynch] and I wanted to put a band together. We were big fans of the Faces. That was our idea, to do something like that."

Tench's first contact with Stan Lynch had been on a corner in Gainesville. It was Lynch's sixteenth birthday. "He was on acid, standing at the corner of Thirteenth and University," says Tench. "He was wearing jeans, had a shag haircut, and instead of a shirt he was wearing a short, blue mini-dress number. Totally glammed out." A few years after that, Lynch had played one show with Mudcrutch, subbing for Randall Marsh. Petty put in the call, asking the Road Turkey drummer to help them out. The show was in Tampa, and the band joined the musicians' union just to do it. As Benmont Tench recalls, "We were told we had to join the union, but that it meant the club couldn't break their contract, couldn't fire us. Then they fired us the first night, and the union didn't do a damn thing about it." But it brought Lynch, Tench, Petty, and Campbell together for the first time. More a child of the rock era than the rock-and-roll era, Lynch felt Mudcrutch was "a little hoppity skippety for my tastes. It was old school rock. They didn't seem to play any new stuff." He was surprised when partway through the Tampa show Benmont Tench went into "Smoke on the Water."

Lynch describes the moment: "I figure, 'Fuck it! We'll do "Smoke on the Water."' Then a guy in a wheelchair comes out onto the dance floor. Obviously a Vietnam vet. And he starts doing wheelies. He's totally like, 'Fuckin' A! "Smoke on the Water"!' Then, as God is my witness, the song turns into 'Louie, Louie.' It's the same organ sound, as only Benmont can do. But the guy in the wheelchair is livid. Like this is an insult to all that is right and good. He actually pulls a wheelie and flips over on his back. Then he's up on one leg. It's just the worst. Cut to, we're fired."

Lynch kept in touch with Tench. And when Road Turkey split up after the unexpected death of Marty Jourard's father, Lynch took the opportunity to make his way to Los Angeles, where the members of Mudcrutch were already living.

"A Gainesville guy let me stay in his basement," Lynch exlains. "It didn't have a bathroom, but I didn't give a shit. It was Laurel Canyon. It was badass. I knew Ron Blair lived next door, so that was a fun contact for me when I'd kind of be scratching my balls and peeing over the rail, and I'd see Ron and go, 'Hey, what's going on?'" Lynch's host was a member of the Gainesville band in which Ron Blair was also a member, RGF.

What exactly the letters meant didn't get registered at Gainesville City Hall. There are those who say RGF stood for "Real Good Friends," albeit a minority, and those who say "Real Good Fuck." Blair, a military kid, had gone to high school in Japan, forming groups with other transients, watching those groups come and go. He'd learned to sew and peg his own pants. But Japan had different cultural logics governing music's transmission, and even the Beatles didn't arrive there on schedule. Blair was a few years behind when he showed up in Gainesville to attend the University of Florida after one year of college in Japan. "It was like a mini San Francisco," he remembers. "People were wearing top hats, incense was in the air, tie-dye chicks were in the streets. And there were tons of bands. Everything had gotten freaky since I'd last been in the States." In a game of catch-up, Blair found his way in as a bass player, recognizing that there was often a need for such a thing amid the glut of guitar players. "I went down to Lipham's," he says, "got a bass, got a tab of acid from somebody, went home and tripped all night, played bass all night, and by morning the gods seems to have OK'd it. I was a bass player."

Blair joined RGF when two brothers in the band started fighting, and one had to go. The group had a lot of gear, played on the heavier side of things, were darker than their country cousins Mudcrutch. But along with Stan Lynch's and Marty Jourard's band, Road Turkey, RGF and Mudcrutch shared a town, which meant the various future Heartbreakers were crossing one another's paths well before they would formalize their relationship. All the bands wanted to get out of town. RGF selected Boston, a choice that marked them as freethinkers.

In a "tripped-out" school bus, RGF made their way to Boston using Abbie Hoffman's *Steal This Book* to instruct them as to how they could scam free gas. In Boston, Blair and his bandmates lived on the bus, though they quickly became disenchanted with the squalor. The drummer found a young woman who took him in, but the others had nowhere to stay. If they hung out with Aerosmith, that didn't mean it was in nice places. In Jeff Jourard's words, it was "Dinty Moore stew on a good night, cooked on top of a can from a previous Dinty Moore stew, with sterno as the stove. The rest of the time it was yogurt or crackers or Cheetos." Two singers, two guitars, bass, and drums, RGF was a lot of mouths to feed, even with a reduced menu. When two members quit to join a budget touring version of *Jesus Christ Superstar,* things fell apart fast. "I was at Steven Tyler's apartment just after one of the singers left," says Ron Blair, "and asked him if he wanted to join RGF. He says, 'No, I think I'll stay with my band.' Good idea. Good idea."

Of the RGF members who left for *Jesus Christ Superstar*, Blair says one left to play, "fittingly," Judas. Jeff Jourard claims otherwise: "He had really long hair and could play Jesus. The other was Pontius Pilate." Either way, it was soon time for the remaining members to go back to Gainesville. "The problem was, we'd made such a big deal about never coming back," explains Jourard, "that we basically had to crawl back into town. We figured we could do that, *had* to do that, and just not tell anybody what happened." The band members managed their shame in different ways, but within the year several of them would be in Los Angeles trying it all again, including Ron Blair and Jeff Jourard, both of whom got calls from Stan Lynch about a session Benmont Tench was setting up at the Village Recorders.

Petty was out in Malibu with Denny Cordell when Benmont called him to see if he'd play some harmonica that night. Ben also called Mike Campbell and Randall Marsh, with Lynch agreeing to a second drummer on the scene. It was like a high school reunion. "I go there," explains Jourard, "and everyone I know from Gainesville is in the room. Six guys I knew from home. We had a good old time *and* did a bang-up job." Without intending to, Tench and Lynch had put the Heartbreakers together. Just a few days later, Jane Petty called Benmont to see if her husband could borrow some of the guys for a session. "Jane and I were really good friends," says Tench. "And Tom didn't really use the phone. I think he wanted to see what it would sound like. He had Jim Gordon playing drums, Emory Gordy on bass, I think. We went down, and the song was 'Strangered in the Night.'" For that recording, it was Tench, Campbell, Petty, Jourard, and the session players. More than halfway there.

When Petty took the idea of a new band back to Denny Cordell, Cordell was ready to consider it, no matter that it was almost the group he'd just dropped from his label, Mudcrutch, largely re-formed. The faces that were different were, it seems, in the right places for Cordell. "Around that time," Petty explains, "Cordell and Leon had a falling-out. Shelter

Records is Cordell's now. Suddenly, you see a big tightening of the belt. Money's not flowing like honey over there. Cordell sees this band, thinks it's a pretty good-looking band, and he feels like it could work." Of course, Cordell, always hard on the drummer, also saw Stan Lynch, not Randall Marsh. Though Marsh had been in on the Tench session, Petty knew what was going to fly with Cordell. And Ron Blair, not Charlie Souza, was on bass: that was noted.

Randall Marsh was out. There would be three guitars, bass, keyboards, and drums. "I knew Jeff Jourard from way back," says Petty. "From when I was like fifteen. He was this kid who had a Gibson Firebird. And he was really good. *Really* good. And trouble." Cordell put the group into Sound City to demo some new material. In Petty's view, it was "just jamming." But Cordell swung by the studio with John Sebastian, who'd just scored a number one with "Welcome Back," and they cut the Chet Atkins–style "I Don't Know What to Say to You." "It sounded really good," Petty says. "I'm thinking, 'This is great. We're really on.' Then John Sebastian says he wants to hire Stan to be in his band. Four hundred dollars a week. And with me it's one hundred dollars a week. I was like, 'Fuck, there goes the drummer.'" But Lynch stayed. It was Jourard who would go. "Jeff was there for the first few things," Petty recalls, "hanging around with us. Finally, we had a band meeting, and I asked, 'Anybody think there are too many guitarists in this band?'"

As Christmas was coming, everyone would be splintering off, heading home or somewhere like it. By that time, they had a name: Tom Petty and the Heartbreakers. It was Cordell's idea. But, still, a sense of uncertainty hung over them. Petty gathered the members. "It was Christmas 1975, and I knew I wasn't fooling around anymore," Petty says. "It wasn't casual shit for me, for whatever reason. We were breaking for the holiday. I remember it was dark outside and cold, and I'd brought everybody together. And I said, 'Okay, is everybody down with this? If you're down with it, let's be down with it. And if you're not, then be out of it.' And they were in."

11

PUNCHING BUTTONS

I think we made the most of not knowing what the hell we
were doing.

—TOM PETTY

Denny Cordell was sending Petty and his band into studios that were costing them
both a lot of money, though Petty wouldn't feel it (or know it) until later. On
top of that, Petty was in a transitional phase, only recently a solo artist, now
in a band. Cordell still had session players coming in, including the ones
who played on "Strangered in the Night," a track that would make the
Heartbreakers' debut. It became clear to Cordell, who was beginning to see
Petty's vision, that it was time to let the band be the band and to stop
spending money on outsiders. So, with the Heartbreakers coming together
and his relationship with Leon Russell coming apart, Cordell decided to set
up a Los Angeles recording studio with gear from Tulsa, a move that would
cut back expenses considerably. He hired two engineers to go out to the
Church Studio, get what was needed, and come back to build and manage
an in-house recording studio, right there in the building next to the Shelter
offices. The engineers' names were Noah Shark and Max. No one was quite
sure where they came from or when they'd leave. But for the making of
the first two Heartbreakers records, they played a critical role in helping
the Heartbreakers get to know the recording studio and its possibilities.

On the trip to get the equipment in Tulsa, Petty and Stan Lynch tagged
along. It was Noah Shark's idea. "We were already rehearsing in the space
where they were going to build a studio," Petty says. "Noah said to me, 'Hey,

nobody's gonna be in the Church Studio when we're out there. Why not come out and cut something before we pull the gear out?' So Stan and I flew out and did a session. We talked our way into a couple of tickets, and we cut 'Luna.' I did it on the Hammond organ that was there. Stan played drums and did the stuff on the Arp string ensemble, playing with that pitch knob. We cut a basic track and brought it back with us. Once we were home, it seemed like the studio went up instantly. And we were under way."

"That was fun," remembers Lynch. "That was a cool trip. But what the fuck was I doing there? Tom and I weren't really tight, didn't know each other that well yet. I had an old girlfriend come up. I remember it was very awkward because we were all sharing a room. That's how stupid I was—I was nineteen years old and figured, 'Well, if she comes up, you know . . .' Tom was like, 'Okay, Stanley. I don't care.' I mean, that's how I did it in Road Turkey."

Mudcrutch had been egalitarian in terms of splitting the rewards and the money passed on to them from the record company, and that spirit remained unchanged. "He was making a solo record," explains Benmont Tench. "Then he got us for his band. But the agreement was that it was all for one and one for all. But the strength lay with Tom and Mike, because even when Mudcrutch broke up, Tom and Mike stayed together to make Tom's solo record. Tom was in charge." Tom Petty and the Heartbreakers could never be a democracy, but Petty was trying to give everyone a reason to stick around. He just didn't know how hard it was going to be to manage that. Trouble is where bands begin. The Heartbreakers were no different. The question is where a band goes after that. With the Heartbreakers, there would be levels of power, and they would begin to reveal themselves.

"I remember Denny urging Mike to write," says Ron Blair. "And he got a little four track. Early on, he was making these great demos. Amazing stuff. I remember him telling me that when he was younger and got the stereo Beatles records, he had to listen to them on some crappy player that could only do one channel at a time. So he'd listen in parts. Right side of the record, then the left. He learned to take in music the way it's constructed. He had a sophisticated kind of mental division in his mind from early on." Campbell, almost painfully shy by most accounts, had a partnership with Petty that informed the band's creative life. Once the new Shelter studio was up, with Noah and Max there to keep it running, the two of them only expanded on that bond, whether they had assurance that it would last or not. But there was some kind of unspoken deal. Some things don't ever get put down on paper.

Campbell still thinks of the Shelter studio as a place he picked up recording's fundamentals. It was an incubation period. "Cordell realized that we were green," says Campbell. "We were lucky, because we were open and learning. We made the first two records there. You can hear some of the excitement. I mean, you can tell we're discovering things, that we're happy to be there, you know? It's frenetic. Tom and I were probably more curious about the recording studio than the other guys. We wanted to figure out how to make records. The rest of the band would play their best and then go home and get drunk or whatever. But we were always like, 'I'm gonna watch this guy for a few hours, figure out what the hell he's doing.' So we became more involved. And we had Noah Shark, who wasn't technical but had a brilliance. He'd say things like, 'Look, you see those speakers there? The bass notes are elephants, and the treble notes are mice, okay? And the mice and the elephants need to get through the speakers at the same time.' Wacky stuff, but it made a kind of sense. He talked in terms of space, color, breath. And he had arrangement ideas, he was a cheerleader, he got us believing in what we were up to. He was the right guy in a lot of ways. And they were on acid the whole time. We'd have a cup of coffee, they'd have a hit of acid."

The next person to join the Heartbreakers' team was Alan "Bugs" Weidel. He'd been a roadie for a few different bands, loading gear and collecting thirty dollars a week unemployment, the lingering effects of an actual day job. One of the bands Weidel worked for, made up primarily of Texans, was called Slip of the Wrist. Stan Lynch had been the drummer. Not long after the Heartbreakers formed, Lynch called Weidel with a job offer. But Lynch hadn't told the Heartbreakers that the Heartbreakers offered Bugs a job. "It ended up being me, Tom, and Stanley, the three of us in this kitchen," Weidel says. "And Stanley's giving the hard sell on me, like, 'This guy, Alan, man, we can't let Alan go. We need somebody like this.' I was confused. I thought I'd already been offered the job. And Petty's going, 'I don't really know . . .' And Stanley just keeps at it, with 'Alan this, Alan that.' Finally, Petty goes, 'Who's Alan?' And Stanley goes, 'Him!' pointing at me. Petty and I look at each other, and it was the first recognition moment we had, you know, where we didn't have to speak. It was like we realized exactly where we both fit into this scheme, like, 'We're both chumps here, huh? I'm thinking I've been offered a job, and you're being set up, with the pressure on to hire me, with me right in front of you.' Nothing was resolved. I just walked away embarrassed. I was surprised when he called offering me thirty bucks a week, what I got on unemployment."

The plan was that each band member would give Weidel six dollars a week out of his pay. By that time, however, Petty and Campbell were *both* husbands and parents. Mike Campbell met Marcie Weiss in the first year after arriving in Los Angeles and married her the following year. Their first child, a daughter named Brie, was born not long after. With Jane and Adria Petty now back from Florida, the Heartbreakers weren't just another young band milling around Los Angeles after dark. Weidel would be taking his collection from young families. "My parents had a big utilities spool in the living room," Adria Petty remembers, "like a wooden spool that was a coffee table. The band would come over, and they'd smoke joints and hang out and talk. We'd all sit on pillows on the floor. Everybody had long hair. They wore baseball shirts and the long, flowy, seventies kind of hippie things. In their appearance and behavior they were not LA—they were very Gainesville, just enjoying California as a new experience. Brie was born a year after me, so there were two little kids crawling around on the floor."

"I remember having to go over to Campbell's house," Weidel recalls, "and there's Mike with Marcie, and the baby she'd just had, and he's just gotten his hundred dollars of pay for the week . . . and I'm collecting for the previous three weeks. Eighteen dollars. Here's another example of why I'm a lucky guy in the music business: none of those guys ever stiffed me. I was getting six percent. Man, if I could've carried on with that . . ." Weidel would become integral quickly and would work as closely with Petty over the years as anyone, getting to know his mind, his sense of humor, his anger, his troubles. But when it came to moving up in management, Weidel wasn't interested. He chose to take care of guitars and one of the guys who played them. He'd be on every tour the band ever booked. You still see him up there, handing off Fenders and Gibsons and Rickenbackers. And cigarettes.

One of Weidel's first opportunities to see the band in the studio came as they were putting Petty's "Breakdown" on tape. Working with Noah

Shark, getting occasional input from Denny, the Heartbreakers had pared the song back to its elements. Phil Seymour from the Dwight Twilley Band had provided an idea for background vocals and done some of the singing himself. Dwight Twilley had zeroed in on a riff Campbell played on the outro of an early take and insisted that *that* was the riff that should be heard throughout. Petty agreed. When Weidel heard the band playing the song, he got it right away. "This was timeless shit. But probably the biggest difference between them and the Slip of the Wrist guys that I had worked with before," Weidel says, "was the sense of urgency. You look back years later, and it's like, obviously, these guys were family men. Tom and Mike were supporting wives and kids. They have a whole different mind-set, not like, 'Let's see what this music business is like. How many chicks can we fuck tonight?' They were a lot more focused. I heard 'Breakdown,' and I knew something was going on there. There was never a doubt in my mind. I was impressed immediately. And they were really funny, and there was that camaraderie. You could tell they were a band. But, also, that it was Tom's band. But that was one of the best parts about it as well. 'Cause I don't know if you've ever been in a band where that [leadership] part's not clear . . . but that can get stupid."

Bits and pieces were already in the can: "Hometown Blues," with Duck Dunn on bass, Charlie Souza on saxophone, and Randall Marsh playing some drums, "Strangered in the Night," with Jim Gordon on drums and Emory Gordy on bass, and the basics for "Luna," which Petty and Lynch brought back from Tulsa. But as new tracks like "Breakdown" came together, there was a feeling that some kind of new energy was carrying them. Noah and Max had educated Campbell and Petty in how to make tape loops, something that would prove meaningful, particularly to Campbell's writing. The first album would open with a track, cowritten by Campbell, that bursts out of the speakers, a drum loop pushing it forward: "Rockin' Around with You." It's hard to say where the track comes from. It's not the first song because it's a single but because it throws off a reckless energy that signals where things are headed. You can hear the band experimenting, hear them learning their way, not sure where they're taking things, realizing that the studio and the stage are two very different places to make music. If Campbell describes the sessions as "frenetic," likely it's because, no matter the band's years together in other contexts and incarnations, they were still coming into being. Anything that worked was allowed. There's an eccentricity to the first album. "It doesn't sound like anything else from the time," says Petty.

If the album defies easy categorization, the Heartbreakers nonetheless arrived at an inadvertently cohesive collection of sounds and songs from straight rock and roll to more eclectic ballads, with layered background vocal parts coming in and out, textures and feels too odd to be the result of know-how or a specific plan. You could hear the Beach Boys in the instrumental sections of "Luna," just as you could hear the Faces and Stones in "Hometown Blues." But it was too strange to feel derivative. Not knowing any better, they weren't refusing any option presented to them. Cordell had shut them away in the Shelter studio. He'd taught them just enough to leave them alone in there. "Mystery Man," "Anything That's Rock 'n' Roll," "American Girl," "The Wild One, Forever"—each cut sounded like it came from a slightly different world, with the band's aesthetic a thread through it all.

Among their many decisions, they chose to include the sound of the process in the record itself. You can feel the recording studio, hear the room and the background talk, the ambient sounds—they leave it all in there rather than tidy it up. If the demo from two years earlier had showed promise, this was the delivery. "Well she was an American girl, raised on promises." Petty had become a writer who could set up a story in a couple words. "She couldn't help thinking that there was a little more to life somewhere else." With "American Girl," he brought home an anthem, without having to dress it up in anthemic trappings. "I think everyone knew," Stan Lynch says, "that there was a little lightning in the bottle on that one."

After trouble of all kinds, his late nights with rock and roll's lost men, elevation and disappointment, Tom Petty made one of rock and roll's great debuts with his new/old band. It was fresh, and it kicked against the door like rock and roll was supposed to. Now it was time to see if they could get anyone to listen to it. It was time for another kind of trouble, the kind they'd need a manager for.

■

Tony Dimitriades was born into a Greek Cypriot family that had transplanted to London. As a young man, he'd gone to see *The Girl Can't Help It*, in order to "get a look at Jayne Mansfield's boobs." Despite his intentions, what stopped him in the film was Little Richard, "this guy at the piano, this primal thing that blew me away." Those who are converted to rock and roll often have their epiphanies; this was Dimitriades's. Years later, when Little Richard was officiating at Tom Petty's marriage to Dana York, the student was able to share the story with the teacher, who was quick to tell him, "Jayne Mansfield's boobs are the only reason I *did* that movie."

As a young man, Dimitriades's plan was to be an English solicitor. Prior to his exams, he aligned himself with an office he describes as a "proper English firm," Leman, Harrison, and Flegg. As one employee informed the young Dimitriades early on, this was a firm that had enough of a connection to the past that Leman's father, an original partner, would occasionally come to work on horseback. There was a hint of Dickens to the scene. But what the situation afforded him was was a firm foundation in law, along with a sense that he wanted to be at least a few steps into the modern world.

After passing his exams, Dimitriades came across a job posting, the phrasing of which stuck with him: "Young solicitor required. Interesting practice. Show business and politics." He applied for the position at Bernard Sheridan and Co. and got it. As described, the job took him into those two worlds, politics and show business. Sheridan was involved in a number of international human rights causes that would give him a reputation, as he simultaneously represented the Hollies, Pink Floyd, Cleo Laine, and others. Dimitriades was drawn to the show business part of things, where it appeared that he could experience politics in abundance, without ever having to go to the other side of Sheridan's practice.

"In those days," Dimitriades explains, "many of the managers were scoundrels, and the record companies were even more blatant in screwing the artists. So Bernard Sheridan and Co. became known for helping artists get out of their contracts. For instance, Fleetwood Mac, the early Fleetwood Mac, was on Andrew Loog Oldham's Immediate Records, which was going bankrupt, and they needed us to get them off the label. There was a group called the Herd, with Peter Frampton. Pink Floyd was another client. I was loving it. I was underqualified, but he threw me into the deep end." The culture of the English music business was at that time more formal. The interaction between the lawyers at Bernard Sheridan and Co. and the artist roster was not social. An air of professionalism dictated that it be so.

Given that, Dimitriades did not know the artists as friends. One particular British Invasion superstar was the only marginal exception, inviting the young lawyer to a show. It fostered enough of a relationship that the artist felt comfortable asking for Dimitriades's help when he needed it.

"He came into the office and said, 'Where's Bernard?'" recalls Dimitriades. "I explained that Bernard was on vacation. 'Well, I've got to get a divorce,' he tells me. When I ask him what he means, he says, 'My wife is in Portugal fucking this other musician. I need a divorce.' I explain that he needs evidence of some kind, of cruelty or adultery, without which nothing can be done. So he tells me to go to Portugal and get some. He gives me the name of the club the fellow is playing in. So I get a ticket to Portugal." Not a great success as a detective, Dimitriades sat outside the adulterous wife's house, waiting, eventually getting enough information to work with, only to return and find that his client was over it. No need to pursue this, the artist told Dimitriades, explaining that he spoke with his wife and they figured it all out. It was a lesson in several things, among them the always urgent yet often fleeting nature of an artist's needs. "I was beginning to see," Dimitriades says, "that they all needed help, of one kind or another."

Rock and roll was an industry of boom and bust, of people hitting the jackpot, hoping to repeat that, and generally failing. It often happened too fast to keep the files in order. Dimitriades made the move to management, where he'd do his best to help the sometimes desperate individuals living in that unforgiving machine. Among his first clients were Terry Reid and Claire Hamill, who got Chris Blackwell's attention early on. There was no schooling for what he would do as a manager, the law background being as good as anything but not exactly what was needed. Elvis's manager, Colonel Parker, came out of the circus, which may have been one step closer to artist management than was the law. "The thing about management," Dimitriades says, "is that you don't grasp the nuances until you've done it. I wasn't very good. I didn't know how to find a producer, how to understand the artist's needs and so forth." But now it was under his skin. Ray Davies approached him about working together, and they launched the Konk label. Dimitriades brought Claire Hamill with him, and Davies produced her second release.

While sharing a flat with session drummer Alan White, Dimitriades helped his roommate negotiate full membership in Yes. And then he heard that Ace needed management. The band had "How Long" in the can, and Dimitriades helped them as they grappled with the reality of having that record go to number one on the US charts. He came to the States, got Ace into rehearsals (they already had a second album completed), and then watched the band fall apart. In a relatively short time, he was in Los Angeles, a manager with no act. He was approached by a fellow Brit named Reggie Locke about forming a partnership. Locke, too, had no clients, having just been fired by Joe Cocker. Dimitriades signed on, each man bringing nothing to the partnership.

In the first week after joining forces, Locke took Dimitriades to the Malibu home of Denny Cordell. Given LA's fuzzy boundary between work and pleasure, no one knew if anything would come of the meeting. Locke was in his element when the cocaine came out, so they stayed awhile. The next day, Dimitriades heard "I'm on Fire" by the Dwight Twilley Band on the radio. The deejay mentioned the label—Shelter Records. "I call Reggie," Dimitriades says, "and I tell him to call Denny right away, to see if the Dwight Twilley Band has management. About an hour later, Reggie calls me back, says, 'Well, they've got a manager, but Denny says he's got this other band that's even better.'

"About a week later we went to the Shelter office there on Hollywood Boulevard to hear the album. It hadn't been released, had just been finished. And I'm really liking it. Now I can't tell you that I knew it right then, that I saw the whole picture. But I knew this was good. I asked a few questions Reggie never would have. And, really, I find out that Shelter Records is suffering. This had been an important label, with twenty or thirty employees in the office, and now they were down to five or six. It was like a little skeleton." No matter, Locke and Dimitriades left the office with a band to manage—Tom Petty and the Heartbreakers.

The idea was to split things up between the two managers. Locke would go out on the road with the group. Dimitriades would stay home, running the business. It was Locke's idea to send the Heartbreakers back to Florida to play some shows there before the record came out. Once an agent was on board, they could launch a tour from Gainesville. "But before Reggie even left to join up with the band," explains Dimitriades, "we had several meetings with agents, and everyone passed. At ICM, the guy came in, heard the album, left, and we never heard from him again. That's what was happening. I also played it for Frank Barsalona at Premier [Talent], but they couldn't commit because they were so busy." No agent, no tour. Then Cordell played the album for Al Kooper, who had played on some of Petty's solo recordings. Kooper, just heading out on an East Coast run, offered the band an opening slot. Then a stand-alone date, opening for KISS, came through Reggie's connection at Joe Cocker's agency. It would be the Heartbreakers' first tour as a band with a record out.

Denny Cordell groaned when Dimitriades came around for tour support. Projections suggested that the band would need fifteen thousand dollars. Dimitriades succeeded, leaving Shelter with a check, most of which went to Florida with Reggie. "They're there a week, maybe a week and a half," Dimitriades explains, "and I get a call from Reggie saying, 'I need more money.'" All of the tour support money, meant to carry them from beginning to end, was gone. And the tour hadn't started. But the worst news was yet to come. "Two weeks later, same thing," Dimitriades says. "He tells me they can't do the tour because they have no money. So I'm thinking, 'What the fuck is Reg doing?' He's my partner, and this is happening. And then I get a call from Benmont, who says to me, 'Tony, you've got to come out with us. We're having so much fun. Last night, there was blow from one end of my piano to the other!' I suppose it should have been obvious. Maybe I just didn't want to believe it could be so. But now I couldn't avoid grasping the situation, whether I wanted to or not."

Technically, it could be categorized as embezzlement, no matter how commonplace such a misallocation of funds was in that line of work. A manager could be sued for this kind of thing, even if his comanager was responsible. And for Dimitriades, there wouldn't be a lot of work in Los Angeles if he got hung up in that kind of legal tangle. He considered quitting while he still could, a move that might protect him. "I really thought about getting out. I didn't see other options. But—and I'll never forget this—I was living with a girl who said to me, 'You can't do that. Do you know how good this band is? You have to find a way.' She really made her point, strongly. So I thought, 'Okay, I have to talk to Tom.' I start thinking what I'm going to say to him. I'm planning the conversation in my head, and the phone rings. It's Tom. He tells me he needs to talk to me. I say, 'That's funny. I need to talk to you.' To which he says, 'You go first.' And I say, 'You go first.' So Tom says, 'Well, Reggie can't be a manager. He needs his own manager.'"

■

For a young band on the eve of its first release, the feeling is often that of a dream coming true. The Heartbreakers were no different. They had a label, some tour support, a roadie named Bugs. They'd waited a long time for this. The anticipation had been building for so long it was like another member of the band. Now something was finally happening. They were even doing blow, thanks to their road manager, who seemed pretty good at coming up with more when it was needed. When they stopped at truck stops for gas, they didn't just look like a rock-and-roll band. They felt like one. They'd been living in two apartments in Gainesville, rehearsing every day in a warehouse in town, and now they were getting out on the road.

When they opened for KISS in South Carolina, they were introduced to the issues that came with playing the arenas. No sound check, limited stage depth because of the headliner's gear. Once up there, in front of a full house, not everyone could hear themselves or one another. Petty recalls having side wedges for the first time, monitors that allowed him to hear better than he could in many clubs, but Lynch says it was a struggle with sound issues back behind the band. It was clear that the KISS audience wasn't there to catch the opener, so the Heartbreakers had something to prove. "We're up there trying to do our thing," says Stan Lynch, "play our album, doing what we do. And all of sudden the crowd erupts in a fucking frenzy. It's almost like they'd just turned the P.A. on or something. I'm thinking, 'Wow, they love us now!' Like something has happened, the tide has turned. I can see Tom out there, feel him getting a little peppy behind it. He turns around, looks at the drums, and then he gives me this look, like there's something to see. I turn around, and there's this giant KISS sign that had been turned on, flashing, 'KISS! KISS! KISS!' Fuck."

The early shows were a source of humility as much as an opportunity to figure out new ways to work an audience. "Nobody had a clue who Tom Petty and the Heartbreakers were," says Jim Lenahan. "But they went out there and played like they were the headliners. They would demand that people pay attention. Eventually, it worked." The Al Kooper shows couldn't have been more different from the KISS experience. The tour was named after Kooper's latest record, *Act Like Nothing's Wrong*. The venues were close to empty, with fewer than ten paying audience members in some rooms. The money was terrible. Radio showed little interest. WBCN in Boston, an exception, picked up on the Heartbreakers record and did a live broadcast of the Paul's Mall show. The bootleg of that night circulates still. Listen to it and you'll hear how few people came out that night. Just like you'll hear the Heartbreakers play as if the room were sold out. But Boston and San Francisco aside, most towns didn't register that Tom Petty and the Heartbreakers were out there. In the first three weeks of the debut's release, sixty-five hundred records were sold. These were numbers that suggested that tour support from the label might soon stop coming. It felt like the end just as much as it felt like the beginning.

■

"The first album was released to little or no fanfare," Tony Dimitriades explains. "But just before I went back to spend Christmas in London at the end of 1976, I saw a great review of the album in *Sounds*, the UK music magazine. It gave me something to work with. So while I was in London, I made an appointment to see the music agent Barry Dickins. I knew him from my time in London, because of the Hollies, I think, and I wanted to play him the album, see if I could get something going in the UK. I showed him the *Sounds* review and played him the record. He was excited enough to bring in a young agent named Ian Wright, who was booking a European tour for Nils Lofgren. They offered us the opening spot on that tour.

"I remember everyone at Shelter Records being very excited when I returned to LA and told them the news. I also recall that someone at the label told some of the guys in the Heartbreakers that they'd better rehearse because Nils was really good. When Tom heard this, he took exception to the fact that they would think he needed to raise his game to come across well as an opener for Nils. He wasn't putting Nils down. Tom just had a belief and confidence in himself and the band. That attitude never changed. We were able to play the European tour despite a lack of financial support from the record companies. Shelter was having financial problems at the time, and ABC, the distributor, was not willing to give us tour support."

England was God's gift to the Gainesville band, a reprieve from the challenge of getting America's attention. "Anything That's Rock n' Roll," never released as a single in the States, was climbing the UK charts in 1977 as the Heartbreakers went on the Lofgren tour. "From the moment we got off the plane," Petty says, "there were journalists there to meet us, photographers wanting to take our pictures. We were on *Top of the Pops* and on the cover of *Melody Maker*." It was a stark contrast to what was happening back home. "It was tight," Dimitriades says, "but we managed to make the money work. Chris Blackwell's Island Records was Shelter's distributor in the UK, and they did a great job. From the very first gig in Cardiff, it was obvious that something was happening. Halfway through the tour, we were asked to stay on after the Lofgren dates to play our own headline tour of the UK. Word got back to the US, and ABC sent an emissary to come with us on the road. She arrived with a check to 'help us and show their support.' Tom tore up the check. We'd gotten that far without them. By the time our headline dates were done, we'd been on the cover of all three UK music magazines, *NME*, *Melody Maker*, and *Sounds*."

They did more television after *Top of the Pops*, including *The Old Grey Whistle Test*. Everything was going exactly as the band and management hoped. "Don't idealize the lifestyle, though," Stan Lynch insists. "It was fucking rough. When we were the opening band, we didn't even get dressing rooms. You'd be out in the snow putting on your clothes, the wet ones from the night before. I suppose it was still a far cry from Boston, when the rat fell on us from above the stage. It was England, so it was cool, at least." The other band members don't remember being without dressing rooms, but every man seems to remember the wet clothes. Mostly, though, it all comes back as their first, sweet taste of recognition. And there will only ever be one of those.

Amid the emerging acclaim for the debut, there were questions in the press regarding what exactly the band was, what musical frontier they'd ridden in from. Playing Holland, Petty ran into a promo record that had the Ramones on one side, Tom Petty and the Heartbreakers on the other. If in hindsight the idea seems ludicrous, Petty's leather jacket on the cover of the first album, worn with bullets strapped across it, was all the evidence some people needed. Obviously, this was a punk band. No matter the category into which they'd be thrown, the Heartbreakers soaked up all the British glory they could. But through it all, they were also learning, for the first time, how to be out on the road and to still be a band, unified, enough so that they could get to the next show.

"I remember," Petty says, "being over there, walking down some hotel hallway, and Ron Blair just jumped on Stan, started pounding on him. I mean, they're going at it. And then, pulled off of one another, they get up, and we all keep walking to the gig or wherever we were going. Not a word gets said. Like it never happened." From the first tour, Stan Lynch emerged as the most complicated character in the Heartbreakers story, in part because he was the lone extrovert in a tribe of introverts. Lynch might have been the one most willing to step up and say what was on his mind. But, as he admits, he sometimes did that without thinking. "We needed him," says Mike Campbell. "Sorely. He was a great energy to be around. He was the one saying, 'Come on, gang!' He had all that, God bless him. I remember doing an interview once, and the interviewer asked each of us what we think about when we're playing. Ben said something esoteric, maybe about Beethoven. I said I was thinking about how to string the next few notes together. They get to Stan, and he says, 'Money. Money and pussy. But mostly money. I did the math and figured out that each time I hit the snare drum I'm getting five hundred dollars. So I put a lot of extra fills in.'"

Stan Lynch could be the band member most ready to go out there and kill it, or the most divisive, or the most enthusiastic supporter of what Tom Petty was trying to pull off, or the most bitter. The problem for Petty came in figuring out when Lynch was going to be which of these things. And what Lynch was saying to whom. And what, exactly, he was after, aside from women. "He was really good onstage," says Petty. "He could read me really well and make a show really exciting. He could also work sex into anything. I mean, we were all as young and horny as he was, I suppose. But I never saw myself as Mr. Love Man. We thought it was great that we could get attention from women because we'd become rock-and-roll stars. But it wasn't my quest. It was Stan's quest."

"I'm a good dog," says Lynch. "Woof, woof! I had fun. I did exactly what you'd expect a young fucking buck to do when he's off the leash. He fucking runs, shits everywhere, and has a ball. You're supposed to go, 'Get 'em, Bosco!' You're not supposed to train him." For the moment, however, this wasn't an issue, and Stan Lynch wasn't the Heartbreakers' biggest problem. America was.

When Denny Cordell and Leon Russell finally parted company, Cordell getting the record label, Shelter needed a new distributer. Previously with MCA, Shelter was saved from stagnation when Cordell made the deal with ABC. In a parallel move, a promotion man by the name of Jon Scott, once a deejay at the powerful FM 100 in Memphis, had left radio to work for MCA before going over to ABC himself in 1977. Fate must have been at work as Scott shadowed the Heartbreakers' move from MCA to ABC distribution, because the band would need him, as much as they would ever need anyone.

On Scott's first road trip for MCA, in 1974, he'd been handed a cassette sampler of upcoming MCA releases to listen to as he drove the highways of the mid-South. Among the songs, a mix of the good and the atrocious, was "Depot Street" by Mudcrutch. If it didn't fill him with the kind of missionary zeal that promo men hope for, he liked the song and managed to get it played in New Orleans and Nashville, though nowhere else. Moving over to ABC, now a VP of album promotion, Scott was relocated to Los Angeles, in a new office, and, as he describes, "twiddling my thumbs."

It was a quiet time in the new position, between waves of releases. Scott had been raised in the wonder years of FM radio, a time when a regional deejay could break an act. "To break acts *was* the goal," he says. It was the work, and it was the high, the way he could leave an imprint that said he'd had been there, his initials in rock and roll's tree trunk. Staring across his office, his life still half in boxes, he saw the Heartbreakers' album. He put it on, listened for a few minutes, and then told his assistant to hold his calls so that he could listen to the whole thing on headphones. Which he did and then did again.

Scott knew not to trumpet his "find" until he first understood its situation. And the situation was not perfect. ABC had tried with this record, but they were done. It had been out eight months, which was already the time span covering birth to bed rest for most records. Only twelve thousand copies had been sold. The success overseas hadn't helped things in the States. It was dead product. ABC, ready to help months earlier when things were happening in England, now wasn't interested in spending more on something that was, by industry measure, over. "That album had come out with thirty-five other albums," explains Scott. "And some of them were very big albums. But it was more than that. Most people in America didn't really know what had happened in Europe. And as much as anything else, Petty was passed over because of the bullets around his neck, because he was perceived to be punk. That jacket." For various reasons, because he was a new VP and because of his persuasive abilities, ABC gave Scott six weeks to "get action on the record." But no money. It was the summer of 1977.

"We came back from England, from that experience, to be unknowns again," Petty says. "And as jarring as the England experience was, coming home was just a bit more jarring. And not in the way we wanted." Even the stations in their hot spots, Boston and San Francisco, would need to be convinced that there was good reason to go back and do more on a record that had already been serviced. Scott called a friend at KWST in Los Angeles, deejay Charlie Kendall, and made him listen to the record. Really listen, with headphones. It worked, and Scott then corralled the deejay into going to the Whisky to see the Heartbreakers open for Blondie. "Charlie told me," explains Scott, "that if the live show was as good as the record, he'd add 'Breakdown' on Monday. After one song at the Whisky, he gave me a firm commitment." Feeling that rush promo men get when they secure an add at radio, Scott made his way backstage to introduce himself to the band, to share the good news, to get to know the group he was working for. "I get to Petty, and I tell him I'm gonna break his record. He looks at me and Charlie and says, 'Bugs, escort these children out of here.'"

On the way out of the dressing room, Scott told Petty that every time the Heartbreakers heard 'Breakdown' on the radio they were going to have to think about him. It may not have been the most original line to come from a promo man's mouth, but within a few weeks Scott got a call from Tony Dimitriades, then an apology from Petty. That might have offered Scott a satisfaction of some kind, but it was not what he was after. He wanted that bigger rush. There was no label president urging him on, no budget to sponsor his passions—Scott was working from instinct alone. He'd fallen for a rock-and-roll record. He wanted to break it.

Los Angeles Times critic Robert Hilburn came into the story from another angle. After writing an initial, tempered review, he went to San Francisco to see the Heartbreakers open for Bob Seger, sensing that there was something more going on with this Florida band than he'd first caught. More time with the record and a live experience caused him to go public with a revised opinion, a second review. He met up with Petty for an interview at a Los Angeles IHOP. It wasn't the kind of behavior you saw in major critics. Hilburn had come around to seeing that this was an important band in the bigger story of rock and roll. He later framed his thinking about that period in music in his theory of "active and passive bands":

> Passive bands can do enticing work (Boston's "More Than a Feeling"), but the artistic heartbeat of rock rests with the more challenging Active outfits: Bruce Springsteen, Elvis Costello, Tom Petty, Talking Heads, Patti Smith, the Cars, Devo and the Clash. While they welcome sales, the primary intent of Active rockers is to say something, and to say it with the individuality that is at the base of all worthwhile art.
>
> The trouble with most Active bands from a commercial standpoint is that you have to pay attention to the music to fully appreciate what's going on. The surfaces can be noisy and intense. You may even have to strain to understand the words. And there isn't always just one interpretation. The aim is to make you feel and consider: get involved.
>
> This involvement was once prized in rock. During the key '50s and '60s periods, Elvis, Dylan, the Beatles, the Stones, the Who, Hendrix, the Kinks, Joplin all teased imaginations. They stepped away from the pop norm in a way that invited you to weigh your own attitudes. But adventure has become a commercial liability in the 1970s. The emphasis is on groups that do all the work for you, thereby taking true involvement out of pop. The God of AM radio is Accessibility. Anything challenging is shunned by program directors. The technique of Passive outfits like Toto, Boston, Foreigner, Kansas and Styx is to reduce all challenge and mystery so that a listener can absorb the music as easily as the handsome photos in a glossy coffee-table book.

In Hilburn, the Heartbreakers had found a critic who grasped what they were doing. It fed the momentum.

Jon Scott went back to the band's first advocates, KSAN in San Francisco and WBCN in Boston. The respective program directors, Bonnie Simmons at KSAN and Norm Winer at WBCN, had already put their muscle and intention behind the album when it came out many months earlier. But to build something real, Scott needed them, even if he recognized that convincing stations to add the Heartbreakers for the first time was a more straightforward task than asking stations that had initially championed the record to give this eight-month-old product a second go. "It was like going to church to ask permission," Scott explains. He spoke with Winer by phone, got him on board, but went further with Simmons, flying to San Francisco to ask for her support. Both stations went along with the plan. "I remember feeling like maybe, just maybe," Petty says, "a dream was starting to come true."

KMET in Los Angeles hadn't added the record the first time around. Scott needed the station to break the spine of the Los Angeles market. His idea was to set up a KWST live, recorded event with the band at Capitol Studios. He would give the recording to KSAN in San Francisco and WBCN in Boston, but he would also bring KMET by the studio to see the line that was bound to form around the building and down the street. A little material evidence. It did the trick. Hilburn, KMET, a string of shows at the Whisky: it all added up to a story about an album that demanded some attention. One and a half years after release, "Breakdown" went into the top forty. Justifiably elated by his triumph on their behalf, Scott was ready to do the same with "American Girl." But two problems kept him from following through. One was the fact that his superiors at ABC expected him to spend a little time focusing on Steely Dan's *Aja*. The second was that the Heartbreakers had a new record in the works. One afternoon at Petty's house, Scott heard "Listen to Her Heart." It helped him move on. Without ever getting the benefit of full promotion, "American Girl" would have a long and glorious life, but not as the Heartbreakers' next top-forty single.

12

OPENING ACTS

This is them when they were in love, see?

—ADRIA PETTY, HOLDING UP A PICTURE OF HER PARENTS

Just as Tom Petty hadn't taken the class that teaches young American men from the working classes to deal with success, neither had Jane Petty been offered any training in how to be the wife of a rock-and-roll star. The shared adventure of moving to California, itself an exercise in adjusting their expectations, was disrupted when she went back to Florida with baby Adria. She was home at her mother's house while her partner worked in Leon Russell's carnival. But Jane was back in Los Angeles in time to see things building for her husband's band. If cautiously, Tom and Jane held on to their belief that something could happen here. They were still together in their vision. But within a year, Jane would start to realize that it wasn't actually her dream—it belonged to him. And she no longer had one.

For the moment, they didn't think of it as his or hers. They just prepared themselves as the dream started changing their lives. The harvest came late, but it was a good one. The money doesn't arrive when the *Melody Maker* cover story hits the stands. But to some degree, the excitement of a burgeoning career masked the disappointment that their material conditions had yet to improve. They were still driving that shitty Opel GT. Even though people were starting to recognize the driver.

Then the Opel—"It looked kind of like a sports car," says Petty. "Like a tiny, bad Corvette, with the lights that flipped up in the front"—started to leak gas fumes into the passenger area. Petty had to drive with the window down and, when it got bad, with his head out the window. The royalty check that came in 1978, the first real check, was for just over seven thousand dollars. A Camaro was seven thousand dollars. He bought one. Not long after, the Pettys were able to rent a small house in Sherman Oaks for eight hundred dollars a month. The place had a grand piano. "There was probably no furniture in it," Petty says, laughing, "but I thought I was doing great. I had a way to pay my rent, and shit, I had a house with a piano in it. The money wasn't my goal. As long as I was comfortable, that was fine. I just didn't want to be ripped off."

For Jane, one thing did come faster than the royalty checks: the awareness of just how lonely this experience would be. A gray wall seemed to be pushing across the horizon line in her direction, just as her husband's party was getting started. He was rarely home. There was more monotony and stillness than she'd ever imagined possible. However much she called on friends like Joyce Lenahan, Jane was often alone with Adria while her husband was out playing shows or recording. She got high, drank a little, cut some hours out of the day that way. But the feeling of being *in it together* was more and more difficult to maintain. And when she described the situation to someone, that person seemed only to hear the part about rock-and-roll success. People got lost in her husband's story. Just as she had.

For his part, Tom Petty had to learn to live somewhere between the highs of his new experiences and the lows of opening the front door to find a wife struggling with a disappointment for which she had no name. At its best, the satisfaction of success gave him the energy to provide Jane with some of the support she needed, as she'd given it to him before the world gave a shit about Tom Petty. At its worst, it meant that everywhere he went someone needed to be taken care of, whether it was a label needing more of his time or a family needing more of his attention. Often, sitting alone in a room at home with his Gibson Dove seemed like as good a solution as any.

"It must have been tough for his wife," reflects Tony Dimitriades. "I mean, she was definitely putting on a brave front, probably overcompensating for not being in charge by leading the way when she *was* able to do something with Tom. But he was getting so busy that I imagine he didn't want to go anywhere or do anything when he did finally get home. And I'm guessing that's probably when she was ready to get out for a while. This is not easy stuff on either side. I do remember that when I had a baby at home, Tom told me how I should take him out in the car, drive around until he fell asleep, that he used to do that all the time. I suppose only then did I realize what Tom was having to do when he got home from the studio or back home from the road. But I was the manager. I wasn't focused on that. I was thinking about the tour, wondering where the new songs were. That was my job, right?"

■

In some ways, the making of the first album wasn't entirely distinct from the slow unfolding of the Mudcrutch years, at least in Petty's mind. The two experiences were part of life before "Breakdown" broke. The debut took a long time to make, just as it had taken over a year to enter the charts, and, of course, some songs on that album preexisted the Heartbreakers. Album number two was another matter altogether. The late success of the first record cramped the space in which a follow-up could be made. Jon Scott's campaign, Robert Hilburn's critical advocacy, the support at radio—it all happened when the Heartbreakers should have been working on a follow-up. Now it was as if they had two jobs, supporting the first record's late success as they also made the second. Youth, adrenaline, and ambition made it all possible.

Their shows had gotten bigger, the dates more regular. Never again would the Heartbreakers see the double-digit audiences of the Al Kooper tour. But that didn't mean that logic would govern the scene on the road. There would still be mismatched bills, like the Rush show in Philadelphia. "It was at the Tower Theater," says Petty. "We didn't know much about Rush at the time, but we were used to appearing on someone's tour for a day or two and then going somewhere else. I remember that it seemed half the room was for us and the other half fervently against. I felt satisfied by the end, like we'd won over a lot of people otherwise set against us. That wasn't the extreme—on another night we opened for Tom Scott and the L.A. Express. We'd never heard of them, but we knew this was not what we should be doing. And we did not win that night."

Hiding away in the Shelter studio, turning knobs on Vox amps while their kids slept, trying to find out just who they were as a band in the studio, couldn't have been more different from trying to find out who they were on the road. One was done in isolation, free of reference points, the other in public. And when they were out there, they were usually assessed in relation to the bands with whom they shared a stage or those with whom the critics grouped them, most of them high school dropouts or misfits of one kind or another. The Heartbreakers weren't Rush or KISS. Neither were they the Ramones, even if they felt a connection. They certainly weren't Tom Scott and the L.A. Express. But there were other acts toward whom they felt a deeper sympathy, bands that seemed to have spent time eating off the same menus at the same dirty lunch counters.

"Mink DeVille," Petty says. "We played some shows with them, and they seemed, *really* seemed like the real deal. I felt like I knew where they were coming from and respected what they were doing." Known for his struggles with heroin and trouble getting to the gig on time, Willy DeVille made two albums with Jack Nitzsche, recordings that seemed like messages from another time, with traces of the Phil Spector sound, and ballads that had all of the New York romanticism of the Brill Building's best. DeVille wrote with Doc Pomus, one of the Brill Building's songwriting legends. DeVille didn't just know the history; he sat down next to it at the piano.

"I loved Willy's stuff, but I'll tell you another band that really astounded me—and when I first saw them I hadn't even heard their stuff, didn't know anything about them," Petty says. "We were playing a club outside Chicago, in Schaumburg, Illinois, and we were going down pretty well at this point. But that night we just didn't get much of a response. The place was packed, we were playing good, but we just weren't getting much back. So I'm talking with this guy afterwards, saying how weird this seemed. And he says, 'This is Cheap Trick's audience, man.' I said, 'Cheap Trick'? 'Wait until you see this,' he tells me. They hit the stage, and it was fucking mind-bending. Robin Zander was one of the most powerful lead singers I'd seen, sang like one of the Beatles. The sheer energy of the thing on the stage was so great. I thought, 'This band is going to be enormous.'"

Seeing Elvis Costello playing a solo show in England, hammering on his Fender Jazzmaster, seeing Bruce Springsteen play solo at the Roxy, Petty felt like there were others out there. And he was right. But the similarities between them all were always more pronounced when the point of contrast was Donna Summer. Otherwise, it was really just a loose collection of artists with a shared affection for guitars and Elvis, Chuck Berry, Van Morrison, the Zombies. But it was enough of a feeling of community to deepen the Heartbreakers' sense of who they were and who they weren't, where they fit, what the mission was, and what the moment was. "Things were happening then," Petty recalls. "There was a changing of the guard. On that club tour, we could tell something was shifting. We'd been playing with Blondie at the Whisky, and suddenly they were getting all this attention. Talking Heads. The Ramones. When we came home from that tour, Cordell called me up and said, 'We've got to go out tonight. You're not going to believe it!' It was like the overthrow we'd dreamed of was going to happen.

"I don't know if I felt a kinship with all those people or some of them," Petty says. "But you'd see stuff here and there that you thought was good. Certainly not all of it." At a Los Angeles club, too drunk to be his own best adviser, Petty agreed to join the Knack onstage. Handed a guitar, he plugged into an amp, turning the volume all the way down on the guitar before he brought the volume on the amplifier all the way up. Then he waited for his moment, watching as the Knack kicked off the song. A minute or so in, Doug Feiger gave Petty the sign, letting him know it was time to solo. And that was when Petty turned the guitar volume to ten, filling the room with feedback before hitting one power chord that if not musical was nonetheless a message. He then stumbled out from the stage, his cord coming unplugged, onto a row of tabletops in front of the stage, kicking people's drinks into their laps. Maybe this was how Petty chose to comment on his membership in the "new wave." Maybe he was just drunk. No matter, the next day a review of the show featured the headline "Tom Petty Digs the Knack!"

Petty bought his red Camaro in cash. It was the kind of thing Chuck Berry and Jerry Lee Lewis had done before him. It was a rock-and-roll move. The Camaro had an eight-track player in it and quadraphonic speakers. Around the time he drove the car off the lot, he got a call from Bruce Springsteen. Petty had seen Springsteen at the Roxy, in the months before *Born to Run* was released, and liked what he saw, recognized a fellow traveler. Petty didn't know the man, but Springsteen wasn't shy in the way Petty was. The guy from New Jersey put in the call, just to hang out, one rock and roller to another. He asked Petty if he had a car.

Petty picked him up at the Sunset Marquis. They went down Sunset Boulevard to the water, stopping at Tower Records on the way, picking up half a dozen eight-tracks. They drove until they'd listened to every song on every one of them. The Stones' *12 x 5* was among the tapes. When "Congratulations" came on, Springsteen raised his arms to the heavens and said, "You can take me now!" Petty loved that. He liked knowing another man out there who went to the same church. But, really, Springsteen was from the other side of the planet—he loved the music hillbillies made, but he sure didn't know what it was like to be one.

Max and Noah Shark played the same role with *You're Gonna Get It!* that they did with the debut album, with even a little more room for input, given Cordell's increased distance. "We realized," explains Mike Campbell, "that these guys had a lot to bring to what we were trying to do. We thought, 'Wow, most of the ideas [Noah] comes up with seem to make things better.' So we just starting listening to him more while we made the first record and *relied* on him when we did the second." Unlike Denny Cordell, Max and Noah had no outside responsibilities. They could focus on the records, coming up with strategies for how to get the best performances out of the band. "They had a flash from a camera," Stan Lynch remembers. "If you weren't playing great, they come out and shoot this flash off in your eyes. It would make you see this white door, and they'd tell you to go through it. I never figured out who the fuck Noah Shark was. I think he was a shoe salesman or something." Cordell, meanwhile, was busy working to keep his label solvent.

"Denny talked with us about the record, but it was more as a supervisor," Petty says. "We were left to make the thing." Some of the songs came very fast. "I Need to Know" was as fine a piece of power pop as the Heartbreakers would ever create. They thought they were cutting a song like "Land of a Thousand Dances," but it came out as a short, tight, two-guitar blast of rock and roll. At two minutes and twenty-three seconds long, the recording didn't linger unnecessarily. Perhaps Cheap Trick had made a dent on Petty's consciousness. "Listen to Her Heart" sounded like a single to everyone but got in trouble with a reference to cocaine. The label wanted it changed to "champagne." "That's not expensive enough," Petty told them. The executives were thinking about radio. Petty was thinking about a song.

"Listen to Her Heart" and "I Need to Know" were worked up on the road, however, before the band started recording. The other tracks happened in the studio, fast. Campbell cowrote "Hurt" and "Baby's a Rock 'n' Roller," with some of his drum loops informing the final recordings. For "No Second Thoughts," they made a loop of the band playing, recording vocals and overdubs on top of that. Everyone wanted to capitalize on the momentum of the first record, so they called it done when they had ten songs in the can, though an eleventh, "Parade of Loons," would be recorded but left off because it had issues with tape distortion.

Going into the sessions, Petty knew he wanted the album to be different from the first. The only problem was that he didn't have enough time to determine what "different" meant. For the most part, the deeper thinking couldn't get done. But the freshness of the debut remained just that in the follow-up. It had the crackle. But not until the third record would Petty make the leap that he knew the band could and, in his mind, had to make. The first two records didn't satisfy his ambitions so much as raise the temperature on those ambitions. Touring behind the second album, Petty was already grappling with this issue. One journalist caught Petty in mid-thought: "We might do some longer things [on the third album]—not rambling—just longer than two and half minutes," he told the writer. "The new album will have a very different feel to it, just like the first two differ from one another. I'm going to try to make the third a double album that sells for a dollar more than a single LP. We're going to record it with a mobile unit—not a live album as such but new songs recorded onstage in a lot of different locations, because there are these little places we really love to play in." He was thinking out loud. All those ideas would go away. But like the best album makers, Petty had to circle in on what he was after.

Denny Cordell wanted to call the second album *Terminal Romance*. The band had done a photo shoot with Annie Leibovitz, already a star in her field, and had something good to work with for the cover. But Noah Shark had Petty's ear, and he was adamant. *You're Gonna Get It!*, both album title and cover image, was as much Shark's vision as anyone's. For better or for worse—mostly the latter—Shark got his way. "I remember Tom say-ing, 'Do you like this picture?'" Lynch recalls of the album artwork. "And I said, 'I don't really care.' He goes, 'Well, that'll be the last fucking time I ask you.' And he meant it. Like, 'If you've got no opinion about it, fuck you.' Not much of an attenuator in Tom. Pretty much a pulse switch." Petty got help where it was available and moved on if it wasn't. Cordell, absent as he was from the sessions, no longer held sway. Noah Shark had been in the room when the record was made and would even get a production credit this time around, along with Petty and Cordell. And ideas raised in the studio, by one like Shark who was deep in the process of creation, had a currency with which outsiders couldn't easily compete. Cordell had become an outsider. As the years ahead would make clear, Petty collaborated best with those who were ready to work alongside him, not in the next building.

As the band moved quickly to finish the record, Tony Dimitriades knew he needed to get an agent who could help build the Heartbreakers' tour-ing operation. Because of his experience with Ace, he had worked with Frank Barsalona's Premier Talent. It was the agency he respected the most. Barsalona was an innovator, a mensch, a principal architect of the touring business in the United States. His vision helped to create a network of promoters and venues and managers that became the backbone of rock era touring. Premier had passed on the Heartbreakers once already, but Dimitriades knew he had to go back again. The Heartbreakers' current agent was pushing him to put them on a national tour opening for Wish-bone Ash. Dimitriades couldn't face the possibility of taking that pro-posal to Petty. Petty's temper came and went, but Dimitriades had gotten a sense for what triggered it. It was things like opening for Wishbone Ash.

Petty refers to these issues as "the adventures of being a support act." When those adventures were over, they were over. But as of the release of *You're Gonna Get It!*, the Heartbreakers were still transitioning. Buses hadn't yet replaced Winnebagos. The band members were sharing hotel rooms. Petty didn't always know when he should exert the power he'd come into or, at other times, if he'd actually come into any power. The band wasn't always sure whether they were rock-and-roll stars yet. Even three decades later, in 2006 during the thirtieth anniversary tour, Mike Campbell encour-aged his bandmates to take a look at the dressing room of their opening band, Pearl Jam, only because it was so much better than their own. In some ways, the Heartbreakers were slow to learn what was within their rights as a major act. On a three-band bill at the Fox Theatre in Atlanta, Blondie opening and the Kinks closing, the Heartbreakers in the middle, Ray Davies helped Petty find his power. Waiting for sound check, Petty saw that the Kinks amps had been pushed so far to the front of the stage that the Heartbreakers could barely fit into the space. Ray Davies was sitting at the piano, playing "Tired of Waiting," though his band had already finished sound check, and it was time for the Heartbreakers to get up there. "He just kept singing it over and over and over," Petty says. "Time ticked by. He just kept at it, 'So tired, tired of waiting, tired of waiting . . .' I finally just said, 'We're not playing. Let's pack it up.' And the crew started taking our amps down."

When Mick Avory, the Kinks drummer, came from the backstage area and grasped what was happening on the stage, Ray Davies's theater of misbehavior, he offered to push back his drums to make space for the Heartbreakers. "He got his roadie to start moving his drum riser," Petty explains, "because there was tons of room to move behind them. That's when Ray came off the piano and decked Mick Avory. A full-on fistfight, right out the back door of the Fox. The last thing I saw was them going out the loading door. Then, a few minutes later, someone comes in and says, 'Okay, it's all right. Move the gear back.' Something got worked out in our favor."

But those kinds of encounters were getting less interesting to deal with, even when they involved heroes from the British Invasion beating the shit out of one another. Midway through touring behind *You're Gonna Get It!*, the album already gold, Petty started thinking a lot about a conversation he'd had with Bruce Springsteen. Springsteen had voiced his own frustrations with the opening slot. His band had faced much of the same trouble as the Heartbreakers, finally making a commitment to pull out of that opening act game altogether. "He told me he'd been through that," Petty says, "and decided he wasn't going to do it anymore, was only going to play to people who wanted to see him. And if he couldn't fill the hall, so be it. His band could make an impression with a club audience, then come back and play a bigger room. I thought, 'That's a damn good idea.' I was okay playing in smaller places if it meant playing to people who came to see us." It wasn't simply a matter of sharing a bill with the *right* act rather than the wrong act. "We were offered Rolling Stones shows, and we just loved them. But if you're opening for that band, once their production kicks in and all those songs go by, no one's going to remember you were even there. I always said no." By the time of the third album's release in 1979, with Premier their agency, the Heartbreakers would be headliners. The audiences they played for were *their* audiences. Their new road manager, Richard Fernandez, who had come on in 1978 and has never left, helped them make the road a better place to be. Something of a legend among those in the touring industry, Fernandez had been with the Faces and the Eagles, among others. He had the band's respect. "From Richard," Petty says, "we found out how isolated you could be from the bullshit. He showed us that. And we liked it."

■

With the band's first major victories not yet fully processed, either by the accountants or in their own minds, Petty was unknowingly headed toward a series of decisions that would be either the making of him as a bandleader or his undoing. If there was a catalyst, it was Elliot Roberts, manager of Joni Mitchell and Neil Young, among others. Roberts had been with Neil Young since 1967, having started a management company with another kid from the lower ranks of the William Morris agency, David Geffen. "Around the time of the second album, work was picking up. We were really touring, had a lot of momentum," Petty says. "That's when Elliot Roberts came in. He'd known Tony for a long time, and they became partners in management. The first thing Elliot did was sit me down and say, 'You can't do this deal where you're giving everybody in the band an equal cut of money, because there's going to be a big problem at some point. You're going to feel really bitter and used. I've been down this road with bands before. It explodes, and everybody walks away. It's going to blow the whole deal. You gotta do it now.' And what he said made sense to me." Within the band, however, no one was going to like it. Some would understand it. Some would come to understand it. Some grumble still.

"It was Tom's vision I was concerned with," insists Elliot Roberts. "Not their vision. So I wanted to put all the power with Tom. Just like we did with Neil [Young]. I don't believe in equal opinion. I believe in best opinion. The drummer and bass player never got called except to tour and record. And they're getting an equal share? When he's giving up his days and nights? All the responsibility of the band's success on his shoulders?" Petty went with Elliot Roberts's thinking: do it now, deal with a pissed-off band, and you may just *have* a band in ten years. Don't act, and you may not have that band. Roberts called the band meeting to let the members know that things were about to change. Petty left it to him, staying home that night. It would be one of the most significant meetings in the group's history, and Petty has no regrets regarding his absence. Some decisions were business decisions, and he felt they should be handled as such. He knew that the management office would be crowded with feelings, and he figured he'd leave space for them.

"The first thing out of Elliot's mouth," says Mike Campbell, "was, 'We gotta get this corn cob out of Tom's ass.' Okay, but what the fuck does that mean? Elliot goes into it, and, yeah, it stung. 'I'm going to make less, and he's going to make more.' But did it piss me off enough to leave the project? It took me a couple days, but I came to grips with it. I remember people were perturbed, though, like, 'Oh, it's the Elliot Roberts star machine. He did it with Neil Young, and now he's doing it with us.' But, look, I loved writing with this guy. That's something I didn't want to walk away from. I'm not *that* into money. And we'd still be partners, not just guys on salaries. I remember I went to Stan and said, 'Look, we've got great managers, we're right on the cusp of doing great things, and there's going to be a lot of money. There's going to be rich, richer, and richest. But we're all going to be rich.'"

There was one problem with the five-way split: there wasn't any money there anyway. "There was nothing coming in!" Stan Lynch insists. "Nothing. I was broke off my ass, driving a Ford Granada. I'm living in a shit-hole but have a gold record on my wall. Five-way split? Of what?" For his part, Benmont Tench was just playing his first Bob Dylan session when he heard about the band meeting. He didn't know what the meeting was about, but when Dylan came up to him, after saying nothing during the session, to ask if Tench could come back the next day, Tench told Dylan that he wouldn't be able to attend because he had a band meeting. "We were told there was this meeting," says Tench. "We get there, find out Tom's not coming, and Elliot's going to tell us how it is. I felt blindsided. I was furious. But you're absolutely fucked, because these are the guys you want to play with. They told us we had to have a lawyer look this over—and the lawyer told us not to do it! But I knew what other bands were out there. I knew what other songwriters were out there. I didn't want to be down at the Rainbow trying to find a band to play with. I wanted to play in the Heartbreakers. But it took years to accept."

■

The band's split wasn't Elliot Roberts's only issue, however. He and Tony Dimitriades saw problems with Petty's Shelter contract. Given his legal background, Dimitriades had already identified its problems. The Shelter deal was something Dimitriades had inherited upon stepping in as manager, not a document he'd helped to draft. But up to that point, he'd put his focus on breaking the band. And at its core, Petty's contract wasn't that different from others signed by young artists long on aspiration and short on business acumen. It was the kind of legal document kids everywhere actually dreamed of signing. It meant you were going to make records. But also that you're giving away the rights to your publishing, without really knowing what that means. Petty thought publishing meant songbooks. But, really, after working for years just to get the chance to be a part of a record label, would any young artist stop the machine because they'd have to give away their publishing? The music business had a kind of cunning. No one ever walked away. Record labels kept pens ready for the next kid coming through the door.

The man who signed Petty, however, also happened to be his producer, Denny Cordell. And that producer also happened to be Petty's mentor. In going after the issue of the bad contract, Elliot Roberts and Tony Dimitriades would be forcing a break between Petty and Cordell. Things were going to get a little Shakespearean, with fathers and sons having to question their allegiances. This third album needed to be something special, but Petty also had to get his house in order, just in case it turned out that it *was* something special. Into that combustible situation walked a man with a can of kerosene: Jimmy Iovine.

■

However different Jimmy Iovine was from Petty, they were good partners. Iovine schemed, wasn't sensitive, and wanted to move up in the world. If you were his focus, you were going to get all of him. And for a while there,

Petty did. "Ambitious" isn't exactly the right word to describe Jimmy Iovine. But neither is "desperate." He was some potent mix of the two—and that happened to be right where Petty was at the time. They were neighbors in sentiment and sensibility.

Iovine was street. His backyard was Brooklyn, and his father a long-shoreman. His story wouldn't work as well if he told you he went to Har-vard and summered in Hyannis Port. It *does* work when he says his first jobs included driving a delivery truck for the A&P and selling jazz rec-ords at Mays department store, when he says he couldn't apply himself in school, that when he heard about "dyslexia, ADD, or whatever that shit is," he was sure he must have had it. He got into the music business when he "pushed a broom around" some New York studios, including the leg-endary A&R Recording studios, which Phil Ramone called home and Quincy Jones used on a regular basis. He got a boost, twice, from a cous-in's friend, Ellie Greenwich, the great Brill Building writer who only a few years earlier had written "River Deep, Mountain High," because she saw something in Iovine, even after he got fired from the first studio she got him into. On his second chance, he survived just long enough to secure the second engineer position on a John Lennon project. And Lennon liked him, which meant that Iovine then worked on the *Rock 'n' Roll* record, with Phil Spector producing. After three projects with Lennon, he got put on a session with a relative unknown. It was a step down, but Iovine would play a bigger role, moving from second engineer to engineer. The artist was Bruce Springsteen, and he was cutting his third record, hoping it would make his career rather than end it.

The way Jimmy tells the story, destiny was in the air. When an *Ameri-can Idol* contestant recently told Iovine that he, as the man behind Beats, was like the next Steve Jobs, Iovine was quick to say, "No. I'm not the next Steve Jobs. I'm Crazy Eddie." The story is better that way. And it's proba-bly more accurate. Ron Blair puts it this way: "Jimmy was kinda scary."

But it wasn't any of this prehistory that brought together Iovine and Tom Petty. The link was Patti Smith, an unlikely, unknowing agent in it all. "Because the Night," Smith's only hit, had come as if from nowhere. But it had a romanticism and a *sound*. Iovine was the producer and the one responsible for getting the song from Bruce Springsteen's hands into Patti Smith's.

That third record of Springsteen's, *Born to Run*, did for the artist what everyone involved hoped it would do. And it meant Iovine would be around for the follow-up. During the making of that next record, however, the sessions changed studios, relocating to the Record Plant, and Iovine was unable to reproduce a drum sound they'd gotten at Atlantic Studios. He tried, and though they gave him time, he couldn't get it. In Iovine's recollection, one band member finally suggested they try another engineer. Iovine went straight to Springsteen's manager, Jon Landau, letting Landau know he was upset. "I told Jon, 'Fuck this! I quit,'" Iovine recalls. "'I've had it. I'm killing myself here, and this guy's gonna bring some other asshole in?' But Jon, who had a very good way of talking to people, says, 'Listen, I'm going to try to teach you something that goes against everything you've ever learned in that neighborhood of yours. It's going to go against every one of your instincts, but it will serve you well if you can possibly listen to me. I want you to look at the big picture. I want you to go in there and be humble and not make this about you. Make this about Bruce. Go in there and say you're going to support him, whatever he wants to do. And see where this goes in your life.' Weeks later, they get rid of this other engineer. Six weeks after that, Bruce gives me 'Because the Night' for Patti. And that song changed everything for me."

"Because the Night" had a sound that was different from what was coming out of California, the echo underscoring the sense of longing that Smith brings to the song. It quickly became a hit on FM radio. On the industry side, no one was quite sure how Jimmy Iovine pulled this from Patti Smith and her band. It was one of those projects that made the producer look good. Denny Cordell heard it. Harvey Kubernik, an LA journalist and record man, heard it. Tom Petty and Tony Dimitriades heard it. What happened from there is a story they all tell differently. Dimitriades says, "Harvey Kubernik had the idea of putting the Heartbreakers together with Jimmy." Iovine says, "A producer manager put us together, said, 'Tom Petty's looking for a producer for his album.'" Petty says, "It was Denny Cordell who suggested we consider Iovine." Almost certainly, one of them is right.

"God bless Harvey," says Petty, "because he was an early supporter, for sure, but I wonder if he had that much to do with it, unless he brought it to Denny's attention. But that doesn't sound likely to me. It was Cordell realizing he just didn't have the time to cut the next record. Even on the second, he'd been less and less available. I remember going into his office one afternoon, as I often did, and he said, 'Have you heard this new Patti Smith record?' I said, 'Yeah, yeah, it's good.' He put it on and goes, 'This guy Jimmy Iovine is very interested. He called and would really like to cut some records with you. I think this could be your man.'" But Petty had already met with Chris Kimsey, who made *Some Girls* with the Rolling Stones, and felt like that might be a way to go. When Iovine heard about Petty being in talks with another producer, he called Petty directly. "He gets me on the phone," Petty recalls, "and says, 'I'm a hundred Chris Kimseys—don't do that.'

"It was when I played Jimmy a few songs on guitar," says Petty, "that's when we really linked up. It was 'Refugee' and 'Here Comes My Girl.' He was ecstatic. He went crazy. Just going, 'Wow, wow, wow! This is gonna be incredible.' I'd never seen such enthusiasm from a producer. And never would again. He was going to die to make this record. His thinking was even more grand than my own. He saw something I hadn't." It didn't even matter that much to Petty that when they first agreed to work together, he thought he was hiring Iovine as an engineer. Iovine worked his way in and got what he wanted, the producer's chair. "Iovine brought an engineer," Petty says, "and found a way to make us pay for it."

■

The making of *Damn the Torpedoes* would be an unconventional affair. The sessions, which started soon after Iovine's role was confirmed, would not be paid for by the record company. They would be paid for out of Elliot Roberts's pocket. Tom Petty was preparing to sue his record company and readying himself to declare bankruptcy. The making of the third album began as a privately funded project.

13

CHAPTER ELEVEN

Fucking producers. Managers. Fuck all of them. The band is
the only thing, in my mind, that makes any fucking difference.
—STAN LYNCH

Petty's mother wasn't doing well back in Florida. She needed extra care. Though
Petty was quick to do all that was asked of him as far as helping, it was done
from Los Angeles. He had a nagging feeling that the live-in nurses hired by
his father were not brought in simply because of their formal training. Petty
worried that his father was looking for a little company. He'd already
seen Earl working the fans, keeping his door wide open should any young
women want to get closer to a rock-and-roll experience. The son knew what
the father was capable of. "He wanted a nurse," Petty says, "so I told him,
'No problem,' and then we'd wonder if he was fucking the nurse. Like, 'Is
this a nurse or is this some chick that Earl is moving into the house?' My
brother and I were suspicious of it. I paid for it, but I never really knew, and
it was so painful to think about I almost didn't want to know." The part that
bothered Petty was the thought of his mother living through that indignity,
no matter that she'd slipped into an almost unconscious state. His old pro-
tector needed some protection, he thought, and he could still fool himself
into believing he could do something about it and also have a career as a
rock-and-roll star.

By the time the lawsuits were under way, of course, there was less time
than ever to be a son, a father, even a friend. Ron Blair recalls sitting poolside at the Tropicana, waiting it out while Petty and his team of managers

and lawyers sorted through the paragraphs and pages that defined the Heartbreakers' contractual situation. For any band member who questioned whether it should be a five-way split, there was now ample evidence that the workload wasn't divided that way. Blair would sometimes see characters milling around the hotel pool, including the Tropicana's poet laureate, Tom Waits, and the members of Cheap Trick. But none of them had Blair's tan. He was a bronzed child of sloth. Not that anyone was asking him to do more. Benmont Tench, for his part, was a regular at the Rainbow Room. The bartenders knew what he was drinking.

For Petty, the almost ceaseless movement between writing, recording, going home to his family, and working through the band's affairs had begun to define who he was. He was a workingman. The old gang wasn't the same because, as he put it, "Someone had to be the adult here." There wasn't a lot of time to give *anything* the focus he hoped to give it, so he cut corners where he could. And that was more on the son and father side of things than anywhere else. No one wanted to see the songs stop coming. They were going to help everyone: family, poolside band members, the crew, his parents, lawyers, record executives.

Petty was in the Sherman Oaks house, had the Camaro, but was still eyeballing yard sales when he passed them. Things improved in fits and starts. For the second time in his short career, he was the object of something like a home stereo intervention. Years before, Denny Cordell stopped by Petty's to play him a record, only to find a "half-broken little player, a child's device." "Where's your shit, man?" Petty recalls Cordell asking. The setup Cordell then sent over from the office was better but not by much. When Jimmy Iovine and engineer Shelly Yakus left Petty's house after their first visit, they did some shopping before going back to their hotel. "They sent over a stereo with two JBL speakers, an amp, a reel-to-reel two-track, a turntable," Petty recalls. "That was them just putting their foot down. They wouldn't work with a guy who couldn't listen to his own recordings on a proper system." Petty's world was being tidied up. The new home stereo was nothing compared to the legal makeover that was about to go down.

Tony Dimitriades was no longer working out of his bedroom, where he'd been alone until 1977, when the band hired Mary Klauzer, the assistant who would stay for the whole ride, a woman Petty says "organized his

life, knew the right people to let in, and along the way became family."
Now Dimitriades and Klauzer had settled into the offices of Elliot Roberts's Lookout Management, where Roberts and Dimitriades were ready to
address as partners Petty's Shelter Records contract, which was in fact the
Mudcrutch contract that Petty had signed years before. "I think I knew I
was in a bad deal after the first record," Petty explains. "It had taken a year,
but we had started to sell significant amounts of albums. There were gold
records. There should have been dough. We hadn't taken a big advance,
and our costs weren't that high. There should have been publishing money,
for sure. Where was the money? That's how it first came up. I remember
Tony saying, 'It's a shame about the record deal. You're still on the contract
you signed with Mudcrutch, and they're using it to their advantage.' So
when Elliot came in, things started to heat up. They made it their mission.
And Elliot put *his* money where his mouth was, bankrolled us during the
recording of *Damn the Torpedoes*, paid all the legal bills. I think he was the
one who came up with the bankruptcy scheme. Elliot's a street hustler.
But he knew that there was no future financially if we didn't get free of
this record company."

Sitting with Dimitriades and Elliot Roberts, the band's lawyers asked
them how they were for cash. The answer: not good. The managers
explained that Roberts was paying for the recordings out of his own pocket.
The lawyers then asked if the terms of Petty's contracts would allow them
to pay back what was being borrowed from Roberts. Answer: not likely.
Weighing the debts against the terms of the recording and publishing deals,
it looked to everyone in the room like the case for insolvency was good. "If
you're insolvent," Dimitriades says, "and there's no likelihood that the
terms of your existing contracts will allow you to get out of your insolvency,
then the court has the right to readjust all of your contracts and deals, and
you can make a fresh start. And *that* is what we were after when we filed for
Chapter Eleven. Obviously, the record companies didn't want to see us win
this kind of case—it would mean a precedent would be established that
could have far-reaching effects."

At the same time, Tom Petty and the Heartbreakers were an act that a
lot of labels would have liked on their roster. For all of the record executives who didn't want to see this Chapter Eleven case fall in the artist's
favor, there were just as many voicing their interest in Petty, should that

be the outcome and Petty find himself a free agent. Rock and roll wasn't a business of sentimentalists or men who got overly attached to their principles, not when there were records to sell. It all made for a strange climate in which to be making that third record. Bugs Weidel, living like he was on the wrong side of the enemy's lines, was responsible for keeping the multitrack tapes in a safe place at the end of sessions. No one knew where he took them, and no one wanted to know, as long as they were there at the next session. The tapes were hidden so they wouldn't become evidence in courtroom proceedings.

"I was at the Troubadour one night, and a guy walked up to me who, I guess, was fairly high up at Columbia Records," Petty recalls, "and he comes up to me and says, 'Hey, we'll give you a million bucks an album right now if you sign.' At the time, that was a lot of money. I was reeling. I called the office the next day and told them about it, because the guy had given me his card. They said, 'Yeah, we know. We're having a lot of those discussions with people.' So in a way, it was frustrating to me. We had a deal where we got almost nothing . . . and there's this buzz going on. But it gave me more energy for the fight for something better."

There was, however, not one legal dilemma so much as a tangle of them. The unexpected upshot of it all went beyond creating a better artist deal. The lawsuit revealed something about just who Tom Petty was, his identity as an artist and a man. What they went through, and the role Petty played in it, helped people understand who this guy was. Up to that point, they didn't know much about him beyond what they culled from a couple of singles. There was no mythology attached to Tom Petty, and he never tried to build one. But this episode gave the audience, the press, even Petty himself something to consider.

Petty had to make a sacrifice in order to take all of these steps forward, and that was his relationship with Denny Cordell. "Denny had always wanted the best for us musically. He was a great guy. I loved him," Petty says. "But there's something about those English guys from the sixties where they can be lovable people, but when it comes down to money, they're just downright crooked. Not so much crooked as selfish, I suppose. They just won't give up the bread." Petty's legal team went after the publishing deal, arguing that Petty had signed under duress, was pressured to sign a publishing agreement as a condition of the record deal itself. They also singled out one aspect of the Shelter contract, which stated that should Shelter be sold by ABC or lose the ABC distribution, the Heartbreakers would be free to go or renegotiate. That clause wasn't an issue they planned to address, at least not until Dimitriades received a letter saying, "Welcome to MCA." Bundle this with the bankruptcy claim at the heart of it all, and Petty was bound to spend more time in court than he had planned. And when he wasn't there, he was in the studio.

■

Petty and Iovine had by that time merged their personalities. "We were both equally driven," Petty says. "He was certainly on the case with this record to the same extent I was. He cared that much. We must have talked on the phone every night for a year. There'd be an hour conference each night about where we were at and what was going on. We were feeling like we were making a record that might be really good, but we were up against something bigger than either of us. I remember one night Jimmy calling me, really down, saying, 'Do you think this will ever come out? What if it doesn't?' I just kept saying, 'It's going to come out. It will.' But for a time there, we really weren't sure that the legal struggles and our work in the studio would come together as we hoped."

In the studio, the band was being scrutinized as never before. Stan Lynch in particular was receiving the kind of attention he preferred not to get. "Jimmy made us bear down and work on our rhythm tracks much harder than we ever had," Petty explains. "He had this dogged determination in the studio. It was a learning experience for all of us. The problem was that the band didn't play as well as they needed to. We'd made a couple of records, but they weren't really the groove-master records. They were kind of garage records. They weren't as elegant as Jimmy wanted it to sound. He had real trouble with Stan. Just couldn't understand why Stan wasn't fired. Jimmy and Shelly [Yakus] were obsessed with the drums. But the Heartbreakers had this all-for-one-and-one-for-all thing. Every day Jimmy is saying, 'You got to get rid of this guy.' And I'm saying, 'This is a band. We don't just fire people.' Jimmy would accept that for a few weeks, and then it would come up again. There were a lot of problems making that record. Groove problems."

"There's a producer," Stan Lynch says, "and as God is my witness, there's all kinds of new dynamics that are entering the game. Everybody's got a plan and a prophecy and a brilliant fucking idea how they're going to take what we've already done and claim that they knew what they were doing. But we were already the architects. We owned the sonic architecture. Everything that you like, everything about this, we owned it. Without those five assholes in the room, you ain't going to make that fucking noise. You could put Deputy Dawg behind the fucking console, and it's still going to sound like that. Shall I list the people who, to me, were hired guns?"

The band did some seventy takes of "Refugee," just trying to find the right feel for a song Petty instinctively believed worth the effort. Phil Seymour came in and played drums. B. J. Wilson came in and played. Percussion overdubs were used to cement the performances. Lynch was fired and rehired. It was struggle and tension. Iovine finds the question of whether the conflict with Lynch was in any way personal ridiculous. "I have to tell you something," he says, sitting on the porch outside his Interscope office. "Right up to today, if you are fucking blazing in the studio, I don't give a fuck if you're an asshole. I wasn't even noticing that with Stan Lynch. I got that he was a bit hard to work with, but that's it. The playing didn't *feel* right to me. That's not a personal thing. I worked with Phil Spector. Phil came behind me with a boat horn and two guns strapped to his chest. I'd never even *seen* a gun before. He shot them off in the bathroom. Stan Lynch? I didn't give a fuck. I wanted one thing: for the record to feel right. I didn't give a fuck who was doing it."

"Iovine really disliked Stan," says Benmont Tench. "I think they didn't like each other. I owe Jimmy a hell of a lot. He gave me a career as a session musician, expanded my life in a million ways. But I think he poisoned the well a little bit with Stan, starting with *Damn the Torpedoes.* Jimmy and Shelly put Stan through the fucking ringer. He's not a session drummer. He's not supposed to be a session drummer. He's a band drummer. Of course, I'm not in charge, and that's probably a good thing. But Jimmy came from the East Coast, from working with East Coast drummers, like Max Weinberg. Now he's on the West Coast, working with a southern drummer who listened to English drummers who listened to black drummers."

Like Petty, Bugs Weidel saw Lynch as having two musical sides. "Live, Stan was a great drummer. He's brilliant. But, especially in the studio, these guys were almost clinical. Over the years they refined it more and more and more. And he was never able to do that consistently. He'd stiffen up. Listen to the live show, and he's out there doing it, brilliant. And when he wanted to—I mean, listen to 'Mary Jane's Last Dance.' I remember Duck Dunn going, 'Ahh, give him a break. That's what the Stones did to Bill Wyman. It's not fair.' But it's not that easy. In everybody's defense, it *was* an issue. I remember Denny Cordell coming in to listen to *Damn the Torpedoes* tracks, which he had to do because of the lawsuit. It was a court thing. It was funny, because he's sitting there, listening to tracks, and he'd be like, 'The rhythm's not right on that one. Good song, but it ain't the take.' He could just peg it immediately. And he walked out of there going, 'Fire the drummer.' That was a tradition from early on, maybe not the second record but by *Damn the Torpedoes*: start recording the record, kind of hit a brick wall, fire Stanley, go a little further, hire Stanley back, make the record. That went on several times."

Mike Campbell had created the demo track for what would become "Here Comes My Girl," a track without vocals Petty could write to, and he'd done it with a drum loop made from the first few bars of Aerosmith's "Walk This Way." Loops, repeating a short sequence of beats, maintained the groove. You could use them like a drum machine, but they often had more human feel. More importantly, with a loop, the tempo didn't drift. When it went to the band, however, that wasn't always the case. "[Tom] would play a demo or play me the song on guitar," Jimmy Iovine says, "then go out and play it with the band. And I'm saying, 'That's making it stiff.' We'd go for days and days. We were drum fanatics, me and Shelly Yakus. I would have stayed there until today to get what was needed. So we just worked until it got to the point where it was cool, but then, if you listen to *Damn the Torpedoes*, there's also a lot of percussion on that record. It's everywhere, gluing things together."

But Iovine wasn't just hounding Stan Lynch. He was on Petty for more material. He wanted more songs. He went to Petty's publisher looking for material that had been shelved along the way. "Don't Do Me Like That" and "Louisiana Rain" were both older demos he turned up in the process. "I was sitting with the publisher," Iovine says, "who said, 'Tom Petty wrote this song for J. Geils.' I heard it and didn't say a word, just asked if I could have a copy. That was 'Don't Do Me Like That.' Then I drove right to Tom's house and said, 'Are you out of your fucking mind? What do you mean it sounds like Jay Geels! It sounds like you. I've worked in a studio next to Jay Geels, and this sounds like you!' I just kept saying it over and over. I could out-torture him. I could. I cracked him. He almost cracked me, but I think I almost cracked him."

If the first two records took significant effort, the third was taxing on another level. It was less about joy than ambition. Mike Campbell recalls walking out the door, leaving the project for a few days. "On 'Refugee,'" he says, "I had a mental breakdown. I just couldn't take it anymore. It was my song, a cowrite with Tom, and we kept playing it over and over and over, changing the thing, changing the sounds. It sounded like Nazis marching. There was no groove. We got into this hole of misery cutting that song. And I said, 'I need to get out of this room for a few days. This is not healthy.' It's the only time I've walked out of a session."

■

In the courtroom, Denny Cordell began to see that Petty's legal team was making headway. As the opposition pressed to expose Petty's bankruptcy case as an elaborate farce, Petty was winning favor in the room. When the lawyers grilled him about what equipment he owned, Petty told them he had an amp and some guitars. When they asked him what kind of guitars, he said, "There's a red one and a black one." The judge laughed out loud. Signs pointed toward a legal victory for the artist Cordell had signed in 1974. For Petty, no matter the angst that went into making *Damn the Torpedoes*, it was starting to feel and sound like the very record he and Iovine had been hoping to make, just as their legal issues were at last finding a sympathetic courtroom audience. On one of the days when Petty was in court and on the stand, he saw Cordell come into the back of the room. "Denny hadn't counted on the bankruptcy strategy," Petty explains. "But we went for it, and on that day in court, I think he knew he was going to lose. It may have been a sham in some ways, the bankruptcy strategy, but I was going to win with it. His lawyers figured we'd out-lawyered him. I don't know what kind of pressure had come down on him from within the industry, but I'm guessing that other record company heads were advising him to not let this happen. I watched him get up from where he was sitting, leave the courtroom, and that was it. He called that night, offering to settle out of court. It was the last day we were in there."

The other lawsuit was with MCA, though Cordell was enmeshed in that as the owner of Shelter. Remembering how little MCA did for the Mudcrutch single, Petty had long harbored bad feelings about the company. When the Heartbreakers needed to play some shows in the midst of the legal battles, what they called the "lawsuit tour," a tour that could only happen after Petty asked the permission of the judge, they made T-shirts that said "Why MCA?" But even the MCA relationship would be reconfigured before the release of *Damn the Torpedoes*.

In 1979, Danny Bramson, who had been booking the Universal Amphitheatre with recognizably good results, was hired by MCA to work for the label. "They didn't have anyone young over there," explains Tony Dimitriades. "They treated him like he was the young kid who knew everything. I think they also felt he could deal with the temperamental artists of the day. So Danny called me and said, 'Look, I can make a deal that will make MCA a better place for you.'" And Bramson did. He got his own imprint at MCA, Backstreet Records, and managed to secure total artistic control for Petty, along with all that Dimitriades and Elliot Roberts asked for, no negotiation. They stipulated that Backstreet hire Jon Scott. A new day had come.

In 2009, Petty sat with Iovine and Mike Campbell, playing back the master tapes from the *Damn the Torpedoes* sessions while cameras rolled. "They were doing one of those shows about the making of a record," Petty says. "So we went back to Sound City and went through the tracks, brought them up on the mains, and we were really kind of moved by it. You could hear all of the care that went into that record. When we brought up a couple of things, it was stunning, like, 'We were really onto something good.' Sitting in those same seats, listening to that record . . . I think it touched us all in a way that maybe we weren't quite expecting. It was a really important time, in the end a very good time. Even with all of the stress we had on the business side, we never let it interfere with the creative part. We were just dealing with the music."

It brought back to their minds the struggles they went through, but they obviously didn't have to relive the anxiety and frustration. Time and distance had done their work in more ways than one. As the cameras captured the scene, Petty looked to be the hippie he is, and Iovine the corporate giant. But *Damn the Torpedoes* was the success that changed all of their lives, giving them the most pronounced before-and-after effect of their careers.

Just before the very high-profile 2014 sale of his company, Beats, to Apple, a three-billion-dollar deal, Iovine said, "I tuned Beats headphones to that album. It's the best-sounding album I ever did. And there wasn't one fucking thing on my mind the entire time we made it. Just that. I was totally single-minded. I've never been the same way in anything I've ever done after. I've never been the same guy. And Tom and I drifted apart, probably because I wasn't the same guy."

14

THE ALBUM CYCLE

The last time I talked to my mother, I remember I was restless.

—JAMES BALDWIN

There are homes in present-day Los Angeles that go out of their way to let you
know you're in them. They announce themselves. For Jimmy Iovine, producing Tom Petty and the Heartbreakers was an early music business victory. There would be many more, and those victories delivered him into
one of those homes. From the foyer to the pool house, the private screen-
ing room to the expansive lawns, it's a grandeur far removed from the
outer Brooklyn that raised Iovine. Tom Petty's place in Malibu speaks in a
quieter voice. The layout of the property doesn't allow for any sense of how
large a parcel of land you're on, and the rooms in the main house stop well
short of mansion or estate scale. You come in through a gate, of course, and
you see a couple of nice cars in the driveway. You know the Pacific isn't far
away but not because of vistas staged to impress. The house is tucked into
the trees and bushes, gardens wild in the way Petty likes them. It's on the
intimate side as far as rock star homes are concerned.

Petty likes to meet in a small lounge area outside of his recording studio. It's open to the air coming off the Pacific, and plants push against the
windows. In that way, it's different from most of the studios in which Petty
willfully caged himself for much of his life, carpeted relics of the seventies. There are some images on the walls—a Shepard Fairey print of George
Harrison, given him by Dhani Harrison, a Dylan painting, a photograph

with Carl Perkins. The guitars that are hanging on the wall and standing in racks tend to get switched out. No doubt Norman's Rare Guitars in Tarzana has gotten a piece of Petty's paychecks for many years, and the store probably still does. There are no gold or platinum records hanging in the room.

When asked about his years living inside the album cycle, Petty drifts off into thought. He's sixty-four and has seen more than his share of success and the trouble that comes with it. But it's as important a topic as any. Petty arrived in the music business when the demands on a young artist with charting records were unambiguous: write the songs, go into the studio, make the record, mix it and master it, set up the release, do press, tour behind the record, write the songs, go into the studio, make the record . . . and thirty years later, if you're lucky enough to *get* that many years, your kids are grown-ups. Petty has spent most of his life at work. "He was gone," says Adria Petty.

No one, Petty himself included, challenges the idea that the work kept him from parenting as he would have liked to. He was always headed somewhere else, minding a movable shop, working closely with management. He'd pick the T-shirt designs and sign the Christmas cards, record the radio spots, and write songs his band could record. And yell a little. Sometimes when he needed to and sometimes when he didn't. "Some days I miss it," he says, "you know, getting up and being Tom Petty. At the time, I was probably complaining about it, but there are days now when my life is so orderly that I miss having to get out of bed with twenty things to do. We were busy for years and years, putting in a pretty good week every week. Bugs was there for all of that. The band wasn't always there. They weren't on that schedule all the time. I think Bugs was probably closer to it than they were. I'm sure he was closer to understanding . . . well, understanding my *life*, what I was living with. I even took Bugs into legal meetings. The lawyers would be arriving, opening their briefcases. They'd introduce themselves, and I'd go, 'That's Bugs.' They'd all kind of have to accept it."

■

Damn the Torpedoes was released in October 1979, just under half a year after Petty had filed for bankruptcy. By February 1980, he was on the cover of *Rolling Stone*. Every time Jimmy Iovine heard "Refugee" or "Don't Do Me

Like That" or "Here Comes My Girl" on the radio, he'd call Petty. Until he didn't. Everyone got busy. The band settled into the realities of success and of the new financial split, which found Petty moving toward a life that would look somewhat different from the others' lives. Of course, everyone was making more and working more than they ever had. And the more they worked, the bigger the band got. And the bigger they got, the more curious people became about Tom Petty. That was the more significant change for the Heartbreakers than any financial split. When fans heard "Even the Losers," they often felt like the singer was looking into their worlds. Good songs have that power. They didn't listen to "Even the Losers" and wonder what was on the bass player's mind. Petty was the mystery, the crush, the mind to understand, the poster on the bedroom wall. The bass player was going to get laid in Baltimore, but, really, how much more? Identities were being renegotiated, in the spotlight and behind it. Some new walls were erected between the leader and his band, just as Elliot Roberts promised. The question was whether Tom Petty and the Heartbreakers would survive this and, if so, what would be lost. "He got exactly what he wanted," says Stan Lynch. "Too bad. You know what I mean? Like, 'You want this? Now it's all on you.' For me, the worm sort of started to turn a little in the whole tragicomedy of being in a band. I thought, 'Hey, dude, you begged for this, actually took it from others to have all this. Accept your Elvis role.'" By most accounts, Petty did. Already had.

"I first heard them during the MUSE sessions," Jackson Browne says, sitting in the living room of his Hollywood home. "I mean, I didn't know them before that." Browne, Bonnie Raitt, John Hall, and Graham Nash were the principal organizers behind the Musicians United for Safe Energy event, the No Nukes concert, as it came to be called. The show, stretched over five nights, included the organizers, but also Gil Scott-Heron, Chaka Khan, Bruce Springsteen and the E Street Band, the Doobie Brothers, James Taylor, Ry Cooder, and more. The Heartbreakers were in with the heavies, a "new act" but, with *Damn the Torpedoes* about to come out and a buzz in the air, not out of place. "They were a band. That was the first thing I picked up on," Browne says. "There was an identity that went deep, kind of a primal thing. I may not have gotten that immediately. After I saw them and heard the record, though, for sure. But also when I met the crew, Bugs and all of them, because we were all staying at the Gramercy. They were hilarious. And they had the same kind of attitude, like, 'We'll see what this is all about, whether this is worthwhile for this band.' So I always felt like there were several rings around Tom. The band was one of them. The crew was one of them. And he was this almost reclusive center."

Browne pauses for a moment, as though searching for the bigger point. "He's very mysterious, doesn't encourage a lot of investigation of his personal circumstances. But because the songs affect us the way they do, because of the intimacy that happens in them, you're looking for a trace . . . maybe that's what he finds unnerving, the recognition that people are peering straight into him, wanting something. But, really, I don't know. I mean, we're friends, but I still can't say I know him well."

When the Heartbreakers came onstage at Madison Square Garden for the MUSE concerts, Jackson Browne was at the side of the stage and warned Petty and his band that they were in Bruce Springsteen's backyard on Springsteen's birthday, that they'd hear people yelling, "Bruuuuce!" But Browne assured the band that this sound wasn't the audience booing the Heartbreakers, just people calling out for Springsteen. Petty looked up and said, "What's the difference?" Stan Lynch, remembering the moment, says, "Without missing a beat! It was like Groucho Marx, that good. With a backdrop of fifteen thousand people screaming, he's just this total presence, total Buddha. Like, motherfucker, he's the coolest guy in the room." Petty could earn his band's admiration or its anger, depending on the hour.

The MUSE show worked out just fine, but what Jackson Browne refers to as the Heartbreakers' "very independent attitude" was, to some degree, manifest as discomfort at being in a super-event setting like that of the No Nukes show. When it came time to approve content for the concert film, Petty passed on the chance to be a part of it. He didn't believe his band's performance was good enough that night. Good, but not good enough. He ran one of the tighter quality control departments, and it was unaffected by the company he was in. Not being in the film wasn't an issue for him. When asked a few years later to be a headliner along with the Police and the Clash at the massive US Festival, a series of concerts sponsored by Steve Wozniak, Petty went along with it. But the million-dollar payday likely increased his comfort. He was a businessman among other things. But, mostly, Petty and his band weren't joiners.

To Jackson Browne's other point, however, there was an intimacy to

Petty's songs that was beginning to bring people around who were looking for that "trace." The success of *Damn the Torpedoes* took the public's
curiosity to significantly higher levels. Stevie Nicks, perhaps because she
was in the band that sold more records than most others in the world and,
as a result, had a measure of access, was the most outspoken of those who
wanted to know more about Petty. She'd already made a few calls to management, but Petty ignored them, not sure that he wanted the association
with California superstars, not right then. "After I joined Fleetwood Mac,
I started hearing Tom Petty on the radio," Nicks says. "And I just fell in
love with his music and his band. I would laughingly say to anyone that if
I ever got to know Tom Petty and could worm my way into his good graces,
if he were ever to ask me to leave Fleetwood Mac and join Tom Petty and
the Heartbreakers, I'd probably do it. And that was before I even met him."
As a member of Fleetwood Mac, Nicks filled whatever room she walked
into, but at the rate of one Fleetwood Mac album every two or three years,
with some four of her songs on each recording, she was a superstar with a
backlog of material. Though it didn't make the other members of Fleetwood Mac feel a whole lot better, she convinced her "freaked-out" band
members that she wasn't out to become a solo artist. She just needed
another outlet for the songs accumulating on her shelf. "I'm not doing a
solo record to turn into a solo artist," she told them, arguably testing the
limits of logic.

To the Eagles' manager Irving Azoff, who was acting as her personal
manager, Nicks said, "If I can't be in Tom Petty and the Heartbreakers, I
want to make a record that sounds as much like T.P.'s as possible." They
went to Petty first through Paul Fishkin, the president of Modern Records,
a label Fishkin and Danny Goldberg had set up for Stevie's solo work, asking if he'd produce Nicks. After some back-and-forth discussion, with
Petty expressing his concern that he couldn't take this on, Nicks and her
reluctant producer went into a studio and cut "Outside the Rain." But the
situation confirmed to Petty that it was more than he could handle, no
matter Nicks's assurances that she'd adapt her schedule to suit his. "I realized I couldn't do this," Petty explains. "There were a lot of hangers-on,
just too much to have to get through. When the Heartbreakers worked,
we never had guests in the studio. I wasn't used to it. So I recommended
Jimmy." Stevie Nicks went to New York late in 1979 and had dinner with

Iovine. "We talked a lot about Tom Petty," she recalls. "I said, 'Really, you know, I want to be the girl Tom Petty.'" Two weeks later, Nicks was living with Iovine—as his girlfriend.

■

While Iovine's career as a producer was getting busier, Petty was out on the road. "Refugee" and "Don't Do Me Like That" were already major songs on the radio, the latter a top five hit. But the audiences that came out to see the band knew more than what radio brought to them—they came because of the album. And *Damn the Torpedoes* was an *album*, with studied sequencing and interstitial material between song matter that connects the whole experience into one event. "Louisiana Rain," "Even the Losers," and "Century City" all have bits of audio scrap leading into the actual recordings, and some of those scraps would become as well loved as the songs themselves. Mike Campbell's wife, Marcie, can be heard shouting, "It's just the normal noises in here!" right in the middle of side one. It was something Petty found in a Campbell demo. "I had a TEAC four-track recorder, and it was right around the corner from the washing machine in our little rental house," explains Campbell. "I was trying to record something, and the washing machine was broken, making this loud noise. I yelled at Marcy, 'You have to turn that off!' And she goes, 'It's just the normal noises in here!' Like, 'Shut the fuck up! I'm living my life!' Next thing you know, we'd be in the car, and there was Marcie on the radio."

Petty pushed Iovine to get the audio snippets on the record. The producer didn't want any of it. "Tom and Mike were Beatles freaks," says Jimmy Iovine. "They wanted that stuff on there, not me. But, really, these guys were already brilliant record producers. The record's perfect. It was number two to *The Wall* for nine weeks. We never went to number one. Talk about *The Wall*." For the Heartbreakers, the problem was no longer about getting gigs and trying to stay busy. The issue now was the pace, the circus that never closed its tent flaps. Girls in the lobby, girls putting notes under their doors, all of it. They could have toured as long as they wanted. They only stopped because they knew, and their label and management concurred, that they needed a new record. They'd have to learn to say no, because the offers kept coming and getting better and better.

Relatively early in the touring, however, Petty came up against unexpected troubles. "We were in New York, doing a promo film for 'Here Comes My Girl.' This was before MTV. It was just a performance they were shooting, but they used those oil-based smoke machines. I was breathing it in all day, and up until that point, I'd never given a second thought to the condition of my voice. Singing was just something I did. It always worked fine, just came out when I needed it. But the next day in Philadelphia at the Tower Theater, midway through the show, my voice started to quit working, started to go. And seventy-five percent of the way in, it was gone. I couldn't make a sound—there was nothing coming out."

At the next night's show, Petty got 90 percent of the way through the set, which wasn't a lot of comfort, knowing as he did that Boston was the following night. In Boston, they'd be at the Orpheum Theatre and had the full support of WBCN, the station that had done so much to help break the first album. It was a night for the Heartbreakers to be *on*. But with the Boston audience in their seats, the band did a vocal warm-up backstage, and Petty opened his mouth to find that nothing would come out.

A local doctor said it was laryngitis and told Petty to take a few days off from singing. The tour schedule was shuffled around, with the Orpheum show rescheduled for two nights later. Petty stayed in his hotel room, not singing, not even talking, just watching TV and sleeping. Bill Flanagan, who would later be the editor of *Musician* magazine, was enlisted to interview Petty and write a review of the show for Boston's *Real Paper*. "I was working in a record store in Providence, Rhode Island, when the first album came out," says Flanagan. "It felt like there was hope, you know? The mid-seventies tended to favor people who had been around for a long time and were just *now* getting promoted to full rock stardom. Linda Ronstadt, Jefferson Starship, Steve Miller Band, Fleetwood Mac. Everyone who had been an opening act in the sixties was getting their moment. Like, 'Okay, it's Boz Scaggs's turn.' We were asking, 'Isn't there anybody new?'" The answer came with Bruce Springsteen, Patti Smith, Graham Parker. When Elvis Costello and Tom Petty showed up, Flanagan says it confirmed that something new was happening, that "the good guys were making a stand." When Flanagan arrived at the Orpheum, however, he found out the show had been postponed. "I didn't get the message that the interview had been canceled, though," explains Flanagan. "And it was a different time. Tom Petty was staying under his own name at the Holiday Inn. So I called the hotel, asked for his room, and woke him up. He's really nice about it but tells me he can't talk. A few hours later, the publicist calls, informs me that he's got laryngitis. I say, 'I know. I just talked to him.' She's like, 'You what?!'"

Better after forty-eight hours of rest, feeling okay to sing, Petty went to the Orpheum with the band. The excitement was even higher. The audience was in, the lights dimming—and Petty's voice was . . . gone. Bill Flanagan wrote something for the *Real Paper* without seeing a show. But with that second cancellation, Petty got something stuck in his head that would be there for years—uncertainty. It was a feeling of never being completely sure that he'd pull it off. Long after the matter was idenitifed as tonsillitis, the mind part of the trouble remained. A tonsillectomy couldn't fix what was beginning to happen in his head. But with a record on the charts and a lot of people looking to him for their livelihoods, Petty didn't make his nerves anyone else's problem. There was a calendar full of dates to play before they got back into the studio. He did what he'd learned to do as a kid: he kept it to himself.

Among those dates were shows that gave the band a chance to return to Florida as heroes. The band that got fired from Dub's was coming back to enjoy their parade. There was some satisfaction in that, and in this case, it was evenly dispersed among the band members. There would be only one first trip back home after hitting the big time. This was it. No other tour stop would mean this much. Not since the Allman Brothers had Florida seen one of its own acts enjoying this kind of attention. And in the case of the Allmans, Georgia seemed to get a lot of the credit. Not so with the Heartbreakers—this one was for the Sunshine State. In Tampa, it felt like everyone was behind them, from the hotel staff and the gas station attendant to the kids smoking dope on the beach. It was a homecoming, and it was, without question, sweet. The day after the show, after only a few hours of sleep, Petty went to Gainesville to visit his mother, for what would be the last time. Bugs drove him while the rest of the band slept it off.

By that time in the *Damn the Torpedoes* touring, the fans would be waiting for them, in hotels, at gigs, after shows. The group's daily itinerary may as well have been a public matter. It was a part of rock-and-roll success that, fun at first, got old faster than other aspects. So Petty was happy to see that the hospital grounds seemed relatively quiet as they pulled into the parking lot that morning. A few people looked their way as he came into the building, interested but giving him space. Petty and Weidel got onto an elevator without commotion. As they would see, Kitty Petty was all but gone from this world, little more than a body. But that wasn't what Petty saw first. Arriving in her room, looking at his mother, Petty saw himself. Several of himself.

"Someone had laid all these magazines with pictures of me on my mother," remembers Petty. "On her chest and across her body. She was just lying there, beneath these clippings from magazines and newspapers. I walk in and . . . it was the strangest thing. I thought, 'Even this moment, *even this* someone had to corrupt with some reaction to fame, or whatever this was.'" A nurse had gotten it into her mind that this would please the famous son of the hospital's dying patient. It was a misguided gesture, innocent but stupid, that left him hollow. Asking a nurse to clear the clippings off his mother, he then took time alone with her.

"I was just beginning to see that there's just nobody that couldn't be affected by fame in *some* way," Petty explains, "like when I walk in some place and my music is playing, because they think I want to hear that. I was starting to see that that's just part of the job. But I wasn't prepared for that in my mother's hospital room, you know? I needed to clear the room of that. I looked at her, and I talked to her. She couldn't talk to me. But she had a kind look in her eyes. It was really hard. I left there thinking, 'I don't ever want to see this again. I don't ever want to see her like this again. That's it for me. She's gone.' My dad had come by, and he rode down the elevator with me. But as we were walking to the parking lot, he goes, 'I want to go down and hit the tracks—do you have any cash?' I said, 'Yeah.' I gave him a thousand bucks, whatever I had on me. But I remember making the clear decision in my mind that I wasn't coming back to this again. There was no point, no way for us to communicate, and it just crippled me. I said to myself, 'I'm not ever going to come around again.' And I didn't. I headed off to the next gig."

Rejoining the band, Petty went to the back of the bus, as had become his practice. He made no effort to explain where he'd just been. The Heartbreakers didn't do that kind of intimacy. "I remember [my father] being super happy when I was young," Adria Petty says, "like he had this charisma and kindness and gentleness. I rarely saw him lose his temper or be any-thing but lighthearted and compassionate, until after *Damn the Torpedoes*, which is when his mother died, like right at the same time."

Kitty Petty didn't live much longer. She went quietly but not without notice. Gainesville did all it could to acknowledge the loss, likely more than was appropriate. Maybe the football team wasn't doing well that year, and the town needed something to attach itself to, so they found a local story. For Petty, he saw it coming: his mother again buried beneath pictures of her son.

"After I saw her last, I went right back onto the road," Petty remem-bers. "Then some months later, she died. And I didn't go to the funeral. My brother told me, 'You come here and it's going to be a zoo. The whole town's already gearing up for when you're going to arrive. They all think you're coming.' So I said, 'Well, then I'm not going. I'm not going to let this be about me. I can't deal with that.' But the truth is that I've always felt conflicted about whether I should have gone or not. I think it's hard for anyone to understand, to see what an extreme position I would have been in. They were absolutely crazy in Gainesville."

Kitty Petty made her way into her son's sleep, waking him in one hotel room or another. She was a complicated ghost, all but lost to her children for so long but always remembered as the one who tried to bring some pure love into their lives. Tom Petty was still in his twenties, a kid with a kid of his own. Keeping it together was the goal. The tasks of a bandleader were lining up to meet him. The pressure to write was palpable, a weight that was always there but building in waves. Iovine was back in LA, expect-ing music. The mourning process was abbreviated. Petty's secret was that he was glad of it.

"Jimmy didn't even want to mention me to Tom," says Stevie Nicks. "Because he thought Tom would think, 'Oh great, now you're all involved with Stevie Nicks, which means you're not going to be focused on this new record we're doing, which is *not done yet*!' And Jimmy was right, knowing Tom, that *is* what he would think. So Jimmy had this house in Sherman Oaks, and I was pretty much living there, but whenever Tom would come over, just to hang with Jimmy and talk about where they were at and what they wanted to do next, I would hide in the bedroom downstairs." Lying on the bed, reading magazines, Nicks would sometimes try to hear what they were saying, but she couldn't pick up much one flight down.

Iovine, not what one might call a romantic when it comes to discussing relationships, attempted a strict division between work and home. He didn't confer with Petty about Petty's wife, and he expected it to cut both ways. "We'd talk about things, yeah, but never about Jane," Iovine says. "I didn't understand relationships. I couldn't help him in that area if he set himself on fire. I had no idea. I was like, 'What's a girl got to do with this?' That's where I was coming from." Of course, that wasn't going to work with the "girl" down in the lower bedroom. Nicks held still as long as she could. Which wasn't that long.

"I started feeling like I was a kept woman, locked down in a dungeon," Nicks says. When Iovine, with Nicks's prompting, finally said something to Petty, by that time in the midst of recording *Hard Promises*, he wasn't entirely forthcoming. "I don't think he said he'd been seeing me for three months!" Nicks says. The idea of collaboration wasn't introduced. But, suddenly, Stevie Nicks was around much more. When she really started work on her solo record, with Iovine producing, Benmont Tench was in her band, Petty was weighing in on the tracks that Iovine played him, was a credited producer on two cuts, including "Outside the Rain," and Mike Campbell was doing some overdubs. The woman from the dungeon was getting her needs met. "Stevie Nicks? Don't even get me started," says Stan Lynch.

Petty insists that the Heartbreakers didn't give themselves over so easily. "We weren't really welcoming to her when she first started coming around," he says. "It wasn't like she received a lot of warmth. We weren't impressed by superstars. It just wasn't our nature. Maybe if it had been Elvis." The closed circle of the Heartbreakers, closed in part because the band was mostly very shy, didn't organize welcome parties for outsiders. Nicks got suspicious looks and a cool Florida wind. But she wasn't a stranger to band situations, and she didn't run back home after failing to get their quick embrace. "She went and worked Jane," Petty says.

Stevie Nicks still sees Petty's marriage to Jane Benyo differently than Petty ever will. But however limited her perspective relative to what Petty experienced at home during the long, troubled marriage, it's striking how different Nicks's picture is. "Tom is a lucky man. He's had two great loves,"

Nicks insists. "And [Jane] was certainly the first. I was around to see it. If you'd met them at the beginning, when I met them, they were like the same person, you know? They even looked alike. She was very beautiful, tall and blond, had these lovely blue eyes that just shot through you. They'd been together since they were kids, really *kids*. And they were young parents. Then he got famous. But I think he was crazy about her."

"Stevie really had Jane in her corner," Petty says. "Because Stevie would indulge her, it took me a long time to realize how genuine and good Stevie was. She was doing a lot of drugs—and she'd be the first to tell you that— but we didn't at the time. We weren't Boy Scouts, but I was afraid of that. Jane embraced it in a big way when Stevie showed up." If it began with mild suspicion, Petty's friendship with Nicks would finally be one of the few human constants in his life outside of his band, management, and crew. She'd come in and out over decades. That first year, however, she got all the way in and planned to see what that meant and what she could make of it. Petty smiles at the thought. "She came into my life like a rocket, just refusing to go away."

Iovine and Petty together arrived at what Nicks calls an "executive deci-sion," concluding that her solo record was missing a single. So Petty wrote "Insider" for her. It came fast. He scratched the words out in a matter of minutes and cut something on acoustic guitar, with just Benmont Tench playing along on organ. The band overdubbed their parts, keeping it spare. Nicks put down a vocal. As the track built, Petty found himself thinking it might be one of the best things he'd ever written. The song was a shade different from his earlier work. He'd managed to get inside the mind grap-pling with loss, and he created a character there, without a lot of exposi-tion crowding the song. Whether there was some received understanding of what an "insider" was or not, Petty had written one of those songs that pins down some human truth. To have *once been close*. Who didn't know that scene? He'd hit on the thing a songwriter is always after. You don't give those tunes away. So Petty didn't. He told Nicks she couldn't have the song he'd written for her.

On record, there was a chemistry between Tom Petty and Stevie Nicks that made people wonder. He'd taken "Insider" back, but her vocal was still on it. And there was something, in phrasing and tone, about the way those two voices lay against each other. Some listeners couldn't accept it as fiction, as something that passed between actors before the curtains closed. And there was truth to what they heard. There *was* a chemistry. Nicks called it "intense, fiery." But the energy the collaboration threw off was going into the work. After cutting "Insider," part of that work now revolved around Petty finding another song for Nicks. That's when "Stop Dragging My Heart Around" came up as a possibility. The Heartbreakers had already cut the song, and there was no plan to give it away to another artist. Even when Iovine raised the idea, Petty thought it sounded too much like the Heartbreakers and that Nicks needed something that sounded more like the singer from Fleetwood Mac. But that wasn't Nicks's aim. It never had been. She wanted to be in the Heartbreakers. This was one way of doing it, to sing to a track they'd already cut as a band, that they'd intended for their own album. Iovine helped broker the deal.

"It was a classic moment," Stan Lynch says. "It was going to be our song, a Petty song. It wasn't a Stevie Nicks record. In my mind, when we were recording it, we were cutting a balls-to-the-wall, great song. I saw an arena. In my mind, it's big. Like, 'Fucking, let's nail this!'" Duck Dunn was covering for Ron Blair on bass. By this time, Dunn was a friend to the whole band, a wise man from the South with a history everyone admired. On *Damn the Torpedoes*, he played bass on "You Tell Me," just as he'd played on "Hometown Blues" on the debut. They needed him. Blair was already drifting away, discouraged by the way his friends changed when their dreams started coming true. Dunn calmed everyone down a bit. They were laying the song down as a band but finding their way to the right feel. "I'm farting around," says Lynch, "making a fool of myself. But on take two something happened. I'm playing the Whitman Sampler, playing every part, changing the beat, and Duck's just following along. We get to the end, and Duck puts a finger to his lips, like, 'Don't say anything. Let the tape roll.' That's always a good sign."

In the control room, listening back to that second take, Dunn sat next to Lynch, close enough for Lynch to feel Dunn's thigh pressing against his own. It was a message for the drummer to keep his head on, stay quiet. At the end of the playback, there was a silence, broken only by Dunn's response. "He looks at the producers," recalls Lynch, "and he says, 'Well, you don't like that, you don't like pussy.'" Benmont Tench confirms the scene: "I think that's a fucking great compliment from the man who played bass on so many astounding records. Duck was a wonder." Lynch insists that if it hadn't been for Dunn, "Stop Dragging My Heart Around" would have been subject to what he believes was the usual second-guessing that got in the way of making music. "Let me tell you what I learned from that," Lynch insists. "A lot of takes that were pretty decent rhythm tracks probably got thrown under the rug. It was validating and beautiful. It made me realize, 'Well, *I* ain't the fucking problem in this room.' Because, at that point, Jimmy had decided that every other drummer in the fucking country is better than Stan."

The other Heartbreakers agree that Duck Dunn was right about the take. That was the one. But did it mean that other usable takes were being scrapped on a regular basis because Stan Lynch was being blamed for not holding down the groove? "No," says Mike Campbell, without a lot of concern for Lynch's theory, "nothing went past us. Maybe once, there might have been a track that we went back to after forty takes. There may be a few places where the generals were looking too far down the field. But, no, we're not going to let something good go by. Nobody wanted to keep slugging away if we already had it."

Talking to *Melody Maker* later that year, Petty describes *Hard Promises* and the shift away from the *Damn the Torpedoes* sessions, when the focus was so much on "the sound": "With *Damn the Torpedoes* they had this incredible sound, with the drums and all that. We were just getting to know each other, so we pretty much said, 'Okay, let's get into whatever Jimmy's got goin' and do something interesting'—and it was. And this time, I think that Jimmy listened to me a little bit more, because to tell you the truth, when I played him the songs he didn't quite understand what I was getting at." Iovine saw the record as "dark." "Even the Losers" typified the spirit of the whole rock-and-roll enterprise Iovine felt the Heartbreakers represented. "Insider" was another species of song. When Campbell brought in "You Can Still Change Your Mind," and Petty wrote to it, they were closer to the Beach Boys than the Stones. "The Waiting," however, did all that "Insider" did but in the opposite emotional direction—it was as complete, as euphoric a love song as Petty would ever write. That was where Iovine got excited.

Iovine came to believe in *Hard Promises*, to the point at which he felt he had even more on his hands this time around. He thought they'd topped *Damn the Torpedoes*. "I'll be honest with you," he says. "That album changed me. I thought 'The Waiting' was bigger than 'Refugee.' So when it wasn't a hit, a real hit, it killed me. It was devastating. I felt it was as good as anything I'd ever been near. That song, I thought that was big. That's why 'Stop Dragging My Heart Around' wasn't important. Because we had 'Woman in Love' and 'The Waiting.'" When asked about "Nightwatchman," "Something Big," and "Criminal Kind," all songs that show Petty going deeper into his storytelling side, with characters moving through and scenes being developed with more detail and stronger internal structure, Iovine simply says, "That's the Dylan thing," and turns the conversation back to his primary concern, the singles.

Contrary to what Iovine wanted for *Hard Promises*, the biggest single he had from those sessions, coolly making its way to number one, was not "The Waiting" or "A Woman in Love (It's Not Me)." It was "Stop Dragging My Heart Around." Stevie Nicks's *Bella Donna* was going to be the record that included the most successful Heartbreakers recording of that period. Radio went after "Stop Dragging My Heart Around" with such unabashed support that the community of FM programmers felt they couldn't give their all to "A Woman in Love (It's Not Me)" *or* the "The Waiting." So they didn't. The three recordings sounded like they were all from the same album. And at one time they had been.

■

When it came time to prepare for the release of *Hard Promises*, MCA knew it had something very good on its hands and decided it was time to apply "superstar" pricing to Petty's new long player, raising the price from the customary $8.98 to $9.98. But no matter his new life as a rock-and-roll star, some cord of sentiment connected him to the teenager who couldn't afford to buy the records he wanted, however much he wanted them. Inadvertently, perhaps, the record company got another fight out of Petty. From his perspective, he'd do what he had to do to be sure it wasn't his face that people saw when they started paying more for their music. His second *Rolling Stone* cover featured Tom Petty ripping a dollar bill in half. He wasn't *looking* for his next battle when MCA tried to raise prices. He was tired and didn't want another struggle.

15

LIFE BETWEEN THE BRANCHES BELOW

Much has been written about the teenager of today—but in every article we've seen, one important fact has been over-looked or ignored: namely, that the teenager of today is the parent of tomorrow!

MAD MAGAZINE, APRIL 1961

Just as Stevie Nicks insists that she saw something real, some deep sense of connection in Tom and Jane Petty's marriage, Adria Petty, though a child at the time, is sure she saw it, too. "I feel like they had a really special partnership," Adria says. "And a real love for the band. Maybe because their own families were so estranged from them, they created this support system, this mom-and-dad atmosphere. But I felt strangely sympathetic towards them when they had their difficulties or when they had failures as parents or in trying to navigate career, relationship, and all of that. I saw them as good people doing their best. And, really, I think my mother was an inspiration to him. She *became* something else. But she didn't start there. She suffered from her own emotional problems. And maybe when the coke came around, it became a catalyst for a one-way ticket into the center of those problems." Rock and roll provided a shaky foundation on which to build a family life. Drugs and alcohol made things more complicated still. But the darkness that lay ahead for Jane Petty didn't come from the outside. The worst of it was within. At a certain point, it couldn't all be explained with recourse to a story about her husband and the good fortune that had befallen them.

Annakim Petty was born in January 1982. She missed out on the years that Adria would later consider her parents' best, when the couple seemed aligned in their view of the strange world they'd entered, when their ambitions for Petty's career neatly overlapped their ambitions for the family. The Pettys were young, young enough to believe that it could all get better if his career achieved what they hoped it would. They'd come from twisted homes, and rock and roll seemed capable of delivering them into something more. For a long time, they were the faithful, holding on to that idea. But Annakim was born into the troubled side of that dream. Just prior to her birth, Petty arrived home from a *Hard Promises* night session to find his wife passed out cold in the hallway of the family's home, with Adria sleeping down the hall. Initially unable to revive her, Petty managed to get Jane up and into the bedroom. But she wasn't making any kind of sense. In a state, he called Alice Lenahan, who had been over earlier in the evening, to see if she knew anything. Alice just said that Jane had been drinking. But this wasn't looking like the result of a few cocktails. It wasn't the first scene of that kind and wouldn't be the last. Tom Petty wasn't even close to questioning his marriage. He was his mother's son, ready to do what he needed to keep his family together. He bitched about it when he had to. More often, he went silent. If there was a plan, at that point, it wasn't an escape plan. He thought maybe a second child was a chance to get things right again. He wouldn't be the first man to believe in such a fantasy. There was some self-deception involved, but the alternative was fear.

If willing to discuss his first marriage, Petty isn't comfortable doing it. "Jane had done a pretty good job with Adria, you know, of being a mom and being responsible," he says. "So when she got pregnant, I said, 'Let's have this baby. I think it would be really good.' I thought it would center her on something. But, yeah, I was probably in denial to a great degree. Because then, suddenly, I had two kids who needed their parents. I couldn't run from that. But, at the same time, I still needed to be Tom Petty. I had a lot of shit going on. I really needed the help of my spouse. Our financial situation had changed, so I was able to do more for Annakim. She and Adria were what I wanted to go home to. We spent a lot of time together in my off time. But work often kept me away. That's when Jane started hiring nannies, which I was against. I didn't want nannies in the house. But I was gone so much, who was I to be saying how things should run when I wasn't there? And so much of what was really going on I didn't find out until later. Jane was surrounded by sycophants who were willing to keep me from knowing more, and other people just didn't want to get in the middle of my stuff. I'd hear later from another parent that Annakim was on a playdate, with a stretch limo waiting for her. She didn't get the ordinary concern a child would get. Am I guilty in this? I guess I am." After stopping for a moment, Petty looks toward the open door in the room. "All of this is not easy to think about," he says. "Annakim had a very hard childhood. It's not the story I wanted for her, or for us. And I don't like to have to tell it." Success was going to keep the family from getting the help they could have used. They were behind a high wall.

■

Thirty-two years old when Annakim was born in a Santa Monica hospital, Tom Petty was also coming closer to the first personnel change within the Heartbreakers lineup, and he didn't know how to manage it or what its effects might be. He would need to wait and watch to understand how it would affect the other Heartbreakers, his audience, and all the others who had invested in the idea of this band. His job, he felt, was to keep it all together. There was a parallel between home and work. And the success he was having was limited on both fronts. He blamed himself. He blamed himself, that is, when he wasn't blaming someone else. And he couldn't be faulted for either approach. There were grounds.

At home, Petty was dealing with the kind of broken love that most families hide from view, like little tombs of silence that gradually gain power over the inhabitants. In the Heartbreakers, however, the problem had a face. Oddly enough, it was Ron Blair's. And the problem *was* talked about— mostly behind Blair's back. The bass player had become the "outsider." There's generally one. It's a basic tenet of group psychology that any band manager could confirm. Or you could turn to Sigmund Freud, who wasn't in a band but must have known someone who was: "It is always possible to bind together a considerable number of people in love, so long as there are other people left over to receive the manifestations of their aggressiveness."

In the case of the Heartbreakers and Ron Blair, the "manifestations of their aggressiveness" came at sound checks, in lounges at the front of the bus, in hotel lobbies. It was the cold shoulder as much as anything else. Sometimes Stan Lynch deflected the scrutiny he was under as a drummer, pointing a finger at Blair. Any rock-and-roll band that has lasted beyond

its first year has had someone in Blair's role. Often the band members alter-
nate in that "outsider" position, with a group leader forming alliances
within a band that shift one year to the next, one month to the next. But
no one in or around the band denies that as of 1981 Ron Blair was drifting. He wasn't behaving like a band member. He'd taken a stroll to the
periphery, and it left him vulnerable.

"I don't know if every band goes through it," Ron Blair says, "but things
had gotten tension filled. I remember early on, at something like our second gig, our road manager telling me never to wear my Levi's shirt, like
we shouldn't appear to be southern. Wearing cowboy shirts with snaps or
growing beards: these were a no-no. Later on, we were back in LA in the
studio, and, hey, I was growing a beard! It wasn't what we were supposed
to be doing. Was I trying to be the sticky wheel? I don't know what it was
I was doing. Maybe I was trying to distance myself. It was just an odd
period for the band. And I wasn't digging it." The Heartbreakers were still
a young act, in what felt like heated competition with their peers. "The
way we'd talk about other people and other bands," recalls Blair. "You know,
'Our gang is better than your gang.' The competition and the gossip. It just
rubbed me the wrong way, the way the game is played." Blair wasn't particularly good at it either. You had to get a little leathery to live through it.
Blair thought there must be another way. Lynch, however, was a master of
that game. And Petty was no slouch. It made for a climate in which you
watched your ass, did what you could to make sure you didn't have a target
on your back. Blair, finally, couldn't get his target off.

"I've told this story probably twelve different ways," he says. "And it
could go anywhere from *If I was fired, I probably deserved it* to *My mind left
planet Band* to *I needed a break*. But there *was* a pivotal moment for me. The
band had been touring all year, playing halls that sounded really bad,
which made for a lot of tension. It was the kind of stuff that would make
anyone sick of it. Month after month of that. Then we had a six-day break,
or something like that, and the idea was, 'Hey, let's go back to Florida, to
the beach house; let's regroup.' It was a friend's place, where we'd all gone
when we were waiting for the first record to come out. We'd bonded and
everything, and so we were going to go there again. But I just couldn't bring
myself to do it." The band members readied themselves to head off on the
retreat, to renew their vows or whatever it was they needed to do to get

connected. "I remember we were in some hotel in some Midwestern city," Blair recalls, "and Stan came by my room. It was like twelve o'clock at night. And he says, 'C'mon, Ron, come with us. It's all gonna be good.' And I just . . . it was a little bit childish, but I was like, 'No, I'm not going. I'm going to go on to the next gig, meet you guys there. I gotta not be around you guys for a few days.' I let the band go on to the beach house to do some kind of recentering trip. But if that caused a rift, I compounded it by showing up to the next gig with my wife, which was not a cool thing to do. Everyone else's wives were like, 'Why didn't I get to do that? Why didn't you invite me on the road?' And we were at a really great resort, the Don CeSar in St. Petersburg, that pink-and-white Moroccan-style hotel. So I sort of set in motion a separation, like, 'I'm kind of going this way, and I don't care which way you guys are going.'" If the band needed something to talk about, Blair was giving them innumerable gifts.

And then there was the studio, where Duck Dunn played bass not just on "Stop Dragging My Heart Around" but on "A Woman in Love (It's Not Me)." Campbell and Petty were also comfortable playing some bass, without a lot of thought as to what it meant for their bass player. Blair hadn't done anything to make himself irreplaceable. Perhaps he couldn't have if he wanted to. Maybe he was just dreaming of the possibility of having two lives rather than one—and that wasn't the phase in which the band found themselves. For the time being, living as a Heartbreaker was all-in experience. Petty describes the *Hard Promises* era as the time in which it "became a job." It wouldn't be long before Blair didn't have one. When asked very directly if he quit or he was fired, Blair says, "Is there something in between?" He got a call from Tony Dimitriades. It wasn't the kind of call anyone would want to get, but it was the call that Blair was half expecting. The conversation was quiet. "Tony phoned me," Blair recalls, "and he said, 'Ron, you probably know this already, but you guys are kind of going in different directions.' I went, 'Yeah, I know.' Then he said something like, 'Should we just call it what it is?'" Dimitriades, not one for shouting across crowded restaurants, delivered it with a gentle hand. "It was kind of on a bro level," Blair says, "not like, 'Here's your pink slip.' And that was it. If I was looking for a change, I got it."

But so many years after Ron Blair's moment as the outsider in the Heartbreakers, no one has a lot to say about it. His is not the name that comes up when the early years of the Heartbreakers are the subject. It's Stan Lynch who gets talked about. "Stan's personality is more complicated than Ron's," says Mike Campbell. "He's got more chips on his shoulder." Blair, passive by nature, was no more than a surface on which tremors of discontent and fear could be projected. After he left, he opened a surf shop, tried to settle into another life, focused on his marriage, and then lost that marriage. In the press, the shorthand made good copy: man leaves internationally successful rock band to open a bikini shop. Really?

Petty had been in this spot too many times to be comfortable with it. He was in it before they found Mike Campbell. He was in it before they found Danny Roberts. A vacancy within the band was a problem with historical reverberations. It made Petty uneasy. Obviously, the process was going to be different this time. He wouldn't have to put up a "bass player wanted" sign at Lipham's. But more eyes would be watching. He needed a member who wouldn't disrupt what had been built. At four albums in, the band had a momentum to consider and an aesthetic to honor. But it was only four albums; they were still building the brand. He'd called the wrong person before, and he knew what that got him. Petty didn't rush to replace Blair, and in the meantime, he pocketed the extra share of band loot, provoking some internal chatter, mostly Stan Lynch's, about "the Ron Blair money" and its whereabouts.

In 1983, a new bass player would be coming into a power structure very different from that of seven years earlier, when the first record was released. Mike Campbell's deputy position within the band had become all but official. Though still a few records away from a production credit, Campbell was without question second in line to Petty. "When you get in the studio with Jimmy Iovine," says Campbell, "you can't have too many opinions. Me, Jimmy, and Tom were on the same wavelength in terms of production decisions, how records should be made. We didn't always ask for other opinions. We had enough going on between the three of us. Ben was like a little brother that didn't get much respect. He's an amazing player, and he gets that respect now. But he was a little more all over the map then. We didn't need two other guys going, 'I think . . . I think . . .' Democracy can be a curse."

Though Campbell had been roommates with Stan Lynch, a situation the crew called "the Michael Stanley Band," no doubt Lynch felt something tighten in his lower intestines as he watched Campbell establish himself as Petty's right hand. Over the next several years, Lynch worked hard on Campbell, talking shit about the boss when the door appeared to be closed. By most accounts, from that time forward, virtually every internal "band situation" involved Lynch in some way. By nature, he was divide-and-conquer in his style, with an emphasis on dividing, when he wasn't being a team player, which he often was. There were two Stans. But since the time he and Petty went to Tulsa, recording "Luna" together for the first record, Lynch's role had become more circumscribed. No doubt it felt like his opportunities were shrinking. And with Blair gone, there was no band member Lynch could use to distract the others, and shield himself, from the painful attention he got in the studio as the drummer who wasn't always giving the band what they wanted.

Who knows how the gods look down on all of this or if they do at all. But they seem to have taken a kind of favor in Ron Blair's case. When the years are calculated, their respective time as Heartbreakers tallied, it's Blair who has been in the band longer than Lynch. Maybe it's how Blair handled things. Just three weeks after that last call with Dimitriades, something compelled him to call Petty. "It was hard," he says. "When something like that happens, you tend to get angry, to start getting mad at life. But after a couple weeks, something in me just switched all around. I thought, 'Man, how lucky was I to have the quality of friends that would stick with me through all that stuff? And Tom looked out for me all those years, with me having no sense about how to have a career.' I just felt a shift. So I called Tom up, and I thanked him. I just had to let him know that we'd been brothers under the gun, and that I couldn't see that except in the highest regard." When asked about it some thirty years later, Petty remembers the call, presumably because you don't get many of those in your life, not when you're the bandleader.

The good sentiments and acceptance aside, Blair was now the-guy-who-used-to-be-in-the-Heartbreakers. He could tell when people were looking at him, wondering if it was painful and in what ways. As Blair would learn, more people can identify with what they think is a fallen man than can identify with a rock-and-roll star. But they don't say much about it, and they definitely don't ask for autographs. He would sometimes wake in the middle of the night from a dream in which he was back in the band, heading out onto the stage, unable to remember any of the songs. He kept it to himself. He played less. However difficult it was, he would go see the Heartbreakers play when they came to town.

"I remember sitting there at the Universal Amphitheatre," Blair remembers, "back before it had a roof on it. Must have been a year or two later. I'm watching the band play, sitting next to Jimmy Iovine. And Jimmy's going, 'Ron, what's it like, man?' To me, his question felt like, 'What's it like, you being a loser now?' I just wanted to hit him. Maybe it's what I was hearing more than what he was saying. I was like, 'Jimmy, it's fine. These guys were my friends. These guys will still be my friends. Just let me enjoy the fucking show.'"

A little over a half year after Annakim Petty's birth, Howie Epstein played his first gig as the Heartbreakers' new bass player. Both the child and the man stepped into fast-moving vehicles. Epstein seemed to fit in, as much as any "new guy" could. He joined as a member rather than a sideman. Of course, there were now categories of membership, and his was entry level. He was a good bass player, even a great one, but more importantly he could sing the kind of high harmonies that Petty had always loved. The Everly Brothers were as well represented in the front man's internal jukebox as Elvis and the Beatles. Southern boys, voices blended as one, born into a world where there was still a farm out back and a church out front. Those harmonies went back to an American past where hillbillies were something more than fuckups. Howie Epstein, a Wisconsin kid who'd gone from garage bands to John Hiatt's, had a voice that gave the bandleader a connection to that musical history, no matter his Midwestern background.

For his part, Stan Lynch had been a steady, often remarkable harmony singer in performance. He could do unison vocals that lay so neatly over the top of Petty's lead that you didn't know they were there, until they weren't. Petty and Lynch, for all their friction, sang like they knew each other as boys. They both remember it that way. But the new band member had a range and a natural gift for harmony that gave the Heartbreakers another melodic layer when a song called for that thickness and color. Petty never tired of hearing Epstein's voice, even after the bass player's death, which was years away and nothing anyone saw coming in the bright, open face of the new Heartbreaker. Epstein found his people with Tench and Lynch, the young guys in the band.

At the time of his hiring, Epstein was in another band, not just out for a stroll by himself when the Heartbreakers found him. That's the way it often goes in rock and roll. The year 1981 was the time of *Hard Promises* and all that came and went with it, including Petty's production role on Del Shannon's *Drop Down and Get Me*, a long player that can be counted among the best Heartbreaker records that don't show up in the official discography. And Del Shannon was the conduit through which Howie Epstein came into the band. Epstein had been Del Shannon's touring bass player and was called in to do some singing on *Drop Down and Get Me*. He walked in the door, high pompadour and Cuban-heeled boots, with no idea that he was walking from one world to another. But the initial connection that set it all in motion, bringing Petty to Del Shannon and a new bass player to Petty was, again, Harvey Kubernik. "I knew what Del Shannon could do. Still. And I knew the stuff Petty loved," Kubernik says. "I hoped Tom wouldn't be able to say no."

Petty may have been busy, too busy to get his own world in order— but Del Shannon was the man who sang "Runaway." Some things were not easily sidestepped. Early rock and roll remained sacred territory for Petty. He knew where he came from and where old debts needed to be paid. Kubernik's instinct was right. "Harvey gave me the call, said he thought I'd make a good producer for Del," Petty recalls. "He'd been in contact with Dan [Bourgoise], who managed Del, and they thought it was worth having a meeting. Harvey knew I was a fan of that era. So we all met at Dan's office in Hollywood. Del played me some demos, and I saw he was writing good stuff. I thought I was too young to be taking on the producer role, but I couldn't *not* do this." The Heartbreakers were Del Shannon's band in the studio, making production easier for Petty. He knew what he was dealing with. Petty managed to take a small budget and put Del Shannon onto the charts once more, where Petty believed Del Shannon belonged.

By that time, Petty had a steady run of hits with the Heartbreakers, and he understood what it meant for Del Shannon to have him produce a "comeback." He wasn't thinking about what it meant to his own career. As a record maker, whether by intuition or not, he lived by something Denny Cordell had told him: "If you're thinking about your career, you probably don't have one." What motivated Petty was simple: an awareness of the neglected, shabby pastures in which the first-generation rock and rollers were often left to graze. Brought out to play their early hits at oldies shows, nostalgia events with hot rods, costume parties of one kind or another, the greats of early rock and roll were imprisoned in a cartoon of poodle skirts and drive-ins, left to wander the set of *Happy Days*, no matter what the Stones and Eric Clapton said of their importance. The problem may even have gotten *worse* for Chuck Berry each time Keith Richards cited one of his early Chess records. From Little Richard to Roy Orbison and Carl Perkins, these guys may have been credited with influencing the Beatles, *by* the Beatles, but they weren't asked to evolve. A new Carl Perkins record? No, thanks. New Roy Orbison? From the time Sha Na Na closed Woodstock, in the slot before Jimi Hendrix, early rock and roll was often little more than an occasion for theater. The collaboration with Del Shannon was something counter to all that and had a quiet but deep significance in the artistic life that Petty was cobbling together.

"I did the best job I could at the time," Petty says. "I don't think I had a vision of Del becoming a completely contemporary artist, but he got some contemporary interest, a song on the charts. And the fact was, I really respected his generation much more than the one I was in. There just weren't that many of my peers that got my attention like the guys I grew up listening to. If one of those artists still had the goods, I was fascinated at the idea of working with them and bringing whatever I could to the table, seeing what happened. And it went both ways, it seems. It's happened a number of times, like some of these guys were thinking, 'I want to find this kid—let's look him up.'

"Making that record really gave me a chance to see that I could do something good with my new position in life. There was a lot of bullshit that came with it. But here was something good."

Petty generally kept the "bullshit that came with it" to himself. It's a small audience that wants to hear about the challenges of stardom. But the fact is: the people around a star often change more quickly than the star himself. And Petty had been dealing with that since "Breakdown." Former Mudcrutch guitarist Danny Roberts recalls an industry function at which Petty, in sunglasses, brushed past him in a crowded bowling alley, pretending to be unaware of Roberts's presence, putting up his arm to shield himself from the photographers that Roberts insists weren't there. It's a story that fits neatly into the rock-star-as-horse's-ass genre. One could read the scene from a number of angles. Maybe Petty didn't think talking with a disgruntled former bandmate was going to be worth either man's time. Or perhaps Petty's head was somewhere very far away from where Roberts was standing. Or maybe Roberts is close to the truth: Petty was a rock star on the town, blowing off an old friend. Who knows? If the trial Roberts is after ever does take place, it will likely be a rather dull affair for everyone but Danny Roberts. The more significant point is that Roberts was only one among a group of people who had watched Petty go from being just another local musician to being the guy looking out at them from magazine covers. Not all of them felt comfortable with it. And some of the discomfort was in Petty's band.

One can say that the change brought about in a person by success and fame is most conspicuous to those in closest proximity as that success and fame first hits. Petty's good fortune could be regarded by some as an unequal distribution of the rewards. Among those who were teenagers hanging at Lipham's Music, some argue that in Gainesville's talent pool there were brighter lights than Tom Petty. But Petty got the job. And once he was up there doing it, even his band would be described as his faithful sidekicks. The spotlight is, obviously, an intrinsic component of the front man's world. "My name, for years," says Stan Lynch, "was 'Drummer in Tom Petty and the Heartbreakers.'" Part of Petty's job was dealing with the effect of his success on the people around him, those with whom he still lived and worked. His new position would sometimes even make him the outsider in his own group. All of Petty's human interactions were touched by his good fortune: at home, at work, and on the street. Because the inner circle felt it most keenly, it could be a chilly place on some days. So he made it even smaller. And then there were the relatives.

Earl Petty saw his son's success as a pretty straightforward benefit. All upsides. He was getting laid. That was right up there with fishing. If the past and the brutal relationship with his son had to be hidden beneath the floorboards, that was nothing new, just family business. No visitor would have thought for a moment that this old guy was anything but his son's biggest fan. Earl wore his satin Heartbreakers jacket all over town. Petty could bite his tongue and let his old man do with local celebrity what he could. When Earl's twin sister, Pearl, showed up, looking for her share, however, Petty came up against his limits.

"Pearl was a right pain in the ass," Petty says. "My father's side of the family didn't handle my fame well. They didn't know me, so I just became an object to them. I remember Pearl coming into a hotel room with my dad, throwing down a notebook, and saying, 'Just sign until you can't sign anymore.' I looked at her like, 'What?' And she says, 'Just sign each page until you get tired.' I wouldn't do it. I looked at my father, and he just kind of shrugged. What was hard though was that she wasn't that far from my old man. He developed an identity from it. God knows how much pussy he got out of it. I mean, my god, it must have been great being him. His house was open to whatever fans rolled up there. You could come and spend as much time as you wanted. Stay for weeks."

When Earl brought one of his new girlfriends backstage at a Florida show, Petty might have been more welcoming if she'd been a quieter presence. Or maybe, for him, his mother was still close by. It hadn't been that long. Several band members recall the moment Earl's friend got thrown out. They all sensed Earl would find another. And so did Earl. He didn't make much of a fuss. "I threw her out," Petty says. "I literally walked her out of the door. He didn't really seem to care. I often think about my father and wonder if I've been too tough on him, but it always comes back to, 'No, I don't think I was.' He was a hard man." Mostly, though, the Earl problem was a Florida problem. He took the dignity out of a trip home. It would be some years before Petty softened toward his father, a result of aging as much as anything. But in that intersection of his own fame and its effect on old friends or family, the harder situation was still to come, as Petty watched his children get old enough to know that they couldn't always trust the motives of the people who came into their lives. "They were both touched by it on a pretty regular basis," Petty says. "They experienced friends who weren't genuine. It took me a long time to really understand that they lived that way. They had to do what I did: put a little bit of a wall up." Of course, not everyone deals with fame the same way. But that's how Petty did it. And he was still a young man. He was becoming an emotional recluse.

16

THE VETERAN IN A NEW FIELD

Think we ought to throw old Spike a bone?

—Tom Petty, "Spike"

"The touring is so seductive," Tom Petty says. **"Rock-and-roll musicians get** something movie actors don't, that instant feedback from the audience. The Heartbreakers absorbed a lot of that at a young age, in very large doses, when other people were out dealing with the DMV and the teacher conferences. You're a visiting prince. That's not the problem, though. The problem is that people get used to it." Not everyone in the band moved easily between arena-wide adulation and a creative process that sometimes felt like a 2:00 a.m. struggle with a drunk. "A lot of people," Petty insists, "not just in this band, are yearning to get back to the tour, so much so that they don't put the work into the songs like they normally would. They just want to get back out there, be free of life, be in *that* world."

When the Heartbreakers were in the studio making records, no one was clapping and no T-shirts were sold. Since 1976, the release schedule hadn't allowed a moment to look up, to look around, and it was beginning to feel like emotional whiplash going between the tours and the recording studios. "I was looking for fun!" Lynch says. "I was looking for love! I was looking for everything. I was on the road, meeting girls, thinking they could be my wife. I was looking for all of that to be permanent. Really. I didn't know that everyone was going to be there the next night for Journey. Here's how fucked up I am: I'm like, 'Why would you even want a recording? Why wouldn't you just want to be a troubadour, show it off one night and move on?' You know, you were either there at the show or you weren't."

Of course, the only reason the Heartbreakers were touring was because of the records they made. Even the best live band, without records, is local. And making records meant more to Petty than anything or, possibly, anyone. He was always readying himself for whatever studio time had been booked. The next record kept him awake at night, watched him from across the street when he tried to take a day off. But he knew that the next record wasn't going to happen if his band wasn't at his side, ready to push ahead to the next place they needed to go. Petty was a student of the Beatles, which meant he believed that every album needed to be different from the last. They didn't make *Rubber Soul* twice.

"I think it was Paul Simon who said it," says Bill Flanagan, reflecting on Petty's situation. "Around the time when Simon and Garfunkel broke up, he said something like, 'When you get in a position where you're in control of everything in your life, like, that tree that's blocking your view? Have someone move it. You want to go skiing out West instead of that trip to the Caribbean? Reschedule the private jet. And then you go into a recording studio, to do that thing you are the master of, that thing that *brought* you the control of everything else in your life, and you've got some guy sitting there going, "No, man, I don't like it. Let's do something else." It's really hard to handle.' And I imagine he's right. Everybody in the world is kissing your ass, and then you go back to the thing that made them kiss your ass—making music, writing songs—and some guy, just because you've known him since high school, is allowed to say, 'No, it stinks.' That could create some problems."

Making *Long After Dark* was a matter of Petty wanting to avoid trouble that might come from the guys he'd known since high school, while recognizing that he'd been in that situation for years. He couldn't have what he thought of as a real band and *not* find himself there. But the fatigue of that and the fatigue of the album cycle itself were both weighing on Petty. The Heartbreakers, too, were struggling with the relentlessness and its cumulative effects. "I think I was lucky," Petty says, "that I was raising a family at that age, because it kept me grounded in a way I wouldn't have been otherwise. I was gone so much, but I made sure I was there when we were off the road. I was home working. I wasn't on the town a lot. I could sit down, put the blinders on, and make sure the songs were going to do the job. You're not always going to have a song fall in your lap. You have to go after them." By that time, Petty and his family had built their home in Encino, a five-bedroom marker of success. "I poured my heart into that place," he says. "It was special." But he still came home from the road, grabbed the Gibson Dove, and went to work. If a song was circling in the San Fernando Valley air, there was a man ready to pull it down. "When I heard *Long After Dark*," Flanagan continues, "I thought it was tremendous. There are great songs on there. I really thought it might be his best. 'Straight into Darkness' hit me very powerfully. But looking back, knowing what we know about all that would come, it feels too much like they're at risk of repeating the formula. They're going to loosen up. But it happens *after* that album."

Benmont Tench remembers the recording sessions as, among other things, another phase in the ongoing drummer conflict. "During *Long After Dark*, the same thing happened," he says. "We brought in Terry Williams, from Rockpile, one of the best drummers you can name. It didn't work. Stanley would come back, and we'd get the track. This dynamic went on for a long time. Like I said, Stan got an undue amount of attention, I think. I also believe we made a great album in the end." Even more than *Damn the Torpedoes*, *Long After Dark* is thick with percussion. Shakers, tambourines, cow bells, wood blocks. Whether those percussion tracks are actually, as Jimmy Iovine suggests, "gluing" the performances together or not is impossible to tell from the final mixes, but there's no question that the producers were putting percussion everywhere on the record. And as a final gesture, Petty got in the habit of speeding up the mixes, which made it all sound just a bit sweeter, the grooves a bit tighter. He may not have needed to. But he did. "They went through the rectum of the fourth dimension," insists Stan Lynch, "and never came back. I say if you want to make a rock-and-roll record, you've got to let some feathers fly. The control issues at that point were way beyond reason."

No matter the other band members' memories, it's Petty who is the record's most unyielding critic. But not for the right reasons. He lost his objectivity somewhere in the middle of it all, before the record was close to finished. He says he doesn't like *Long After Dark*. But what he doesn't like is the world he was living in during that period of time. The songs tell the story of that place, more directly than the material on any previous recording. Hopelessness, loss, lust, the impossibility of love. A man who didn't want to be in his marriage but didn't know how to leave it allowed his feelings to leak onto a recording, without a lot of symbolism to hide behind. "There was a moment when I really loved her / Then one day, the feeling just died." No bride and groom were going to make their way to the dance floor while the wedding band played these songs. "Straight into Darkness," "We Stand a Chance," "You Got Lucky," "The Same Old You": love's splendor wasn't the point. But, together, the songs comprise another of Petty's beautiful collections. His aim wasn't to write what he thought we wanted to hear. But the emptiness and the anger he brought to it somehow left a little more room for rock and roll. Among other things, it's a true rock-and-roll guitar record.

Long After Dark would also be the last full album on which Jimmy Iovine would be credited as producer. "It was that album when I felt he'd betrayed me," says Petty. "He failed to mention that he was working on a Bob Seger record. As I saw it, I'm a full-time job." At one point during the recording, Iovine was making so many phone calls that someone in the band cut the cord on the studio phone. Jimmy, it seemed, needed to be somewhere else. But, no matter, the record went to stores, and people fell in love with it. "You Got Lucky" and "Change of Heart" made it to the radio. "You Got Lucky" also became the group's first MTV hit, in part because the new network needed content, and Jim Lenahan had been making what the industry called "international films" some years before the dawn of the MTV era. It was all in motion, once again. The Heartbreakers got on a leased plane, a Phantom, with a line from *Long After Dark*'s "The Same Old You" painted on the side: "Let That Sucker Blast." Off they went, into America to play those songs. And in his head, Petty was thinking about the next record.

■

After months of touring behind *Long After Dark*, the Heartbreakers were going to get a break, the first stillness after eight years of making records and supporting them. And it wouldn't go well. Keith Richards isn't the only man in a rock-and-roll band to note that the real trouble doesn't come on the road—it comes when you get home and *live* like you're on the road. That's a paraphrase, but it's an idea that gives some sense of what was coming for the Heartbreakers. Mike Campbell calls it "the dark period." Petty says a little more: "We took a lot of shrapnel that year. It taught me a lot. We had never been allowed to grow up. We'd never been in a situation where it was even expected of us. You know, you're bouncing everything off the same four or five people you've been around since school, and you have children, you're married—most people would have been conducting themselves differently. We suddenly had to deal with maybe not being around much longer." Whether that means as a band or as individuals isn't clear. But mortality hovered in ways it hadn't previously. The death of Katherine Petty came to her son almost as if it had been waiting for him to slow down. Mike Campbell went into the hospital with exhaustion. Petty went into the hospital for surgery on a broken hand, self-inflicted in a fit a rage. Benmont Tench worked his way toward recovery from drugs and alcohol, without getting all the way there until 1988. When asked about *Southern Accents*, the album that was released next, Petty says quietly, "When I hear that one, I can taste cocaine in the back of my mouth."

■

Petty spent good parts of the *Long After Dark* tour looking out the windows of his bus, particularly during the southern swing. He was seeing places, people, and images that triggered thoughts of his southern upbringing. More depressed than other regions, the South couldn't have moved on if it wanted to. The past was right there, in the rotting barns and peeling billboards. Apart from truck stops and strip malls, it looked to him like the South couldn't afford to be the future, so it remained the past. And it was his past. Backward, beautiful, fucked up, often forgotten, sometimes violent. People who knew music seemed to be aware that most American song traditions came from down there, but they often didn't know much more about the South than that. It was a place with an incomprehensible character, America's dirty secret. Somewhere between Walker Evans's photography and *The Dukes of Hazzard*, in the trailer parks Petty saw out the bus window, there was a place that he recognized as having a heartbeat of its own. He thought of Randy Newman's *Good Old Boys*, a meditation on the South that is as much a book of short stories as it is a song cycle. Petty wondered how far he could go in Newman's direction himself before losing his audience. That, he figured, was just about how far he *needed* to go.

It's not easy to construct a chronology of the making of *Southern Accents*. Robbie Robertson had asked Petty for a song to include in Martin Scorsese's *King of Comedy*. That may have been where it started. Petty loved the Band recordings and Robertson's part in them as much as the next man, so he did some digging and found a song from the *Hard Promises* sessions. He played "The Best of Everything" for a few people, Nick Lowe included, and felt good about passing it along. Robertson took the multitracks into Village Recorders and went to work. Far from asking for Petty's input, however, Robertson requested that Petty stay away, even stopped him at the door when Petty happened to be at the studio one day.

"The Best of Everything" came back transformed. The spirit of the basic tracks remained—the difference was in the layers of horns and in the beautiful harmony vocal sung by Robertson's former bandmate Richard Manuel. Listening along with Robertson, Petty didn't say much. Manuel's voice brought an emotion to the recording that drew out the song's ache. If Petty had already been thinking about Randy Newman's *Good Old Boys*, Manuel's voice illuminated some deeper connection between "The Best of Everything" and the American South. The South haunted the early Band recordings. No doubt Manuel's voice was triggering some association. Though Petty said nothing to Robertson, he felt he'd been given another sign. And horns? He'd never thought of brass as a thing that could emerge in such a central way, not on a Heartbreakers' record. But to his ears, it worked. Regardless, it was a song for a movie, so there was no reason to worry that it didn't fit directly enough with the Heartbreaker aesthetic. He approved the mix and sent it into the world, not knowing then that "The Best of Everything" would return to him when MCA refused to allow it in a film released by another company. Even before the song came back to him, however, the horns had already sent a signal into Petty's creative unconscious.

If it started there, "Rebels" was the song that gave Petty permission to fully engage the idea of a concept album. It freed him from writing about his own life in Encino. He was going somewhere else for his material. "I think I was also trying to become a better writer," says Petty. "I felt I had enough going for me that I could do that. I'd touched on it, but my focus had been on writing good rock-and-roll songs. This was the first time, I think, that I started to push beyond. And I found a way to do that." The songs that were coming had particular characters, people who had far more to do with Earl Petty's North Florida than they did his son's Los Angeles. "Honey, don't walk out, I'm too drunk to follow"—the opening line of "Rebels" tells you that things are going in a different direction than with *Long After Dark*. "The first time I heard 'Rebels,'" says Mike Campbell, "it blew me away. I thought, 'This is one of our best songs.' Those lyrics and that imagery, only Tom could write that. You can't write a better song than that." Like Campbell, Petty quickly understood how important "Rebels" would be to the album, establishing its sense of place, bringing in the region's lost people. They started thinking of it as an album opener before they even had a take that worked. But if "Rebels" initiated the story, it was "Southern Accents" that arrived as the album's centerpiece.

"There's a Southern accent where I come from / The young 'uns call it 'country,' the Yankees call it 'dumb' / I got my own way of talking, but everything is done / with a Southern accent where I come from." The song came quietly, with Petty alone at the piano in his new home, his family asleep upstairs. It showed up almost complete. A middle-of-the-night encounter, "Southern Accents" went beyond "Rebels" as an example of what Petty could do as a writer capturing not just emotion but time and place. It was epic poetry in three and a half minutes, a reminder as to why he was laboring to chase this album in the way that he was. The recording features strings arranged by Jack Nitzsche, which are, apart from the vocal, the track's fundamental texture, with a simple piano sitting just behind them. It's a case of the material getting what it deserves. The production is as good as the song. "I had no desire to be on that," says Stan Lynch. "I played a wood block, I think. That was one of those songs I was proud *not* to play on live. It's so good, it isn't even a song. You can just etch that in a piece of granite and walk by it. I felt like saying, 'You don't ever have to write another song again. You owe me no more good songs.' It's like it's from a prayer book." In the song's bridge, as transcendent as anything Petty would ever write, is a visitation, a moment of pure beauty in which Petty's mother, at that point years deceased, arrives to her son. "For just a minute there I was dreaming / For just a minute it was oh so real / For just a minute she was standing there, with me." It's the album's moment of deepest longing. And as the song came to Petty, so, too, did a little peace, however fragile. Songs were the place he took his loss and turned it into something else. Which may not have been the same as grieving, but it was something.

■

At the outset of *Southern Accents*, Petty had installed the recording studio in his family's Encino home, further damaging the already broken gate between work and home. Then, without giving it a lot of thought, he allowed himself to believe that the Heartbreakers could make this record without an outside producer, an idea most of the band liked. The inner sanctum of the Heartbreakers' creative world was a place generally closed off to traffic, except for producers. Now it was entirely closed off. Or would have been, if there weren't drugs on the table. And somebody had to sell them to the band.

The home studio became the scene of a party as much as it was the scene of a production. But it wasn't always a particularly pleasant party. When Petty set out to cut "Rebels" with the band, he felt like the recording he heard in his head wasn't coming back to him through the studio monitors. His response was to bear down, put in more time, record more takes, to keep trying—until it hurt. It was the Iovine school of record making without Iovine present. But the song deserved it, demanded it.

"It had gotten unpleasant," Petty says. "The thing I loved the most, making this music, had become so difficult, more a fight than what it should have been. Something needed to give." At the rate Petty was going, he'd kill the joy off in a matter of months and be left with nothing but a job. What saved the situation—and what also threw it off course—was the arrival of Dave Stewart, cofounder, songwriter, and producer of the Eurythmics. He was a dose of levity, a shot of positive energy and impulse. For the rock-and-roll fan, he was surely the enemy. The Human League, ABC, the Eurythmics—the British synthpop bands seemed to be everything the Heartbreakers weren't. And Petty was responsible, if inadvertently, for Stewart's arrival, no matter that he never intended to be the one to usher the Englishman through the door.

Some months before the trouble with "Rebels" had begun, Petty received a call from Jimmy Iovine, a request for material for a new Stevie Nicks album, which Iovine was getting ready to record. Petty didn't have anything to offer. It may have been too soon after "Stop Dragging My Heart

Around." But he did have some advice for Iovine: find the guy from the Eurythmics. On the basis of hearing "Sweet Dreams (Are Made of This)" on the radio, Petty knew this guy could write. No matter that the Eurythmics' recordings were underpinned by drum machine and synthesizer, Petty knew good writing. If he was a slave to anything, it wasn't a particular sound—it was the song. Iovine made the call and brought Dave Stewart in.

Aware that Tom Petty had gotten him the job with Iovine and Nicks, Dave Stewart phoned the Encino house to see if Petty would come down to the studio where he, Iovine, and Nicks were recording. Nicks and Iovine were no longer seeing each other, but they'd managed to keep making records together. Working on a song built around one of Stewart's drum programs, they were at a standstill, not sure where to take the song lyrically. "I had no idea he was in town, that they were working, none of that," Petty says. "But I was at the point where a field trip was always welcome. Just to get out of the house." Nicks left not long after Petty arrived. It had been a long day already. Stewart and Iovine stayed, and the three men worked through the night, until they had something. Petty sang a lead vocal as a guide. They were ready to play it for Stevie, and then she could sing it.

"Tom had come down, and he liked what we were working on," explains Nicks. "I was writing madly. I had my little book, and I was just writing, writing, writing. Tom, Jimmy, and Dave were sort of talking. But it was five in the morning, and I was really tired. So I said, 'I'm going to go. I'm leaving you guys, and I'll be back tomorrow.' I left, and when I got back the next day, at something like three p.m., the whole song was written. And not only was it written; it was spectacular. Dave was standing there saying to me, 'Well, there it is! It's really, really good.' And they go to me, 'Well, it's terrific, and now you can go out and . . . and you can sing it.' Tom had done a great vocal, a *great* vocal. I just looked at them and said, 'I'm going to top that? Really?' I got up, thanked Dave, thanked Tom, fired Jimmy, and left. That went down in about five minutes."

When Petty left that afternoon, it was with a basic recording of the new song in his pocket. It was his, not hers. The track was undeniable. It was as good as anything he'd done in the past several years—and altogether different. Petty had watched with admiration as Prince, in the midst of his *Purple Rain* years, moved around the musical landscape, no concern for the laws of migration that either the business or the *Billboard* charts imposed, and he wanted to keep moving himself. "I saw Prince doing what looked like an attempt at psychedelia," Petty says. "And I loved it. It inspired me." The recording in his pocket sounded like movement. It wasn't clear what it all meant, where it fit. Petty had certainly let a stranger into the Heartbreakers' midst. This wasn't the Del Shannon collaboration. It wasn't even having Duck Dunn come in to play bass. This was Petty slipping out in the night to create something great without any of the Heartbreakers involved or, really, even knowing. This was infidelity. And the drum machine on the track only made it worse. Petty was out sleeping with a tramp. And it felt good to him.

There was one Heartbreaker who knew something was going on. "I just happened to stop by Tom's house that day," recalls Mike Campbell, "and he's packing up his bass to go to a session, kind of acting like he's been caught with his pants down. He tells me, 'I'm going with Dave Stewart.' So I talked to Stevie, and she said I should just go down. I called the studio and said, 'What's going on? Can I come by?' They tell me, 'We have to ask Tom.' I ended up going down, but this hurt my feelings a lot. I felt from his energy that he knew he should have told me. But he didn't tell me, and he didn't expect me to come down. It was awkward." From there on out, Mike Campbell went everywhere Petty did. From a musical angle, it was always worth it. And Petty needed that collaborator and ally in the band.

The other Heartbreakers behaved like bands do. If "Don't Come Around Here No More" was a victory, it wasn't theirs. Feeling suspicious at least, betrayed at most, they took a few shots at Dave Stewart, his dandy-from-overseas flamboyance. The Heartbreakers knew how to laugh long and loud, but it was often at other people. They were skeptical of Stewart. Mike Campbell was the most immediately open to him—but even Campbell had his moments. And he told Petty as much. The others muttered behind Petty's back—to no avail. Petty needed a break from the "band bullshit." "Don't Come Around Here No More" sounded more interesting to him each time he played it back. And the songs were the one allegiance that stood above that with his band.

As far as the infidelity went, it didn't hurt that Stewart was a lot easier to be with than the Heartbreakers had been in some time. Petty and Stewart bought cowboy hats, had a tailor make custom suits with rhinestone skulls on them. Stewart drove around in a Cadillac with massive fins, went after the fun, never waiting for it to come to him. His working approach had as much to do with creating environments for songs as it did creating songs. Sometimes the material came a lot easier when a place was made for its arrival. The band would have to give in if they wanted to be a part of Stewart's engaging madness and the new recording. He broke them down, grinning through it all. After Petty brought "Don't Come Around Here No More" back to the Encino studio, the Heartbreakers came onto the recording. For two weeks Petty, Stewart, and the band worked on the track, feeling like they had a single. Benmont Tench's string parts, played on a Yamaha DX-7 keyboard, heightened the theater of the whole musical scene. Campbell's wah-wah guitar on the track's outro brought back a sound that had fallen out of favor among guitar players. It felt bold, unguarded, a step in another direction. By the time the recording was done, Dave Stewart had made an impression on them all.

"Dave put on the best parties in the eighties," Petty says. "Somehow, there were always midgets involved. At one, Timothy Leary reached out to me with a hit of acid, and when I declined, he said, 'More for the rest of us,' and put it on his tongue. I had to escape Dave's house that night. I locked the bathroom door and went out through the window, since my house was only a block away. I knew Dave wouldn't want me to leave. Dave could just keep going, and he wanted us all with him."

Petty figured there were more songs waiting where "Don't Come Around Here No More" came from. And he was right. They just weren't as good. That first cowrite was the lucky one. And it worked in relation to the album's conceptual theme. The singer of "Don't Come Around Here No More" belonged among the characters of Southern Accents. It was the way Petty leaned into the lyric. "I don't feel you anymore / You darken my door / Whatever you're looking for / Hey! Don't come around here no more!" The speaker may as well have been some southern misfit, stringing up barbed wire at the edge of his property line. "Beat it!" It showed just how wide Petty could go musically without losing the thickness of his identity. But the next two Stewart cowrites didn't prove so successful. "Dave was a breath of fresh air," says Mike Campbell. "And he was at the top of his game. We were like, 'This Dave Stewart guy is great! Let's do whatever he says.'

Then, after a couple more, 'Okay, that's enough.' It was 'Make It Better' and whatever the other one was."

Stewart distracted Petty from the concept album he'd set out to make, but Petty was a full collaborator in that distraction. "Make It Better (Forget About Me)" and "It Ain't Nothing to Me," the other two tracks born of the Petty-Stewart collaboration, pulled the project away from its origins. Stewart's guitar playing, featured on both, had a seventies R&B feel that seemed closer to the spirit of Nile Rodgers than it did to the Rolling Stones. That wasn't bad, but it was out of place. The songs would have gotten more affection as B-sides, but as album tracks they were scrutinized and, ultimately, blamed for the misdirection of *Southern Accents*. They felt like something else—fun afternoons at the studio that shouldn't have been allowed to be more than that.

"The bigger picture there was we were all on a lot of coke," Benmont Tench says. "On the *Long After Dark* tour, I discovered how much cocaine there was in the world. And then I came home and went straight on tour with Stevie Nicks, and, boy, did I discover how much cocaine there was in the world. *Southern Accents* was a great idea for a record. Tom started writing the record, from what I understand, by just writing words associated with the South. 'Rebels,' 'Trailer,' 'Apartment.' Then, somehow, out of those three words that become songs, two are left *off* the album. How the fuck do you leave 'Trailer' off *Southern Accents*? And 'Make It Better' and something else—I can't remember—*are* on the album. It'd be like leaving 'No Second Thoughts' off *You're Gonna Get It!* or 'You Tell Me' off *Damn the Torpedoes*. I think if it weren't for the drugs, better music would have come out. Better decisions would have been made." As the focus shifted from the original idea, there were songs that not even Tench knew much about, that didn't get past Petty's notebook. One of them was called "Sheets," a stark look at the racism that so often structured life in the American South. "It was a really scary song," Petty says, "but one that would have had to be included, if the original idea for the album had been carried through to its conclusion."

Instead, Petty had begun to think of it as a double album. With "Rebels," "Southern Accents," "Don't Come Around Here No More," "Trailer," "The Best of Everything," and "It Ain't Nothin' to Me," a collection, meandering, often beautiful, sometimes schizophrenic, was coming together. But it wasn't done. "Rebels," the song that started it all, was still a problem. Petty put horns on it. But the horns fought for space with the twelve-string guitar. He wanted the sound of *more* but without losing the sense of space that the song's mood needed. He played with the panning, pulled instruments in and out, messed with the EQ and compression, mixing and remixing, never getting the results he wanted. The absence of a producer was conspicuous. There were no late-night calls with Iovine. In the midst of trying to mix "Rebels" one more time, Petty went back to his original demo of the song, looking for some kind of clue, and he heard something that made him crazy with frustration: the demo still beat the recording he'd been laboring on. Too angry to think, he expressed himself in the way he knew best. He went back where he came from, hitting a wall with his bare fist, pulverizing the bone. It would take eight months to heal. Would he call it rage? "I'd just call it stupid," he says.

Though a doctor managed to re-create the bone structure that Petty had destroyed, he couldn't help Petty finish the record. It was the first time Petty's anger made the news. Up to that point, it had been a family secret. Tony Dimitriades knew it best, only because he caught it more than anyone else. But Petty went ahead and told the truth. He'd hit a wall. It wasn't the most flattering story. He was beginning to see that things were out of control. Finally, he called Jimmy Iovine, asking for help.

Iovine demanded a few things of Petty. First, that he get out of that recording studio in his house as soon as possible. Second, that he forget the idea of a double album. It was the quick imposition of some structure. The double-album idea had crept in without a lot of scrutiny; it was the cheap way out of having to choose which tracks should stay. Iovine did what was asked of him and got things moving. But even Iovine missed the bigger point. Years later, he realizes this was so. "What happened with *Southern Accents*," he says, "was Tom had an idea that he should have stuck with." The concept album that had been Petty's original vision was sacrificed. "Trailer" was relegated to a B-side. "The Apartment Song," a loose, pre–*Full Moon Fever* version with Stevie Nicks singing harmony, was weeded out and cast aside. Covers of Nick Lowe's "Cracking Up" and Conway Twitty's "The Image of Me" went on the same pile. "Sheets" never got recorded. The point was to finish. So what if the album sounded like an identity crisis played out across two sides of a long player—why shouldn't it? Even the Beatles made a few of those. And the fact is, Tom Petty *was* having an identity crisis. Those who were ready to lay flowers at the grave of a masterpiece that *almost was* weren't factoring that in. Whatever else it was, *Southern Accents* was the necessary door into an experience of searching that would carry Petty through a few albums. It was the shaking of the tree—and he would be gathering the fruit for a number of years, not always sure what he should eat and what he shouldn't.

■

Mike Campbell had four cowrites on *Long After Dark*. He had only one on *Southern Accents*, "Dogs on the Run." During the making of the record, he'd given Petty a number of cassettes with music on them but, as Petty surmised, nothing that fit the project. No doubt Dave Stewart took up some of the space that might have been Campbell's. But Campbell had a gift for watching what happened rather than stewing or confronting. His demos piled up. The ones he'd passed along to Petty were, as always, fully produced, minus the vocals. He'd always been a guy with something cooking in the closet, the garage, the living room, the bathroom. All he needed was a closed door and a little magnetic tape. He didn't write songs so much as he wrote records, less a folkie than a Brian Wilson. He used loops and drum machines, mandolins and lap steels, synthesizers and sequencers— whatever got the idea across, and maybe a little extra.

Petty would listen through the Campbell demos, see if there was anything that made him sing. It was all done by feel. If Petty couldn't make it his own, there was no point in chasing it. With Campbell, there was always more where that came from. "Mike once said to me, 'I work in bulk,'" says Petty. "He'd send me twenty things on a cassette. More than enough for an album. I'd go through them, see if I could turn something into a song rather than a track." When one of them struck him, Petty started to work with it, sometimes asking Campbell to pull everything out of a section but the drums so that he could write new chord changes. But he often took the demos as they were. It tended not to happen exactly the same way twice.

Among the demos Campbell brought to Petty around the time of *Southern Accents*, there was a track that seemed good but not all the way there. The chorus didn't feel right to Petty. He worked on it a bit but finally set it aside without a lot of thought. They were in the middle of the album, and if a song wasn't happening quickly enough, there were others demanding attention. Campbell waited for a verdict on the demo, but Petty's mind was elsewhere. "I played that one for Tom and for Jimmy," says Campbell. "But when it got to the chorus, instead of going major, I had some jazzy minor chord thing. Jimmy goes, 'Jazz?' Tom thought the chorus should go to a major key. I remember thinking, 'Yeah, I can see their points. The chorus could be better.' Then Jimmy called me and said, 'I spoke to Don Henley, and he's looking for a song.' I figured I'd fix the chorus before I play it for Don. From there, it all happened fast. I played it for Don, and he wrote to it, put down a vocal, quick. We were in a *Southern Accents* session when I brought in the mix of 'Boys of Summer.' That was the day Tom broke his hand."

After hearing Campbell's demo, Don Henley had moved things quickly, getting to a finished recording in a matter of weeks. Campbell was out jogging shortly after that when he heard it on the radio. There were still artists who could turn things around that quickly, if they wanted to. Henley was one of them. Whether or not the song was right for Petty, only Petty would know. But after Henley worked on it and rush released the recording, you couldn't escape the song. It was playing everywhere. What Petty heard was a demo he'd passed on. In the middle of trying to finish "Don't Come Around Here No More," he and Campbell went to check a mix in Campbell's car. "We go out there," Campbell says, "I turn the car on, the radio comes on, and it's 'Boys of Summer.' It's at the end, and the deejay starts going on about how it's the best song and all this. Tom just sat there. You could tell he was bothered. I put our cassette in to check the mix, and it sounded like shit. You know, it wasn't finished. But still. Big difference. At the end of it, Tom says to me, 'You did really good on that. I wish I had had the presence of mind to not let that song get away.' It was a moment. It felt good to me. It was good for my confidence. It was nice that he didn't go and break his other hand." Albums were coming and going, but Petty and Campbell kept finding ways to work together. Close but never too close. The same couldn't be said for everyone in the band.

"My two best friends in the Heartbreakers," Benmont Tench explains, "were Stan Lynch and Howie Epstein. Stan is like a year younger than me, and Howie was a year younger than Stanley. This band, we tended to let each other have our own emotional experiences. Me and Stanley, or me and Howie, may have gotten into that stuff. I'm not saying I want to go into therapy with these guys, but Tom and Mike . . . maybe it's southern men of a certain age. In spite of growing up in the sixties, in spite of all the liberalism, it's like there's some very old-school southern thing in Tom. I don't know if it comes from his father. I don't know if it comes from working really, really hard to make it and being like, 'Nobody's taking this shit away from me.' He's created this thing. He's created him. And he's protective of it."

"We learned to split into our own camps," says Petty. "But Mike and I usually didn't. We had to carry the flag. We were in the trenches, trying to prepare the music for the next project. But no one in the band knew what was going on at home for me. I thought it was all my fault. I'd turned into a rock-and-roll star and turned my family's life upside down. But by '84, around *Southern Accents*, I knew I was out of there. I knew I was gonna leave my marriage. I was just biding my time." Petty's life at home made the band more important to him than ever, and the fissures within the band more troubling. "When you're in a creative relationship," says Adria Petty, reflecting on the Heartbreakers of that era, "when it's men, and they're deriving their self-confidence and identity from that, that's a very delicate thing. You really need to know that you're bros, like you're in 'Nam and you're gonna have each other's back. The Heartbreakers often say, 'I wouldn't send that guy out for ammo.' That's their joke. 'I wouldn't send *him* out for the ammo.' But that's the reality. You have to surround yourself with the best, and it's hard to find them and harder to hold on to them."

Shifts in power, trouble cutting rhythm tracks, and differences in income were the most difficult issues to get around. Stan Lynch felt like he was watching Jimmy Iovine and Tom Petty count money as a hobby. He recalls his discomfort when Iovine showed him a picture of a place on Long Island, saying, "That's the house 'Refugee' built." He got the same uneasy feeling upon entering Petty's new place in Encino, though he didn't end up there very often. "It wasn't until 1984 that I made actual money," says Lynch, "where I went, 'That's a nice check.' And even then, it was only go-out-and-buy-a-car money." True to Lynch's nature, he couldn't keep his thoughts to himself. He vented to his former roommate on the road, Campbell. Being so close to Petty in the work, Campbell was Lynch's connection to power. But it often got back to Petty, who was more sensitive to the chatter than Lynch may have assumed. The effect was the opposite of what the drummer was after.

"I'm sorry Tom didn't feel he could discuss what was going on at home," says Lynch. "No man should have to feel that kind of pain at home." But the younger Lynch wasn't the one Petty would have turned to if indeed he was to turn to anyone. However cold it may have seemed, Petty didn't take chances in relationships. And because of the chatter, he'd learned not to trust Lynch. "It was like Stan was always trying to figure out how to get more out of us than he was getting," says Petty. "One day he came to me and said, 'Cinderella's drummer has a yacht.' I said, 'Cinderella's drummer has a yacht? Wow. Who is Cinderella?' It was this popular heavy metal band, hadn't been around long. I said, 'I don't buy he's got a yacht.' Stan's like, 'We should have yachts. I should have the same kind of money that fucker's making.' I said, 'You should join that band.'"

17

THE BACKING BAND

Coyote's wits are sharp precisely because he has met other wits, just as the country bumpkin may eventually become a cosmopolitan if enough confidence men appear to school him.

—LEWIS HYDE

Dave Stewart convinced Petty to bring a horn section and backup singers on the road when the Heartbreakers went out to support *Southern Accents*. It was another decision that would be talked about with some regret just a few years later. There were those who could only see Tom Petty as a meat-and-potatoes rock and roller. Petty had already released a major single that didn't simply use a drum machine—it *featured* a drum machine. To those who wanted him to stick closer to the rock-and-roll formula, the brass and the singers of the *Southern Accents* tour felt like something from *The Tonight Show*. Horns had been a staple before R&B was called rock and roll, but the British Invasion made the four piece an institution. "It was fun at the time," says Mike Campbell. "We did it. We survived."

The live album that was released that year, *Pack Up the Plantation*, mixed the big band Heartbreakers of that tour with some older cuts. The WBCN live recording from 1978, which had traveled widely as a bootleg, provided "Don't Bring Me Down," the Goffin-King song made famous by the Animals. "Rebels" and "Southern Accents" made the collection, but the notable absence of any other songs from *Southern Accents* was the giveaway that this live album was much more a career retrospective than a tour souvenir. The point *Pack Up the Plantation* made, that the Heartbreakers were one of rock and roll's best live acts, seemed to be generally accepted by the critics. The fans had always known it.

The closing track on the collection, the album's emotional center, was a cover of John Sebastian's "Stories We Could Tell." It's a simple thing, tossed off as much as the Heartbreakers tossed off anything. Petty strums a loose acoustic guitar, the Fabulous Poodles' Bobby Valentino provides fiddle accompaniment, and Stan Lynch sings a harmony. But it's the best version of a song recorded by a number of acts, the Everly Brothers among them. It shows a side of the Heartbreakers that doesn't always get the spotlight, that comes out in originals like "Mystery Man" and "No Second Thoughts." And it's a song that takes as its subject the melancholy of a life spent making live music, sitting on the edges of hotel beds, playing something before going out to play something more. "Stories We Could Tell" is a meditation on what compels a person to give up so much in exchange for a life that's a mix of monotony and transcendence, in unequal portions. For touring musicians, the song is a reminder of why you do it. And Petty himself needed the reminder.

"Don't Come Around Here No More" allowed certain among Petty's critics another reason to give him good but not great grades. Every review Robert Christgau ever wrote on Tom Petty gave with one hand and took back with the other. It had begun to seem that if the Heartbreakers' string of hits filled the arenas, the same chart success made the band vulnerable to critical backlash. Neil Young didn't move a lot of units when he released *Landing on Water*, but his seeming disregard for the marketplace got him points with critics. Young had earned some freedoms—he could pay the bills with *Harvest* when *Trans* didn't move at the record stores. Much of his audience was already comfortable paying little attention to the latest release. Most of them wanted "Old Man." For Petty, the situation was different. He was still building a legacy. And he never wanted to think of a release as something people accepted but didn't celebrate.

Still, as early as the band's third album, Petty was frustrated with the downside of hits. "I remember one of the most heartbreaking things was going to the Whisky right after *Damn the Torpedoes* had come out," Petty says. "Everybody treated us different, almost like we were sellouts or something. There was that vibe. We had a hit. A *hit*. It was as if they were couching it as this integrity versus popularity thing. But I wanted to have hits. That was the point. Jerry Lee Lewis had hits. I didn't want to *not* get the music out there." In 2002, *Billboard* named Petty the all-time leader on the Mainstream Rock charts, with forty-six chart appearances. That kind of thing was good news. But some people looked askance at the artists who were too regular in their visits to the charts. "Some of that goes on to this very day," Petty says with a shrug. "It just matters less. But back then? It bothered me. A lot." A collaboration with an artist like Bob Dylan would put Petty in the company of a man who had set up a very productive shop at some distance from the *Billboard* charts. Dylan was another teacher who showed up when Petty needed him.

■

Tom Petty had met Bob Dylan before. With only two albums out, Petty had gone to see Dylan play at the Universal Amphitheatre, and Dylan, much to Petty's surprise, had introduced the younger artist from the stage. Why he did that, Petty didn't know. But by 1985, they'd become closer still, sharing a manager in Elliot Roberts. When Tony Dimitriades joined up with Roberts, Petty was on a roster that included Joni Mitchell, Neil Young, Devo, the Cars, and Bob Dylan. In that regard, he was close to Dylan, which made him almost as close as anyone else.

At Live Aid, Petty had watched from the side of the stage as Dylan, introduced by Jack Nicholson, walked out with Keith Richards and Ronnie Wood for a forgettable, sloppy performance. Some would say that it was just what Live Aid deserved. For all of its noble intentions, Live Aid carried within it all the hubris and bloat of the mega-event. But in the midst of that unfocused performance, between songs, Dylan made a passing comment that, for most among the massive audience, drifted unnoticed into the nighttime air:

> I'd like to say that I hope that some of the money that's raised for the people in Africa, maybe they can just take a little bit of it, maybe one or two million maybe, and use it to, say, to pay the mortgages on some of the farms, what the farmers here owe to the banks.

Dylan's words worked their way into Willie Nelson's reefer-infused but agile mind and, as a result, brought about the launch of Farm Aid. Nelson, Neil Young, and John Mellencamp took the lead in putting the event together, and as spiritual father to the idea, Dylan almost had to show. Perhaps because of Dylan's sloppy Live Aid performance, Petty got a call from Elliot Roberts, asking if the Heartbreakers would back Dylan at Farm Aid. "When I came up with the Dylan/Petty thing, that was just a dream I had," Elliot Roberts explains. "I told Tony that I wanted to put Tom with Bob, then called Tom and said, 'I have this great idea.' Tom tells me he'd kill to do this. So I tell Bob, 'Hey, Tom's willing to do this, to be your band, and not charge you anything.'"

Not charge anything? "It wasn't quite like that," Tony Dimitriades says. "For Farm Aid, possibly. We might have done that for expenses only. But we weren't going to go on the road without meeting our needs. Dylan meant an enormous amount to all of us. He was and is a giant in our collective estimation. But, as manager, I didn't leave the practical dimension out of consideration." Dylan's Farm Aid performance, while loose, was transcendent when compared to that of Live Aid. Because Petty was untethered from the microphone, he got to play some lead guitar and smoke more cigarettes. Benmont Tench was smiling. Dylan even smiled.

"Bob really liked Tom a lot," says Roberts. "He thought he was a great player and a great singer, had great songs. So following Farm Aid, the idea of a tour came up." After confirming the dates with Dylan, however, Petty had second thoughts about it all. He was feeling less comfortable about leaving his kids at home. Things had gotten worse in Encino, for everyone. Without knowing just what he was dealing with, blaming it on the drugs, Petty was watching his wife come apart. She was losing a fight with a mental illness. It took Stevie Nicks to push him to follow through.

"Tom was sitting there on the chair at his house," Nicks remembers, "and he says, 'I'm not going.' I told him, 'Oh yes, you are going! You can't cancel on Bob fucking Dylan! What, you're going to call up Bob and tell him it's off!?' Tom just goes, 'I'm not doing it.' 'Okay,' I say, 'Why?' He tells me, 'Because Jane won't go.' Now this is where the Floridian parts of these people really come out. I said I was going to talk to Jane, but he insists that she's not interested, just doesn't want to go. So I turn around and say,

'Well, do you want me to go? Do you need a sidekick, is that what you're saying, someone to be with you and to make you laugh, and to be there when you're lonely? This is obviously the thing that is scaring you on this tour, and *you're* not afraid of anything; you're not afraid of alligators.' What the fuck, you know?"

By Nicks's account, she didn't get a response out of Petty. But that mattered less to her than getting an answer out of his wife. "I had only rarely taken Jane on tour," Petty says, "so I don't know why I would have said I wouldn't go without her. I was probably throwing a fit. That kind of thing happened. But that tour, having Stevie along, was very good for me. It changed the channel. Stevie was lighthearted. And she *so* loved music. She figured out before I did that we had a blend as singers. She'd come over, and the guitars would come, and we'd sing old songs, and it could sound so good. But right then she also knew, probably better than most people, that I was in a really delicate mental spot. I was just shattered emotionally. I was just going back and forth from one extreme to another every day, completely freaked out. She kept me focused on what I had to do, where I had to show up, got me on stage."

Stevie Nicks had a bond with Jane Petty. Nicks's song title "Edge of Seventeen" inadvertently came from Jane. When they were first getting to know each other, Jane Petty was telling Nicks the story of the early days in Gainesville, how she met her husband at "the age of seventeen," which, filtered through her North Florida accent, sounded like "the edge of seventeen." What Nicks heard had the right poetic resonance. It didn't hurt their friendship that they both loved cocaine. And Nicks kept her inventory in good supply.

Nicks played the go-between with Tom and Jane. "I said to Jane, 'He's not going to go without you. Do you want this tour to be canceled?' And she said, 'He can do this. He's Tom Petty. He's perfectly capable of going on the road and backing up Bob Dylan. *He* made this decision. He's a grown man.' I looked at her and said, 'Well, he's not going without you, so do you want me to go for you?' 'Sure,' she tells me, 'you go.' So I marched upstairs and told Tommy, 'Guess what? I am your wingman. I'm going to get my passport and get my assistant Rebecca, and we'll meet you at the airport.' He said okay, and off we went."

"Not exactly," says Petty. "There *was* this moment when Jane went to

Stevie and said, 'I want you to go to Australia and keep an eye on Tommy.'
I found it kind of unusual but not *that* unusual. I'd heard her say this to
people before, you know, 'Take him away and keep him involved.' Basically so she could party on her own, without any supervision. I had limits
as to what I thought was appropriate. I thought, 'Yeah, that sounds good
to me.' It was weird times. I remember going over to Stevie's house and
talking about it, and she needed to get her passport renewed real fast or
something. But we did it. And we really got to know each other better on
that trip. Everybody liked Stevie. She was just part of the entourage. I mean,
we weren't a couple or anything."

The press saw it otherwise. Stevie Nicks had a single out and should
have been home supporting it. The David Letterman show was calling her
manager, Irving Azoff, asking for her to perform on the show, unable to
grasp why an artist would release a single and then disappear. "Letterman
wanted me to come on, to sing 'I Can't Wait,'" Nicks explains. "But I was
gone, out of touch with the world. It got into the papers, and they got pissed.
And I'm in Australia with Tom Petty and Bob Dylan, having a great time,
oblivious. This is how important Tom Petty and the Heartbreakers are to
me. I was completely willing to get in the way of my own single." When
Dylan waved to her from the stage at an early show, Nicks didn't think to
do more than wave back. But he was signaling her to join them onstage,
which she did, and would have for the whole tour, but for the fact that she
had no work permit. But it was no matter. She hadn't come with the intention of performing and was happy at the side of the stage.

The connection Petty felt with Nicks would carry them for years, though
it had its own volatilities. "She got really mad at me one night in Australia," says Petty. "We were talking about Fleetwood Mac, something about
the band, and I said, 'Yeah, but the Heartbreakers are a rock-and-roll band.'
She kind of lost her mind, saying, 'I'm in a rock-and-roll band!' 'Not really,'
I told her. And she said, 'How dare you say that to me?' And this long
debate ensued about how you get those credentials. And I love that band,
have the greatest respect for Lindsey and Mick, but I didn't see them as a
'rock-and-roll band.' I thought her journey was different than mine. There
was a rub, like I didn't always agree with her musical taste, and she didn't
always agree with mine. My frustration with her was, 'You need somebody
to remind you what you're capable of. You get too easily distracted by

bullshitters that want to make a hit. I don't know why you're doing all this synthesizer rock.' I was probably an asshole when I think about it. But I felt free enough with her that I could do that." When told that he and Nicks certainly *sound* like a couple, Petty appears to be a man who can't argue the point. "Well," he says, "we were close . . . We were never what you'd call 'an item.' But we certainly had our times."

■

When the subject of Bob Dylan comes up among the Heartbreakers and their camp, no one says a whole lot, beyond stating their love and admiration. Mostly it's the safe stuff. Respect for Dylan, among those who have worked for him or still do, is shown in the silence that follows the mention of his name. No one interferes with the mystery around Dylan, which may be his greatest creation. When asked what Dylan was going through during the tours with the Heartbreakers, a period Dylan writes about in great detail in *Chronicles*, Elliot Roberts says, "That was unique to Bob, going through that . . . I don't really like to talk about him, frankly. I'm still good friends with him. And that's probably why."

But those passages in *Chronicles* are quite remarkable. Dylan describes being at some kind of creative low, lost, as the tour moved sluggishly toward its last weeks:

> I'd been on an eighteen month tour with Tom Petty and the Heart-breakers. It would be my last. I had no connection to any kind of inspiration. Whatever was there to begin with had all vanished and shrunk. Tom was at the top of his game and I was at the bottom of mine. I couldn't overcome the odds. Everything was smashed. My own songs had become strangers to me, I didn't have the skill to touch their raw nerves, couldn't penetrate the surfaces. It wasn't my moment of history anymore. There was a hollow singing in my heart and I couldn't wait to retire and fold the tent. One more big payday with Petty and that would be it for me. I was what they called over the hill. If I wasn't careful I would end up ranting and raving in shouting matches with the wall. The mirror had swung around and I could see the future—an old actor fumbling in garbage cans outside the theater of his past triumphs.

Dylan's description of what came next relies on a language and imagery that suggests nothing short of a conversion experience. It's stuff that recalls Tolstoy's Ivan Ilyich on his deathbed. A sudden psychic and spiritual shift, an epiphany as much of the body as the mind, an opening onto the next part of his creative life and immediate awareness of its significance. It happens onstage, at a show with the Heartbreakers in Locarno, Switzerland:

> Everything came back, and it came back in multidimension. Even I was surprised. It left me kind of shaky. Immediately, I was flying high. This new thing had taken place right in front of everybody's eyes. A difference in energy might have been perceived, but that was about all. Nobody would have noticed that a metamorphosis had taken place.

By all accounts, most of the Heartbreakers *didn't* notice, with the exception of Petty. "I remember seeing that," he says. "I remember having a shock when he went to sing and nothing came out. He just kind of took a deep breath and came back, full-voiced." The other Heartbreakers were more likely wondering what key the next song would be in.

"Bob's performances are what he lives for," Elliot Roberts says. "His whole day is based on eight o'clock. I don't know if that's how people relate to him now, but in those days, that's how it was. Every show, didn't matter if it was Cincinnati or LA." Talking with Bud Scoppa for a *Creem* feature in 1987, Petty describes the rehearsals themselves as being particularly stimulating. "'But more than the tour, I think it was the rehearsals for the tour that inspired us,' Petty adds. 'They were long rehearsals—five hours sometimes, where we played a hundred songs in a night. We played so many songs every night—it was *really* inspiring. 'Cause Bob was excited— everybody was excited. We were just havin' a great time. And then, when we started realizing how to drive that thing, we really started getting excited.'"

Among the band members, the Dylan tour registered differently. If they all agree without reservation that the experience took them to the next level as a band, the *not knowing*—not knowing how a song might be played, what key it would be in, what feel—wore on them differently. Benmont Tench, as Dylan points out in *Chronicles*, wanted to explore Dylan's catalogue with him. The spontaneity, the almost careening beauty, engaged the keyboard player. Petty, too, felt like he was learning something about what it meant to approach songs as Dylan had learned to early on. Dylan's relationship to his material reflected something that had become rare in the pop tradition. "Bob works in the way a true folksinger works," Petty insists. "You can drop sections, make changes on the spot. It's part of the very idea of folk music. Onstage, I felt like he had the same spontaneity of a great jazz player." The Heartbreakers would be talking about what they saw up there from that point forward in their lives as musicians.

Dylan's spontaneity wasn't restricted to the stage. There was something to be learned from him in that regard, too. At one of the first rehearsals, even before full production, Dylan showed up late. The band was only able to rehearse some ninety minutes before Stan Lynch let Petty know that he had to leave. "Tom was like, 'Fuck. Where do you need to be?'" says Lynch. "And I told him, 'I'm going to see Frank and Sammy tonight at the Greek.' The whole band just starts backing away from me. I mean, literally, it was like, 'We don't know him.' This might have even been the first rehearsal. Bob's got his shades on, kind of noticing the conversation but not a part of it. Two minutes later Bob says, 'Frank and Sammy?' The room's still dead quiet. 'I love those guys,' he says. I go, 'Well, I have two tickets. Fourth row. And I don't have a date.'" Lynch and Dylan left in the drummer's Jaguar XJS, a twelve-cylinder two-seater. There wasn't room for Dylan to bring security. "I thought Stan was getting brownie points with the new boss," says Mike Campbell. "I was kind of jealous."

Stan Lynch had seen Sammy Davis Jr. several times in Las Vegas, had what he referred to as a "Sammy museum" in his house. He knew much more about Sammy Davis Jr., in fact, than he did about Bob Dylan. "I wasn't really sucked into the whole vortex of Dylan mythology yet," says Lynch. "Bob Dylan was, to me, this guy who was really cool, and 'All Along the Watchtower' is a great Hendrix record. I'm still that fucking stupid. So I'm trying to strike up conversation with Bob Dylan, and it's going pretty well. 'So, you think this tour will go out on the road?' I ask. 'Yeah, we'll go on the road,' he says. 'Where do you think we'll go,' I ask. 'We'll probably go all over,' he says. 'Do you like having a band?' 'Yeah, it's fun having a band.' Right? He's just a fucking guy. Then we get to the Greek Theatre, and he tightens his sweatshirt hood around his face. We make our way to the fourth row. He looks like the Unabomber. But by that point, a few people are realizing that Bob Dylan is there. You can sort of feel the energy. The show starts, and it's fucking great. But I kinda got one eye on Bob, one eye on Sammy. Like, 'How's Bob reacting to this? How's Bob reacting to me loving Sammy so much? What's happening here?' The whole thing is odd, with the people around us reacting to how Bob is reacting to Sammy."

At the end of the set, after a standing ovation, Dylan made to leave. Perhaps all the talk about Sammy Davis Jr. had confused things. Lynch, not knowing what else to do, grabbed Dylan by the back of his sweatshirt as he started heading toward the aisle, reminding him that Frank was still due to perform. "But now it's intermission," says Lynch, "and I'm pressed for more conversation. Then Cheryl Tiegs, the supermodel, walks by, and it's a perfect opener. She's hot! Musicians can only talk about a few things, right? I go, 'Cheryl Tiegs, man.' He goes, 'Huh? Who?' I say, 'Right there in front of you.' I say something like, 'Nice ass.' And this is where I knew we were going to be friends. He says, 'That's way after my time.' I go, 'What?' He says to me, 'I like Ann-Margret, Elizabeth Taylor.' He starts naming chicks like that. I say, 'Really?' He looks at me, takes his sunglasses off, and says, '*Really.*' I finally start catching on, like, 'Right. Bob Dylan. *Life* magazine and shit. I'm in another league tonight.'"

No one in the Heartbreakers went away from working with Dylan without feeling like they'd been to the very best school. Dylan's relationship to the song affected everyone else's. But like most of the men who came into Petty's life, Dylan didn't have a band in the way Petty did. Dylan had road bands and studio bands and some that stayed with him for long periods. But Dylan was a solo artist who brought players in. As bandleaders, the two men had different job descriptions. Petty was a member of a group, even if he was struggling to remain one. "I remember one night on the Dylan tour," says Petty, "getting into an argument with Stan onstage. I don't even know what it was about anymore. We were doing the Heartbreakers section of the show. I looked at him, not to communicate something, just looked at him for some reason, and he took his drumsticks in one hand and just shot me the bird, mouthed the words 'Fuck you!' I don't know what it was, but something about it made me so mad. I went into a rage, just pushed my guitar off, walked from the stage, shut myself in the dressing room." Sitting there, too angry to talk, Petty told the managers to go away, said that everyone needed to stay out. It caused obvious concern among the production team. Onstage, the Heartbreakers kept playing. Petty could hear as Al Kooper got up and started jamming with the band, a blues thing.

"Finally," says Petty, "the door opens, and it's Bob. He comes in and goes, 'Hey, man, I heard you got mad. Don't be mad. Let's go back and play.' I was so angry. I said, 'Stan gets . . .' But Bob stopped me, said, 'No, no, don't go there. Everything's okay. John Lee Hooker's here. We're going to play with John Lee Hooker. C'mon, you don't want to miss that. Let's go play.' So I went with Bob and John Lee Hooker, went up and finished the set. But Stan, he had the power to get under my skin. I don't only want to knock him, because he was a tremendous part of our success. But he could get under my skin." Between Petty and Stan Lynch, though, there was still Mike Campbell, Petty's number two. For a long time, Campbell had been the link keeping that band from falling apart. Lynch was regularly putting Petty down behind the bandleader's back. Petty, for his part, didn't have to say much for Campbell to know how bad it had gotten. Campbell knew. From both sides. But he wouldn't be in the middle for long.

■

After months of touring, the Heartbreakers were deep in a kind of in-betweenness—they weren't entirely themselves or, really, Dylan's. To be Dylan's band was not to experience oneness with the man. You didn't get to move into Dylan's head and take a look around. He had a band, but the show was his, as was his experience of it. As that account in *Chronicles* more than reinforces, Dylan was sometimes detached, a front man living in a different hemisphere than his players. Though the Heartbreakers were doing their own set every night, the Dylan part of the show remained an experience so different from their own that, at times, they were having an almost schizophrenic musical experience. They were working out of someone else's office, so the pressure was less in some ways—but they were also becoming disassociated from their own program. What, Petty finally had to ask himself, were they really doing? It was a question that came only toward the end of the first Dylan tour. But it was Petty's responsibility to answer it. And making a record was the most obvious way to do that.

Given that the Heartbreakers had been out on stage chasing Dylan night after night, Petty chose to let the looseness borne of that enter into the process. When they got off the road from the True Confessions tour, with time booked and their gear moved into Sound City, Petty started writing in the studio, calling out chords to his band, not sure himself where he was going. It wasn't how he'd worked in the past. On the rough mixes, you can hear him barking out the changes, letting intuition carry him. Everyone involved knew that the Dylan tour had heightened the band's capacity to move as a unit, to build something without a blueprint. An already agile group had become something more, a rock-and-roll outfit as fleet-footed as the great studio bands they'd listened to growing up.

The album they created had a top-twenty hit and went gold without a lot of trouble, but it wasn't the kind of success the band had gotten used to. Petty still says that the title, *Let Me Up (I've Had Enough)*, is the best part about it, if only because it's fitting. No one is harder on a Heartbreakers record than Heartbreakers. And not everyone outside the band is in agreement, of course, even if the Heartbreakers lit the funeral pyre on *Let Me Up* some time ago. There are critics who don't fully understand why everyone would be content to write that album off. Bad sales? That hasn't stopped a slew of other recordings from being viewed as classics. A disjointed collection? Some of the best albums fit that description. The idea that *Let Me Up (I've Had Enough)* was a failure seems to be one of those things that everybody agreed on in haste, moving on before a fair trial could take place.

Benmont Tench has always suggested that the album's problems stem from the disconnect between Petty's loose, written-in-the-studio approach and the tracks Mike Campbell brought in, meticulously crafted pieces built around programmed drums and layers of overdubs, most of it made in isolation, not with the band. "Runaway Trains," "My Life/Your World," and "All Mixed Up": the Campbell recordings were the opposite end of the spectrum from the Dylan experience. They were tracks built in a studio, not found on a stage. In 1987, on the eve of the tour supporting *Let Me Up (I've Had Enough)*, Tench was already quick to brush aside any compliments that might come his way regarding the record. "You should hear how good it was when the band played those songs live," he said. "That's how they should be heard." The Heartbreakers' contracts didn't say they had to recite the superlatives from the press release when asked about a new record.

In some way, "The Boys of Summer" was still a scent that came into the air. And, for record makers, any occasion on which another recording enters the control room is trouble, whether it's a demo or some previous success. Or someone else's previous success. You can bet that there weren't any other recordings crowding the room when the Kingsmen finally put their cover of "Louie, Louie" onto tape. But for the Heartbreakers, it was difficult to completely ignore the background noise of "The Boys of Summer." Of the songs on *Let Me Up*, "Runaway Trains" pulls toward that recording more than any other. Not that anyone talked about it that way. But it was the same Mike Campbell who built "The Boys of Summer" track who created the music for "Runaway Trains." And there was little doubt that Petty preferred not to watch one more Campbell demo become another man's hit. As the song evolved, particularly when Petty's vocal went down, it became a Heartbreakers recording. "Runaway Trains" remains one of the great, underrated Petty-Campbell songs, largely because Petty's instinct was right: this was a Campbell demo in which he could make a place for himself. He wrote to it as naturally as he did "Refugee" and "Here Comes My Girl."

But Petty feels he let everyone down. Usually meticulous, focused, willing to leap off some cliffs, fastidious in knowing the inner life of the songs so that he could guide their evolution as recordings, Petty got distracted. For the first time, he'd moved out of the family house. He got himself an apartment at the Sunset Marquis. He was getting ready to end his marriage. After being there for a few months, however, he got a call from his wife, frantic, saying that Annakim had broken her arm. He rushed back. It wasn't a broken arm. But he didn't have the heart not to stay. "There were records that were hard to make, records that got confused," he says. "But I was always there to watch them go off the rails. With that album, though, I kind of stepped out to the back alley for a smoke and didn't come back, just as we were finishing recording. I was ready to hand it off. I talked to Iovine, and he felt Mike Shipley could take what we'd done and turn it into a record. It was the first time, the only time, I handed a Heartbreakers record over to someone else to bring it home. I shouldn't have. No one knows a record as well as the people who made it. You don't just give it over to someone who wasn't there when it went down." Previously, Shipley had worked with Def Leppard.

1987

My band, the Del Fuegos, finished our third album. There was talk at the time about what that third record could do for us if we didn't fuck things up. We started our touring in Europe. We'd already been invited to open for Tom Petty and the Heartbreakers on the US leg of their upcoming tour supporting *Let Me Up (I've Had Enough)*. The idea was that we'd do Europe, build momentum, and return to do the States. It was a good plan, and it would have made a lot more sense . . . if our record made sense. Instead, the reports started trickling in while we were overseas. Radio wasn't playing it. Our managers tried to sprinkle good news in with the bad, but there wasn't a lot to work with. Simultaneously, the Heartbreakers were facing their own disappointments: weak album sales were translating into weak ticket sales. Someone had an idea: put another band on the US tour and call it the "Rock and Roll Caravan." And make sure that third band had something good going on.

The "caravan" meant we were no longer opening for Tom Petty and the Heartbreakers—we'd be opening for the Georgia Satellites, a rock-and-roll band that had just found their way to the top of the pop charts with "Keep Your Hands to Yourself." A few months prior, the Satellites had opened some shows for us. Reversals of that kind didn't always go down easily in the digestive tracts of young bands. But the Satellites had made a record that was everything ours wasn't. It was pure rock and roll. Onstage, they were even better. Here was a band that did what so many others failed to do: they recognized that sometimes the best innovation is to play straight-ahead rock and roll very, very well. They plugged into vintage Marshalls, avoided fussy gadgets. And they were having the time of their lives. They were doing what they did far better than we were doing what we did. We weren't even entirely sure what it was we did.

The attractive young women on the Caravan tour, the ones experienced enough to make their way into an arena's backstage, were generally asking directions to the Georgia Satellites' dressing room. Knowing that we'd be facing a small fleet of tour buses at Caravan venues, the Del Fuegos didn't even have the strength to downsize. We, too, arrived by tour bus, losing some hundred thousand dollars in order to be on tour with Tom Petty and the Heartbreakers for the summer. By that time, we were neither the accountant's nor our own best friends. Every night, we had to watch not one but two rock-and-roll bands go up there and do it right. Not that Tom Petty and the Heartbreakers were having the kind of fun the Satellites were having.

Only days before the Caravan tour, someone burned down the Pettys' Encino home. Even today, when Tom describes getting out of the house, making sure his family was okay, grabbing what he could, he recalls the scene with the lingering shock of a man who has told a story many times but still doesn't fully understand it. The fire was quickly classified as arson. The family stood on the street in Encino, the sun just up, as the firemen went to work. But the media got there before the fire trucks. Annie Lennox, a neighbor at the time and a friend, went out and bought clothes for the Pettys, bringing them to the hotel that would be the family's home for the next few days, before the Rock and Roll Caravan tour would begin.

The Pettys went on the tour as a family. Or something like a family. The girls scattered into the backstage areas, hotel rooms, and tour buses. Mike Campbell also brought his kids for some of the tour, so Adria Petty had a companion in Brie Campbell, but she also spent significant amounts of time poking around the less-than-child-friendly environments of the opening bands. She had a foot in both worlds. On one evening early in the tour, Adria brought Brie into our dressing room, and only moments later Mike Campbell was in the doorway, asking what in God's name his young daughter was doing in our dressing room.

Jane Petty was not as much of a fixture backstage as Adria. I remember her being welcoming, somewhat aloof, but also frequently absent. There was an uneasiness to the tour that I wasn't able to fully understand. How much was my own discomfort, I don't know. Just prior to the tour, I started dating a woman who had recently been involved with Benmont Tench. It wasn't the kind of move that members of opening bands are encouraged to make. But I was young, and I think it gave people something to laugh about for a few moments before they forgot about it. And Benmont may have viewed the whole thing as me helping him move things along. I don't know. There was music, too. I watched the Heartbreakers every night.

By the final week, I was more than ready for the tour to be over and done. At the last show, the Heartbreakers invited all of the bands to join them onstage, with Roger McGuinn also a part of it. I was as uncomfortable as I would ever be playing music in public. I remember Mike Campbell putting his arm around me as we played, and he seemed surprisingly large, as though his body were three times the size of my own. It was a psychological effect—I'd been mistaken for an adult, mistaken for a musician, and I wanted it all to end before the truth was uncovered.

With the Caravan tour finished, the Heartbreakers went back out with Dylan, for their final adventure as his band. The Pettys rented Charo's house in Beverly Hills, where their marriage would continue its descent into disconnection. *Let Me Up (I've Had Enough)* settled in as the unqualified low point in sales for the Heartbreakers.

The following December, I was invited to the Pettys' Christmas party. It was one of the last times I'd see Tom for many years. As a Christmas gift, he gave me a Beatles fan magazine from 1965. It was Los Angeles, so it was no surprise that there were some celebrated faces milling about. When George Harrison came in, he avoided the main room and went into Petty's office, but a buzz still went through the place. A Beatle. I felt compelled to mention to Jane Petty that the gift they'd given me would look nice with Harrison's signature on the front of it. "Of course it would!" she told me, taking me by the arm and leading me down a hallway, where she opened a door and all but pushed me in, with a very brief mention to the occupants of the room that I had "something impending I needed to address."

George Harrison, Jeff Lynne, Tom Petty, and Mike Campbell were in the middle of playing a song, cut off by my entrance. Jane was gone, so fast it must have appeared that I had barged into the small office space of my own accord. Harrison, always ready to entertain his friends, stopped what he was playing and said, "Look, it's Brian Jones, back from the dead!" He then proceeded to play another song, about a dandy, which had everyone laughing, except for the very uncomfortable fan holding a Beatles magazine from 1965. When it was over, Harrison took a marker and signed the cover, "To Warren of something impending," adding the signatures of every Beatle. Petty, perhaps seeing that I was stunned, quietly let me know that I was welcome to stay, that I could hang out in the office with his friends. If I wanted to. I did. But I didn't. I left as abruptly as I'd come. When I later heard about the Traveling Wilburys, I understood that I had been witness to a moment, surely one of many, but a moment nonetheless. And it was clear in that office that Petty seemed as close to comfortable and as close to happy as I would ever see him.

18

GONNA LEAVE THIS WORLD FOR A WHILE

Though I prize my friends, I cannot afford to talk with them
and study their visions, lest I lose my own.
—RALPH WALDO EMERSON

The onstage awakening that Bob Dylan describes in *Chronicles* came with only nine shows left in the Temples in Flames tour, in Locarno, Switzerland, on the Piazza Grande, a cobbled city center encircled by rows of town houses, all hundreds of years old. It was a gorgeous location, but beauty and history were no longer as compelling to the traveling musicians as they might have been a few weeks earlier. It was the point in the tour when one could hate the sound of the next man's breathing. The stores in the Piazza Grande were too crowded to enter, and the small Locarno apartment that the band used as a dressing room didn't offer much as a refuge. Everyone was ready to go his own way. Egypt, Tel Aviv, Jeruselum, Australia, back and forth across the States, Europe. It was more than the band had ever taken on. Two years of it, with the Pettys' Encino house burned down by an arsonist in the middle of it all. The bandleader went from being ready, at last, to leave his marriage to feeling like he had to do all he could to protect his family. Nature had taken over. He didn't even know the kind of trouble he was in. And the band was following at a short distance. "We'd been on the road a long time," says Stan Lynch. "And there's a little stress involved. I'm getting lonely. I'm getting a little freaked out."

Mike Campbell's family had joined him in Europe, renting an apartment in Lugano, Switzerland, on the Italian border. "I wanted my wife and kids to come to Europe," says Campbell. "They could stay in Lugano while I went out and did gigs. But they weren't on tour. They were on their own tour. I knew I was traveling with the band. Mixing family into that was generally frowned upon at the time." If the rigorous separation of band and family on the road could be explained in many ways, perhaps the best explanation relates to the everyday culture of touring; it's not easy for the touring musician to find a space or a moment of his or her own. The road experience involves most everyone trying to limit what is already an abundance of group activity, noise, interaction. Hotel rooms are places the musician is too often wrenched from in order to perform, to travel, to eat. The bus provides the most consistent sanctuary. And even there you're going to find other bodies. Put families into that picture and the complexities increase. Only after his family's home was burned down did Petty bring his own wife and children on the road.

By some accounts, the challenge of taking a family trip in the midst of a Heartbreakers' European tour found Marcie Campbell and the kids more connected to the band's world than originally planned; the Lugano apartment didn't get as much use as had been envisioned. And the band and crew felt like they hadn't been given a lot of notice about the change. The truth was, Campbell hadn't gotten much notice himself. Family trips generally involve some spontaneity. Not so rock-and-roll tours. In this case, the two worlds were bumping up against each other. It put Campbell in an uncomfortable position. Behind his back, more than one crew member likened the guitar player's family to the Griswolds. It might have played out differently if it hadn't been the end of a few years on the road, but everyone was tired, if not on edge, and the Campbells provided one more element to contend with. The show immediately following Locarno, Switzerland, was in Paris, and the Campbell family planned to go. The bus ride, however, was one of the longer ones on the tour. Many of the performers planned to fly. But not all of them.

"This is before the G4 [private jet] era," says Lynch. "It's pretty real. You're on ferryboats. That kind of thing. But for that trip my plan was to take the bus. It was fourteen hours or something. And there were girls involved. You know, I'm leading a different life. I'm having an alternative lifestyle, *right in front of you, right now*! I'm not on the Mister Rogers fucking tour. I'm a single guy. This is what you do when you're a Viking!" The tour manager, Richard Fernandez, informed Lynch that the Campbell family would also be on the bus for the ride to Paris. "I'd already given up some fun for Mike's family," Lynch continues. "And no one thanked me. Mike never went like, 'Thanks, man, for not having the time of your life tonight and putting up with this shit.' Richard sees the problem and says, 'There is another way. Maybe they could go on another bus.' Without missing a beat, I went, 'Fuck it. Put them on the other bus.'"

"I think there were some girls involved," says Petty, chuckling. "They were going to have a rolling orgy to Paris or something. It sounded like a good time. I understood what Stan was talking about. Then there's Mike and his kids, who were quite young at the time, and Mike's wife, Marcie. That kind of killed the party idea. But the background singers had a bus, and they were going to fly to Paris. Richard Fernandez thought he had solved the problem when he got that bus. But he hadn't. Someone was going to have to give. Someone was going to have to take the other bus." Petty walked into the Locarno apartment with Roger McGuinn just as Campbell and Lynch were beginning to address the issue. Howie Epstein and Benmont Tench were also there, but got up to leave as things got heated. Petty and McGuinn went to the back of the room, initially unaware of what was going on.

"I felt I'd gone to great lengths to separate my family from the band," explains Campbell. "Here's *one* ride where I needed them to come with me. This one leg. I think I went to Richard and said, 'I want Marcie to ride on the bus with me from here to Paris. This would really help me out.' Richard went, 'Oh, okay.' He was just trying to please everybody. Unbeknownst to me, Stan had made plans for a hooker fest or something. The way I remember it, it created a lot of bad energy from Stan toward me when I said I wanted to bring my wife. It became an impasse. It was like he was saying, 'How dare you do this, spoil my plans?' And I felt like, 'You're spoiling my plans. This is my *wife*.'" It wasn't the first occasion the issue had come up.

"There were other times," Campbell says. "Once in Florida, Marcie came out by herself for a few days. And there was a ride from Tampa to Miami. So I told her to come along on the bus. Then the word came down, 'No, no wives on the bus.' I had to rent her a car. I felt like I was peer pressured by the group. Like it was okay if someone was bringing his girlfriend, but if you're bringing your wife, that's not cool? It was lame. I'm not proud of that. I can't believe I did it. But what happened in Locarno didn't come out of nowhere. There was some history." When the subject is raised, others have asked why Campbell stayed on that bus in Florida rather than joining his wife in the rented car that followed—*that* wasn't the band's decision. Clearly, it's a complicated history, with a collision of narrators. But the Heartbreakers weren't the only band out there struggling to find the boundaries between home and work when rock and roll was the job. "In Stanley's defense," Bugs Weidel says, "there were some of us going, 'Thank God somebody said something.' It's complicated having a family on the road, and it had gotten over the top." Some in that world look at it from a black-and-white perspective. As onetime Heartbreaker and former Motel's guitar player Jeff Jourard insists: "You can't tour with your family, for God's sake."

"I think Mike was really worn out and had been drinking pretty heavily, just wasn't himself," Petty says. "I understand he felt caught in the middle. But I'd never really seen him that difficult. Stan was Stan. And the argument got ugly. Really ugly. In such a small space, with everyone just worn down to nothing after so much touring. The rest of us had no involvement in the argument at all. But it would have been impossible to step in and try to negotiate things. Maybe somebody said something to them, but nothing was going to stop this. It got bitter. Quickly. I remember looking over at McGuinn at one point and I realized he was tearing up, looked really upset. It was that mean. And then Stan, hearing Mike tell him that he wouldn't even see the kids on the fourteen-hour bus ride, finally just exploded." With Dylan and his singers in the front room of the apartment, Lynch yelled at Campbell, "It's not you! I can't stand to hear your wife's fucking voice!" And something between the two men shattered.

"It was awful," says Benmont Tench. "It was quick. And it was a decisive moment. It did horrible damage. Just horrible." The already delicate structure of the band was transformed. "From that point forward," says Campbell, "I felt like, 'This guy's not on my side.' I don't remember the words, but I remember the energy was unforgivable. And I just said to myself, 'I'm not with him. I'm with her.'" Mike Campbell was no longer the one in between Petty and Lynch. Now there was nothing holding Petty and Lynch together. Campbell didn't speak a word to Lynch, or listen to one, for more than a year. "With that, they're done being friends," says Bugs Weidel. "They're done everything. For life."

■

Petty talks about it in terms of weather. The Dylan tour hit England, and the final shows came like the end of a period of penance. In the days prior, those buses carried angry, confused, or just lonely men. Then everything lightened. For three nights in Birmingham and four in London, it all got a little better. Jeff Lynne and George Harrison showed up in Birmingham, and then returned for every Wembley Arena show, bringing Derek Taylor and Ringo Starr with them. Mick Avory from the Kinks came around. Denny Cordell, proud to see the Heartbreakers with Dylan, came to share in it. The collective spirits lifted the proceedings high above the struggles of recent weeks. On Petty's birthday, Harrison, Lynne, Starr, and Taylor were among those singing to him. "We were laughing and drinking and, really, never had such fun," Petty remembers. "It felt good." And then it was over. All except the weather.

"I went home to my room after that last show, and a hurricane hit London, with no warning," Petty says. "Meteorologists hadn't predicted anything like this. I didn't know hurricanes hit England. But one damn sure hit London that night. I remember getting up in the night, hearing the rain hit the window and thinking, 'Man, it really rains here in England.' And then I walked out in the morning, and huge oaks were toppled. The hurricane came through, wreaked havoc, and moved on. But after the fact, I thought, 'You know, ever since that hurricane things have been different.'"

Petty was back home after the last gigs, the Dylan tour finally over, driving his car, when he saw Jeff Lynne at a stoplight. He had new neighbors now that he was on the other side of the hills from Encino. "I'd just finished doing George Harrison's *Cloud Nine*," Lynne says. "And I'd seen the Dylan shows in London only days before, and Tom actually stopped me on the street in Beverly Hills. He kept honking his horn, and I thought, 'Who's that?'" Only days later, Jeff Lynne *and* George Harrison were in a private room at a French restaurant where Petty spontaneously stopped for lunch with his daughter Adria. Harrison had just asked Lynne for Petty's number when he found out that Petty had entered the restaurant, so he had the staff bring his new, surprised friend back to where he was sitting with Lynne. Harrison asked if he could follow Tom and Adria back to their place after lunch. It all unfolded with the kind of choreography that seems possible only when fate is moving the pieces around.

Harrison drove behind Petty through Beverly Hills to the Pettys' rented home, where the two men had a chance to be alone for the first time. Picking up a guitar, strumming "Norwegian Wood," Harrison said, "You know this one, don't you?" Struck by the ease and detachment with which Harrison played with his own legend, Petty was quickly drawn into Harrison's confident, warm charm.

"Almost as soon as we met them, we spent more time with Tom and Jane Petty than with anyone but the Keltners," says Olivia Harrison. "They were family. We had Christmases together. They came to Friar Park. We'd just hang out, for hours and hours, with Dhani and Adria and Annakim playing together, staying up way too late, probably. Tom and George playing guitars and ukuleles. Between George, Tom, and Jane—a lot of cigarette smoke. But we had fun. We got very close. I think it was a lot of fun for Tom. And George had never met anyone quite like Tom. George with his Liverpudlian accent and Tom with his drawl, there was something connecting them, some common element."

If right then Petty needed someone to step in and throw him a line, George Harrison was perfect for the task. Life with Jane had little comfort left in it. The Heartbreakers were men he respected as musicians, his traveling partners, but Petty didn't go to them with issues unrelated to work. "I think I needed a friend really badly," Petty says. "My friendship with the band was a different kind of friendship. And it was frayed. I'd become very lonely. George came along, and we just got so close; it was like we had known each other in some other life or something. We were pals within minutes of meeting each other. I remember him saying to me a couple of days after we'd known each other—he's just hugging me, holding me, and saying, 'Tommy, you're in my life now whether you like it or not.' It was like I'd been sent the very person I needed. He healed a lot of wounds."

Though not a man who saved everything along the way, Petty has kept a stack of letters, sent by fax, filled with words and pictures from Harrison. "Some weeks I'd get one every day," Petty says, laughing. "He liked

that fax machine." Harrison was a master of friendship, cultivating a connection. Not a father or brother figure, but someone who had learned to
enjoy most of what he'd been given. Harrison wasn't the first, and wouldn't
be the last, but he may be the man who got the closest and stayed the longest. "I know that Leon Russell was very generous to my dad when he was
young," says Adria Petty. "And I know that when he was in the studios with
producers, certainly Denny Cordell but even a Jimmy Iovine or someone
like that, when there were other men that believed in him, Bob Dylan or
Johnny Cash, I think it gave him an incredible sense of confidence. I even
think Jeff Lynne nurtured him. It's a lot of men, powerful men that came
into my father's life. But George Harrison was something special."

"The number of heavyweight dudes who really connected with him is
striking," Jeff Jourard says. "You know, George Harrison, Dylan, Johnny
Cash. But he delivers. He's got the goods. And when he's with his peers,
he's fun and funny. I suppose so many people are looking to get something
out of him for their own enhancement, it must be depleting. With the
heavyweights his tank's not being drained. He was probably getting his
tank *filled*. That's what it seems like. Not everyone is getting in there,
though. He's got tinted windows on his soul."

■

Jeff Lynne was by that time a part of George Harrison's world. "I think
George felt he had to court Jeff for a while," says Olivia Harrison, "before
he could ask Jeff to produce a record. He wasn't that presumptuous. George
wanted Jeff to trust him and to feel comfortable with him. So George took
him all over the place. They went to Formula One races, concerts, played
music." It turned into a collaboration that went on for almost ten years.
"And it would probably still be going on now, I'm sure," she adds, laughing, "because they were wicked together in their criticism of everything
that wasn't pure." By contrast, Petty and Lynne fell together quickly, without any courtship, on the strength of the Harrison connection, and the
work began. Without any thought as to what it meant.

"Around *Let Me Up (I've Had Enough)*," Mike Campbell recalls, "Tom
called me and said, 'We're done. I think we're done.' I couldn't believe he
wanted to stop the band. But I think he really meant it. He said, 'I've had
enough of this whole scene.' It kind of broke my heart. I said, 'Not now,

man. What are you saying?' He called me up later, said he was sorry, that he'd been in a mood. But it hit me that maybe he didn't mind giving up. I remember feeling like we were kind of lost. *Let Me Up* didn't sell well. The Stan stuff. I can't speak for Tom. He's the songwriter and the leader of the band. But maybe he felt like he just wanted to get away." Working with Jeff Lynne gave Petty some of that but not with a clear sense of purpose attached. At least at the outset. They simply got in a room together, with a few instruments around them, and things started happening. It wasn't the carnivalesque atmosphere Dave Stewart brought. Jeff Lynne was in love with the work of making records. His approach to that, however, left limited space for the Heartbreakers to be a band, even if they had been called to participate.

Bands weren't Lynne's primary concern—songs and recordings were what mattered. He wasn't interested in the groupthink, not if it didn't lead to the record. At Petty's house, sitting in the office with guitars, Petty showed Lynne a song he couldn't quite finish, "Yer So Bad." "I couldn't figure out a way from the verse to the chorus," Petty explains. "And Jeff figured something out right away. Things happened fast with him. So I asked him if he'd produce the track. I loved what he'd done with George."

Lynne came back to Petty's house the next day. He played "some Casio thing" that Bugs Weidel bought for Petty. At the time, Petty wasn't sure just why the keyboard was there or why Weidel bought it, but Lynne reached for it as they sat down in the outer living room of Petty's rented house and started fooling around. In Petty's telling, he was just trying to make Lynne laugh, playing some simple chord changes, throwing out images and phrases. Then, as Petty was strumming and singing, Lynne said, "Free falling." Petty grabbed it. When Lynne said, "Take it up an octave," Petty did that, too. A fragment began to feel like a song. "The cost of that keyboard was covered, I believe," says Weidel. Something in the song signaled a shift, to a greater degree than "Yer So Bad." "It was so light, so removed from struggle," says Petty. "I hadn't felt that in some time. It was like I hadn't taken a deep breath in I don't know how long. But I think you can hear me taking one in there." Lynne had little interest in sitting on what they'd written. He told Petty they should cut the two songs. Since Petty no longer had a home studio, he suggested they use Mike Campbell's place to record, even though it was, in Campbell's description, a "kitchen-sized bedroom with a board and a tape machine."

"My friend brought me into the fold," says Campbell. "He didn't have to. I got the call, and I was in. I loved it from the first day they showed up at the house. It was like going to musical college. But I really thought they were just cutting a demo." There was no deliberation, no waiting to find out what it was they were doing. "I guess I was showing Tom and Mike a way of making records that wasn't about just laboring all day going over the same thing," says Lynne. "You just get it done, and really quite quickly. Not quickly and stupidly, of course. But by the time you're recording, you've already put quite a lot of thought into it. I think what Tom and Mike liked was having a record almost done at the end of the day. There was no second-guessing, no *Let's come back tomorrow and see if it sounds any better*."

It wasn't going to be the recording of a performance. It wasn't going to be about playing the song down until there was a good take. It would be about building tracks—quickly. They'd find a tempo, put down a kick and snare or hi-hat on Campbell's drum machine, and begin layering. The drum machine, acting as a click track, would be pulled out of the mix when the layering had evolved sufficiently. The elements were simple: guitar, bass, drums, some keyboards, vocals. Nothing new. But several of those elements came in multiples. For Petty and Campbell, who had spent years in studios chasing the best single performance of a song, sometimes wearing themselves out, losing the spirit of the thing, Lynne's approach was striking. Lynne doubled and tripled and quadrupled guitar and background parts, while leaving open space for a single lead vocal with little or no reverb on it. Petty and Campbell watched as Lynne turned the new songs into something thick but airy, not weighed down by the layering but lifted by it, perfect pop. "I was just watching him do it, watching how he went about things," says Petty. "I found it fascinating. I was learning stuff that I had always wanted to learn and nobody had ever really taught me. This really talented guy was showing us a whole different way of working. He wasn't a producer like, say, Jimmy, who was concerned about what exactly we're saying here, or Rick [Rubin]. Jeff wasn't worried about that. He thought a good record said it all."

"I don't usually work out a guitar part in advance," says Campbell. "I put the track up, get a sound, and start playing along with what I'm hearing. Jeff doesn't do that. He works out a part. We needed a guitar part here or there, and Jeff would go home and work out parts. He'd come in the next day and say, 'Have you got any ideas for this?' And I didn't have ideas until I was playing along. So he'd go, 'Well, I have a couple.' By the second song we did, you better believe I came in with some ideas."

The chemistry between Lynne and Petty may not have been obvious to everyone at the outset. The dilemma in having a band as good as the Heartbreakers is that when Petty didn't use them, there would always be a chorus of doubters, thinking more about what Petty wasn't doing than what he *was* doing.

"We were supposed to make a Heartbreakers record," says Benmont Tench. "I called the main guy on our crew about a week before we were supposed to start, just to ask what time we were coming in. He just said, 'Uh . . . *ummmm*.' He hemmed and hawed and finally told me they were making a solo record. Nobody told me." The Heartbreakers, Campbell aside, were among the doubters. Again. Tench and Stan Lynch, even Howie Epstein, didn't stop short of shitting on Jeff Lynne's approach and its results. But something undeniable was happening. Lynne's production was bringing Petty's vocals forward in a way that they hadn't on previous recordings. The eccentricity and economy of his lyrics came to the front. The world was about to get to know Petty in new ways. Lynne productions favored the voice, in part because he would have Petty record a lead early in the process rather than when the basic track was nearing completion. It allowed the music to be more consciously geared toward that vocal performance. Then, in the mix, Lynne put the singer in the front, pointedly avoiding what could sometimes be the gauze of echo and delay. Listening to "Free Fallin'," you feel like Petty is across the table. "George [Harrison] used to say," explains Lynne, laughing, " 'Tom's a lucky bugger, because he's already got the twang built in. He's got a head start on us.' It's really hard to be from an industrial city in England and get a sound like that."

But it was more than twang that Lynne drew out. His records threw a little more light on the beautiful tension between Petty's voice and the words he wrote. The sadness, the juxtaposition of images, the release—it all came out more explicitly. "She's a good girl, loves her mama / Loves Jesus and America too / She's a good girl, crazy 'bout Elvis / Loves horses and her boyfriend, too." There was an assurance to the way Petty handed the story over to the listener. He was the narrator at a distance one minute and the main character the next, sliding between positions. There was a sophistication to the writing and an ease with which he handled it. And the emotional life within Petty's songs was as vibrant as ever. Part of what connected Lynne and Petty was a shared appreciation for voices like Del Shannon's, with which both men had experience as producers and fans. "[Del Shannon] was my favorite singer when I was about thirteen, fourteen," says Lynne. "I went to see him at Birmingham Town Hall. It was the first concert I'd ever been to, and it blew my mind. He sounded great, looked fantastic. Then by chance, I got to meet him at a club in Birmingham, in about '72 or '73. It was just when ELO was starting to come to America. We became great friends, and we wrote a couple songs then." The other voice at the top of Lynne's list was Roy Orbison. "Del's voice was like a powerhouse. It was so loud, and his falsetto was so strong, he could knock you over with it. Roy's was a different thing altogether, the subtlety of those velvet tones when he was in the mid-range—then he'd swoop up for those big notes. I mean, nobody in pop has achieved anything like what Roy did." Both voices had what Lynne describes as "a plaintiveness, tinged with sadness in some way. Like there's a story in there."

In Petty's voice and in his writing, Lynne discovered something of what he found in Del Shannon and Roy Orbison. Not technically, but in another way, in that *tinge of sadness*, that suggestion of some story "in there," which not every voice has, but Petty's always had. The Heartbreaker was heir to a tradition Lynne loved. "I think Tom's voice was one of the things that knocked me out when we first sat down to write," he explains. "It was the sound of his voice as we made the tune up. I thought, 'This is going to work great, because it's already there. It's coming out of his mouth, so all I've got to do is record it properly.'" They made most of *Full Moon Fever* in Campbell's garage, with the owner of the place acting as engineer. "The control room was that spare bedroom," Lynne says, "while the studio was a big old garage with a few motorbikes in it, some oil drums, stuff you'd find in a garage someone's been using for a number of years. I'd only known Mike Campbell for his brilliant guitar. But as an engineer, he gave me everything I wanted, got it going as quickly as I needed, you know?"

Whether it was the informality, the spontaneity of going from writing to recording with hardly a pause between, Lynne coming off a few records that had him in top form, or just the absence of a band hanging in the background, the record worked. But surely part of the achievement of *Full Moon Fever* had to do with Petty's feeling that he wasn't sure where he was headed.

"There's nothing like having nothing to lose in order to create good music," he says. "I felt we'd made *Let Me Up (I've Had Enough)* in a hurry. We'd been around the world with Bob Dylan, and then we made *Let Me Up* without a lot of thought, and it didn't do what we hoped it would. I had higher expectations. I remember coming home from the Rock and Roll Caravan tour and having a bit of a cold feeling, thinking, 'Wow, this whole thing could be on its last legs. If this happens again, we may not be able to maintain the stature we once had.' So *Full Moon Fever* was about just having a little fun on my own, a break from the pressure of thinking about where the Heartbreakers should go next. It was a little bit of a lark, really, done very quickly. But then, as we were making it, it felt so good to me. There was a looseness there that you can't force. You can only hope that it comes around every now and then. And it did. I was so pleased. And then something happened that had never happened before in my history in the business: the record company rejected it."

Petty had made what he felt was a great record, only to have the doubters at his record label be among the first to hear it and pass judgment on it. The rejection knocked him down. It hadn't ever happened that way. That anyone at MCA felt they were in a position to respond as they did left Petty stunned. At a dinner at Warner Bros. Record's chief Mo Ostin's house, with Jeff Lynne, George Harrison, Warner Bros. president Lenny Waronker, and some others in attendance, Harrison started fooling around with "Free Fallin'" on guitar, then insisted that Petty play the song for the group. Under the vaulted ceilings in Ostin's living room, it sounded transcendent. Hearing that this was among a collection of songs that had just been rejected by MCA, Waronker said on the spot that he'd sign Petty to Warner Bros. However good the idea sounded to Petty, he still owed MCA several albums. Waronker told him they should do it anyway. And they did. Years before Petty would make *Wildflowers*, his Warner Bros. debut, he was a Warner Bros. artist, with a signed contract hidden away in a vault for almost two years. MCA knew nothing of the deal. But it changed Petty's future even if it did nothing for his present.

The necessary short-term relief came only a matter of weeks after, from within MCA. When Irving Azoff left and Al Teller came in to run the company, *Full Moon Fever* got a different set of ears. Teller and a few others at the label got behind the record. It was that simple. Now, the only complaint was that the album was too short. "They wanted me to add a couple of songs," explains Petty. "So that's what I did. And they put it out. And it was a huge hit. It was kind of part two of this whole thing. We were rebirthed."

■

Between MCA's initial rejection of *Full Moon Fever* and its subsequent release, the Traveling Wilburys were invented, a George Harrison creation using the artists he most wanted to work with. The conversation started with Harrison and Lynne but quickly included Petty. "Once George met Tom," says Olivia Harrison, "he wasn't going to let him go. He really enjoyed Tom's company and loved his musical sensibilities." Then it was Bob Dylan and Roy Orbison. "The night we all went to Anaheim to see Roy perform," she continues, "I think they approached Roy, got down on their knees, and said, 'Please be in our band.' Barbara Orbison and I weren't allowed in the dressing room when they proposed. We all went to Denny's on Sunset that night after the show. There were some Goths hanging out, and it was all we could do to keep George from jumping in that car with them. They looked like they were having fun. That's where 'Zombie Zoo' came from. It was an amazing time, everything happening at once. George always missed that element, I think, of a band, a group dynamic. Whether he would admit that or not."

A web of admiration held the group together. Lynne and Petty were enamored of Harrison, just as they were raised in a world where Bob Dylan mattered to everyone. But no one was a bigger fan of Dylan than George Harrison. And *every* Wilbury looked to Roy Orbison with a kind of reverence. Orbison, for his part, understood that he'd just been invited to the hippest party in town. Every member was getting something. The spirit of the project was as light as the quality was rich, and it caught the public off guard, its humor in the foreground and little trace of pomp. It was a big hit, without a trace of the desperation that so often pushed records up the charts. Then, two months after the album's release, Roy Orbison died. Harrison called Petty as soon as the news came to him. "Aren't you glad it wasn't you?" he asked Petty.

"Here's the thing," says Olivia Harrison. "George would skip all the small talk. 'Did you hear about Roy? Oh, isn't this terrible?' They knew all that. They had a shorthand. They didn't have to have the initial five-minute conversation. Eventually, they'd get to, 'Aren't we lucky to be here?' That's what George's comment meant. Life is fragile. George used to say, 'In a moment, everything changes.'" A second Wilburys project would come out a few years after, but an element was missing. And it seemed that Roy Orbison, a quiet personality, a different generation, had provided something that gave the Traveling Wilburys a balance they needed.

19

PLANNED COLLISIONS

One could say that whenever one is in a group one has to
hide one's best nucleus, or very rarely let it come out. One
has to draw a veil over a part of one's personality . . .

—M. L. VON FRANZ

Jeff Lynne's name is on a lot of hit records. You're going to hear them when you
leave your home in the morning, maybe at the supermarket, the bar, or
laundromat, maybe as a sample on another record—"Strange Magic," "Evil
Woman," "Don't Bring Me Down," "Mr. Blue Sky," "Handle with Care,"
"You Got It," "Free Fallin'." He seems to know what makes people reach for
the volume knob. Born into pop. But for all that Lynne has done, he
acknowledges that *Full Moon Fever* earned a special place. "It's probably my
favorite album I've ever worked on," he says, after considering for a moment.
"Yeah, I would say so. Every song feels spot-on for what it's supposed to
be." A garage recording, the album has what Lynne calls a "sparkle."

For whatever wasn't right in his life at the time, Petty certainly felt some
satisfaction as the album became the biggest of his career. In the year after
it hit, describing how he felt about its success, the word Petty reached for
more often than any other was "happy." At the 1990 Grammy awards, *Full
Moon Fever* was nominated for album of the year, up against the debut of
Petty's "other band," the Traveling Wilburys. Of the other three records
nominated, one was Don Henley's *End of the Innocence*, an album with songs
cowritten by both Mike Campbell and Stan Lynch. On the music side of
life, abundance surrounded Petty and his band.

Petty never used the success of *Full Moon Fever* as an excuse to leave his band at home. He could have, of course. It was a solo record. But the idea never crossed his mind. Instead, he focused on how the touring for *Full Moon Fever* might require modifications to the band. It wouldn't be the big band of the *Southern Accents* tour. No girl singers, no horn section. But neither could it be what it had been when the Heartbreakers supported their early releases. Musically, the group needed a little more onstage to cover the changing sound. The stacked acoustic guitars that Lynne favored, together with the layered background vocals that punctuated his records, meant that more hands and more voices were needed. And though the point was not to find another guy to put on album covers, Scott Thurston came in to help and never went away. He was a utility guy, could play anything— guitars, keyboards, bass, harmonica—and hit the high notes. Eventually, years later, some photographer mistook him for a band member, and everyone else went along with it. Or something like that. In the beginning, however, Thurston was a hired hand brought in from Jackson Browne's band.

It was Stan Lynch who suggested Thurston. The sideman's background was rich in strangeness. He'd played with Ike and Tina Turner, Iggy Pop, the Motels. It would be fair to say that Thurston was prepared for anything. If you couldn't learn it from Ike or Iggy, it probably wasn't worth learning, not if playing in a rock band was what you planned to do with your life. Indeed, the fit between Thurston and Petty indicated that Thurston's education prepared him well. Exactly which among his earlier jobs had given him the tools he most needed to be a Heartbreaker is a question worth asking. Perhaps what he picked up as a musician on past gigs was second in importance to what he picked up regarding diplomacy. Or maybe Thurston was a quiet enough guy by nature and managed to stay that way long enough for the other Heartbreakers to realize he had no master plan, was no threat to *their* master plans. He just liked to play rock and roll. And he could play whatever was needed. "He had the skills," says Stan Lynch. "And he had a totally laissez-faire attitude, like, 'Who gives a shit? What's the worst thing that can happen? You fire me?'"

Early on in Thurston's tenure, Petty, a little lonely on the "star bus," welcomed the new guy into riding with him. Petty had kept his doors open for the others, but no one in the band walked through them. This time it was Thurston's idea, and it was an act that involved what Petty says was "the risk of being the teacher's pet." "I don't know why it was like that,"

Petty says. "And, really, it hurt my feelings. It went on for too long, me being pitted against my own band. But Scott called bullshit on that. And I think he even helped bring the band together, eventually, through that kind of freethinking." Bugs Weidel points to Stan Lynch as the primary architect behind the walled cities within the Heartbreakers. "The dynamic with Stanley, for years," Weidel insists, "was Stan against Tom. Tom was the boss, and Stan was like, 'We gotta be united against the boss. We're a band, we gotta watch this guy.' The only power he had in the past was Campbell. He'd go, 'Come on, Mike, you gotta look after your guys here. You got this advantage, Mike.' It created this weird thing, this deep, lasting schism."

With Thurston in the picture, the first signs of change arrived—and if Thurston's entrance wasn't the most dramatic harbinger of a new era, his choices as a band member were nonetheless beginning to register among the others. Petty and the new sideman would sit up for hours, analyzing the condition of planet Earth and its inhabitants. "Scott came up like I did, in garage bands," Petty explains, "and he had a hundred million rock-and-roll stories." Even when the bus pulled up to a hotel or venue, Thurston and Petty would often stay on the vehicle, as if still in transit. It couldn't have been anyone but Thurston. There was too much time between Petty and the other Heartbreakers to make that kind of looseness possible.

"I considered him my best friend for a long time," says Jackson Browne of Thurston. "He was my closest friend at the hardest time in my life. He was a very big part of what I did. *Produced* several albums. So Scott was in both bands for a while. Two years, I think. He was Tom's best friend. There's probably twenty of us out there, thinking we're his best friends. You'd be surprised how many. But it came to the point where he couldn't sustain doing both. The gig with Tom paid better. They traveled better. Played to more acclaim. But he didn't want to leave my band. He was at a breaking point, though. So he says he's going to retire. I ran into Tom at some thing, and he was like, 'How about that Scott Thurston, retiring like that?' Then I looked at Tom, and I got it. I was like, 'Okay, I think he should . . . I think he should come out of retirement. He doesn't have to do that.'"

Had there not been a series of hits to enjoy with *Full Moon Fever*, and Scott Thurston to bring a lighter mood, the Heartbreakers' grumblings may have worn on Petty more than they did. Not that it was always easy to play with musicians willing to publicly dismiss some of the music they were performing. "Before the record came out, Stan went all over town telling people that the album sucked," says Petty, "that what I was doing was terrible. I think the Heartbreakers were insecure because I did *Full Moon Fever* and then went into the Traveling Wilburys. They were pissed off. But I wasn't quitting the band. I had no intention of quitting." But it was hard to argue with the success of *Full Moon Fever*. The good results made the detractors look more like sore losers than anything else. Lynch bitched openly in *Rolling Stone* when asked about the tour, saying, "That was the first time a tour ever felt like work to me—I never want to feel like I'm in a cover band." Of course, by that time Lynch, too, had cowritten songs with Don Henley and was feeling the satisfaction of being recognized for talents beyond those utilized in the Heartbreakers. "Tom's never asked me to write with him," Lynch said in the same interview. "And that's one party you do not invite yourself into. He obviously doesn't see me in that light." Lynch wasn't alone in expressing discontent. Howie Epstein, at first listen to "Free Fallin'," let Petty know that he didn't like the song. Benmont Tench showed up for some work that was offered, but grimacing. Insecurities and fears weren't addressed openly—blaming the music was the masquerade that hid all that. Not well, of course. In the face of it, Petty let go of the idea of bringing the band in to play more. Only Mike Campbell took the full ride with Petty.

When it came to thinking about a follow-up, Petty showed himself to be a man who wanted it both ways. Traveling with a band that wavered in its support of the bandleader had its effects. He'd had a remarkable run with Jeff Lynne that included two Wilburys albums, *Full Moon Fever*, and cuts for Randy Newman, Del Shannon, and Roy Orbison, including the hit "You Got It," written by Petty, Orbison, and Lynne. But Petty felt he had to try bringing his two worlds together, to make a Heartbreakers record with Jeff Lynne producing, however much Lynne's approach was antithetical to the idea of recording a band in the studio. As Campbell says, "We felt bad for the other guys." The truth Petty was perhaps not willing to confront, however, was that there *was* no going back. He wouldn't really have a band again. Not that band.

Having Lynne produce the Heartbreakers was a puzzle Petty could deal with. The more abstract conundrum was the success of *Full Moon*

Fever. Gone was the freedom of having nothing to lose. The object was to follow a smash with a smash. Al Teller at MCA was now a fully inculcated believer. There's nothing like a multiplatinum record to make a man in the business your biggest champion. Very quickly, the fresh, direct, unencumbered character of the *Full Moon Fever* sessions, the looseness that allowed the producers to work quickly and effectively, was gone. The "sparkle" wouldn't be as easy to find. They'd left the garage.

"*Into the Great Wide Open* maybe lost the simplicity that *Full Moon Fever* had," says Jeff Lynne. "*Full Moon Fever* was a kind of blatant, this-is-what-it-is-so-take-it-or-leave-it feeling. The sound was so concise, just one sound that belonged to itself. The next one, *Into the Great Wide Open*, maybe it was just thought about too much. It wasn't as simple or straightforward. *Full Moon Fever* songs were so clean, just moving along. When I did that, it was basically me, Tom, and Mike doing everything, including background vocals." Lynne doesn't point to the involvement of the band as the problem. Not directly. He went about things as he needed to. Any forked-tongue comments from the band were generally made behind his back. By the time they'd finished it up, however, fully absorbed in their creation, Lynne thought he might have a very big record on his hands. Al Teller at MCA was *sure* he had something that would double the sales of *Full Moon Fever.*

■

Rick Rubin knew Al Teller from the days when Teller was at Columbia and Rubin's Def Jam had Columbia distribution. Already viewed as being among the most important record producers of his time, Rubin was fast becoming one of pop music's great crossover acts. In metal and hip-hop, he was a star. Now he was setting out on a kind of expansion campaign that would release him from any genre-bound future. "The album [of Petty's] that got me was the first Jeff Lynne album," Rubin explains. "It wasn't even one song that did it. I remember hearing, probably, three. And by the time I heard the third single, I thought, 'This just sounds like it's going to be an incredible album.' That was my first Tom Petty album experience. And I listened to it a million times. It lived in my car. In those days, there were no CD changers. I had a one-disc slot, and *Full Moon Fever* was in there for at least a year. Every day, that's what I listened to."

Rubin sought out Al Teller at the time *Into the Great Wide Open* was being set for release, just to tell him about the record he'd fallen in love with. "I called him and said, 'Al, there's an act on your label, and I just want to put the word in that if there's ever an opportunity to work with him, I want to do it. He made my favorite album, and nothing would please me more. And he's like, 'Oh, great. Who's that?' And I said, 'Tom Petty.' And he said, 'I'm sorry, Tom Petty makes his records with Jeff Lynne, and that won't be changing any time soon.' And that was that."

Tony Dimitriades describes Al Teller's faith in the *Full Moon Fever* follow-up as unflappable. Perhaps Teller was even a bit drunk on the thing. "He thought it was going to be even bigger," Dimitriades says. "I remember we had lunch with him, me and Tom, and he said, 'This is going to sell six million albums.' I couldn't believe that he said that. I thought, 'Why would you even go there? Why say that to your artist? Now if you sell four million, you've failed.' He could have said that he'd do everything he could for the album, that he's fully behind it. But, no, he said it's going to sell six million. And it did well, but it didn't do that. In relation to *Full Moon Fever*, it was a disappointment." What Teller didn't know was that his artist, his MCA artist, Tom Petty, had already signed that contract with Warner Bros. Petty had somewhere to take his disappointment.

Mo Ostin entered the music business as Frank Sinatra's accountant. He then turned Sinatra's Reprise Records into something legendary, bringing it together with Warner Bros. Records along the way. A look through his early desk calendar reveals a meeting with Sinatra for lunch, Jimi Hendrix in the evening. Ostin had the kind of pedigree reserved for the heavies of the industry, without the gas that some of them gave off. It suited Petty to have a Mo Ostin in his life. But it was on Dimitriades to figure out how he was going to get his artist from one label to the other—now that Petty had contracts with both. As Dimitriades says, in his gentle style, "I eventually had to take Al Teller to lunch. But it didn't unfold exactly as any of us planned."

In some respects, Teller knew that Tom Petty's relationship with the record business as a whole was fragile. Perhaps the executive should have seen it coming. Back when *Full Moon Fever* was first getting notice, Teller had gotten a taste of Petty's character. MCA had paid for the Heartbreakers to go to New York for a *Saturday Night Live* performance. "I Won't Back

Down" was the track the label was promoting. Petty, however, felt that the song wasn't yet working as well as it needed to with the band. For the *Saturday Night Live* performance, he instead decided to do "Runnin' Down a Dream" and "Free Fallin'." "I Won't Back Down" had been out for some time, had already had a good life as a hit, so Petty thought he'd introduce something new. He didn't consult with MCA on the matter, because that's not how he worked. "I then had a meeting," Dimitriades recalls, "to thank Al Teller for the money to do the show. Those were the days when they wrote checks if it was important enough, which SNL was. Al just went off. 'What do you mean by not doing the single? I'm paying all that money, and he doesn't do the single?' I did my best to smooth things out. And I guess he was entitled, as the head of a record company, to want to promote his single. So I left, then called Tom to discuss a number of things. And on that call I mentioned that Al Teller wasn't happy that the band didn't do 'I Won't Back Down' on the show. Tom immediately goes, 'What do you mean he's not *happy*?' I say, 'Well, you know, he's paying for this.' But Tom says, 'He's not happy? I'm promoting the record, but *he's* not happy?' I realize quickly that I've given Tom more information than he needs. After all, Al didn't force us to do anything. He was simply *not happy*. But then Tom asks me for Al Teller's phone number, says, 'What's his number? I'm calling him right now.' I say, 'Tom, don't do that. It's fine.' He says, 'I want the number.' To which I reply, 'Tom, I'm not giving it to you.' Then he hangs up on me. Only a matter of minutes later, I think to call Mary [Klauzer] at the office and say, 'If Tom calls . . .' But she cuts me off and says that he already called. 'What did he want?' I ask her. 'Al Teller's number.'"

By the time Dimitriades put in a call to Al Teller it was too late, and Teller let him know it. "Al tells me, 'Don't ever put me in that position again,'" Dimitriades recalls. "I explained that I'd tried to stop Tom. But I had to ask Al what exactly Tom had said to him. And he tells me that Tom, who knew Al had been at Columbia Records, called him and said, 'Did you ever tell Bob Dylan what to play when he went on TV?' I said, 'Well, that seems fair enough. What was your answer?'" Petty remembers the call but only says, "Sometimes you have to consider what you think is right and act on it. But, yeah, I really sandblasted his hood over that one."

For the most part, though, Al Teller got behind the records, pushed for their success, and enjoyed the rewards when they came. But he was unknowingly up against a situation that was hard if not impossible to compete with. Petty was already somewhere else in his mind. He wanted the kind of relationship with an executive that would be along the lines of what George Harrison had with Mo Ostin. Harrison and Ostin were in business together, but they were also friends in business. "When George just didn't feel like making records for a while," says Olivia Harrison, "Mo didn't push him. Mo simply waited, stayed in the background, let George go do what he needed to do. And when George came to him with *Cloud Nine* and the Wilburys, it was worth that wait. Mo didn't look at George as a product, you know?" Petty wanted some of that same culture, even if it meant coming to Warner Bros. late in the Mo Ostin years.

Tony Dimitriades wasn't there when Mo Ostin and Lenny Waronker offered Petty a secret deal. "Tom called me and said he met someone from the music business at a dinner," Dimitriades says. "I'm thinking, 'Interesting.' He didn't have a history of mixing with the industry types. I asked who it was, and he told me Mo Ostin and Lenny Waronker. He says, 'They're fantastic guys, and I want to be on their label.' I said, 'Well, Tom, you have two more records to deliver on your MCA contract.' He says, 'Well, you've got to get me out of it.' No one found out for several years that we had a deal." Almost no one.

"Six to nine months after I went to Al Teller about my interest in Tom," says Rick Rubin, "I was having lunch with Mo Ostin one day, and he said— in the context of everything else we were talking about—he said, 'It's a secret, but guess who we signed? You can't tell anybody.' I said that's fine. And then he says, 'Well, we signed Tom Petty.' I said, 'Tom Petty made my favorite album. I love Tom Petty. That's incredible.' Mo is like, 'He's making one more record for MCA, and then he's coming over to Warners.' I said I thought this was great and that if they ever needed someone to work on a record with him, I'd love to. And that's how I got to meet Tom."

There was too much at stake for this to be an easy handoff, with Warner Bros. and Rick Rubin stepping up to usher in the next era. MCA was enjoying what Tom Petty brought to them. Why would any record label allow one of the biggest acts in the company's history to walk away, just to watch another company count the millions? No one was going to make a move in the name of Art when old man Commerce was looking down on the scene. Why should MCA? But things began to unravel when the "secret" contract was no longer a secret. Just as Rick Rubin had heard about the Warner Bros. deal, so too had others within the industry. When Tony Dimitriades received a phone call from one of them, he knew he had to inform Al Teller that Petty had plans to move on to Warner Bros. when the MCA contract was up for renewal. There was one more album to be delivered after *Into the Great Wide Open*. Petty could make the jump after that. But Dimitriades had to inform Teller. Teller couldn't hear it on the street. That's not how Tom Petty and the Heartbreakers did business.

Knowing he should move fast, Dimitriades called Teller to set up a meeting. But Teller was heading off to Hawaii. It would have to wait. By sheer coincidence, Dimitriades was also going to Hawaii. And on the flight back to Los Angeles, the two men were only seats away from each other. Aware that this wasn't going to be an easy conversation, Dimitriades spent the flight pretending to be asleep. As far as he was concerned, it wasn't going to go down in first class, with the manager trapped above the clouds, an angry label president in close proximity, and a full bar to make the good times better and the difficult times worse. When he finally sat down with Al Teller the following week, it was hard enough. But he got it done. Al Teller was pissed.

But that wasn't the end of it. And the drama that followed is the Tom Petty part of the story. Something bothered Petty, even after Teller got the news about Warner Bros. Maybe Petty had some feeling in his gut that the next record was going to be an important one in his artistic life and it had to have the right home. Maybe Petty was operating on pure intuition. Maybe he felt record labels were complicated enough when fully in support of a project—and if MCA knew it was about to be stood up for Warner Bros., how could it be fully in support of the next record? Maybe he knew himself well enough to know that he had already moved on from MCA. He was gone, and he couldn't go back. He called Dimitriades and told the manager to schedule another meeting with Al Teller, that it was time to leave MCA. No last album. The contract couldn't be the final word.

"It was just the two of us," says Dimitriades, remembering when he let Al Teller know about the bigger change that would be coming. "We were talking, and I said, 'Look, Al, Tom's really not happy with how *Into the Great Wide Open* is doing.' Al says, 'I know, I know.' And I just get to the point and tell him that Tom doesn't want to give him the last album. Al says, 'What do you *mean* he doesn't want to give us the last album?' I say, 'He's not going to give it to you. He wants to leave. He's unhappy.' We're in this restaurant, you know? And Al says, 'You can't do this to me!' But I could. The artist we were talking about was a guy who chose to file for bankruptcy rather than deliver an album." Teller ended up negotiating, with part of the deal being that the Heartbreakers would record an extra original track for the *Greatest Hits* album that MCA had planned. Petty hated the idea but wanted out. "Why," Petty railed, "would a new recording, one no one knows, go on the *Greatest Hits* album? It makes no sense." The problem fixed itself. The extra song they recorded was "Mary Jane's Last Dance," which, conveniently, became a greatest hit. And the collection went on to sell twelve million units, a windfall that MCA didn't refuse.

■

Though some viewed putting the Heartbreakers together with Jeff Lynne, a producer who didn't need a band to make records, as a failed experiment, *Into the Great Wide Open* had songs that would appear and reappear on the Heartbreakers' set list. "Learning to Fly" would always have a home in the live shows. It became one of those songs that an arena could sing. "That record," Petty says, "gave us some of our most evergreen songs. It's our biggest album in Europe. But suddenly we were in a business where you could feel bad about selling only a few million records and recording some songs that live forever." But even as he says it, shaking his head at the strangeness of the predicament, Petty acknowledges that he had tried to make the Heartbreakers something they weren't. The solo album had caused long-term trouble among the Heartbreakers, as did that Lynne-produced "band album." In *Rolling Stone*, Benmont Tench spoke candidly about it all. "I was pissed off and hurt. I was also worried [that Tom would] split up the band because there was conflict within the group at that time. There wouldn't be anybody coming to blows, but Tom and Stan would have disagreements, and Stan would leave the band, or get fired, and then come back less than a week later. Stan was always worried that Tom would go [solo] or just grab Mike and pack up. So when he did that [solo work], that's how it felt." No matter how outspoken, though, Benmont Tench was not the band member that tripped the wire in Petty's brain.

"I could always look around the room," Petty says, "in the studio, say, and know right where I stand with everybody there, except Stan." Lynch's ways of handling his fears about Petty breaking up the band generally found the drummer doing more to ensure that the band did break up than anything else. That Lynch had more skills than were being used in the Heartbreakers hardly set him apart within the group. He'd gotten a publishing deal with Warner/Chappell in the early 1980s. He had ambitions. "Stan was more talented than just being a drummer," says Petty. "He was quite a bright guy. He wrote music, though he never approached me with any. But he was a songwriter, a producer. There was a lot he was capable of. But there never would've been that outlet for him in the Heartbreakers." Petty says Lynch was kicked out of the band "two or three times." Others see that as a low estimate. Lynch's decision to move back to Florida shortly after *Full Moon Fever*, leaving Los Angeles for good, was the geographic symbol of an emotional divide that the band and crew had been living with for years.

By the time Petty and Rick Rubin had begun to commingle their ambitions for what would become *Wildflowers*, and Petty had entered into a writing phase that would be richer than any other in his career, the question came up again: is this going to be a band record? "I said to Tom, 'Do you want to do it with your band? Do you want to put a band together? Like, how do you want to do this?'" recalls Rubin. "I was completely open to however he wanted to approach it. The album that I was a fan of was not a Heartbreakers album, so I wasn't tied to that. It was really more up to Tom. And he talked a lot about not wanting Stan to play on *Wildflowers*." Which meant that Petty was again weighing his own ambitions in record making against his loyalty to the band. It wasn't a place he liked to be, but it was a place he often found himself. Loyalty, which seemed unambiguous as a virtue, was bringing him a lot of trouble. He resented the people with whom he had to work the hardest to remain loyal, which meant Stan Lynch but also his wife, Jane. How could they not feel it? Surely they did. Some days they hated him.

"I think people need to feel that their place in the world is something *they* found through their own actions," says Adria Petty. "Or they don't know who they are. In some cases, if another person helped them to find their place in the world, they can actually feel *angry* about this. The person who helped becomes far too important, and they resent it. In my dad's case, he had people around him that didn't completely know how to handle that he's not just Tommy and that their identities are almost reliant on his. I think it began to look like the dynamic had shifted in his favor. But he didn't create that situation. It's just his situation. I think it affected Stan, and I think it affected my mother in some way." As *Wildflowers* was being created, Petty felt like he was living under the weight of both those relationships. The relationship with Lynch would be far easier to negotiate than the one at home. He would choose to make a solo recording. "I didn't want to find myself writing things," Petty says, "limited to what Stan could do. It almost got there. I was almost on that path. He was really good onstage, a great singer. But the studio was a different place." There was somewhere Petty had to go in his next batch of songs, and he didn't want anything in the way of his getting there. There was a story he had to tell. He needed to know what it was, and he had to make the record to find out.

20

A BOAT OUT AT SEA

Freud suggests that the subject in mourning simply converts
the lost love object into an identification, in effect becoming the object that it can no longer have.

—Diana Fuss

Steve Ferrone was a tap dancer from age three. He's among a handful of notable
drummers who did tap before they got behind a kit, including Earl Palmer,
who at six years old was the tap-dancing mascot to a New Orleans pimp,
the two of them dressed in matching formal wear. In Palmer's case, he'd get
off the streets and into the recording studio soon enough, making records
with Little Richard at New Orleans's J&M studios, Sinatra at Capitol in Hollywood. Buddy Rich was a tap dancer, and Steve Gadd still is. Tap is a
school for syncopation that's also a school of song. "There's a dynamic that's
used in tap dancing," explains Steve Ferrone, "that's the same as what you
use when you're playing the drums. You build into the chorus. You have
the introduction, the verse, all of that. I tap danced to 'Georgia,' slow. And I
won a car doing it."

The sentimental education of Steve Ferrone distinguishes him from his
Gainesville bandmates. Different teachers, different schools, but the same
lessons. In a way that never could have happened in the American South,
British-born Ferrone didn't even recognize himself as black until it was
pointed out to him. "It just never came up when I was a boy," he explains.
"I mean, I was born five years after the end of the war, and people were
still talking about *that* more than anything else." His mother, who Ferrone
describes as "an English rose, blond hair, very, very fair," was from a

different world than that of his father, who, when Ferrone first met him at age nine, was "the blackest man [he'd] ever seen in [his] life." His father had been in England, on a cultural exchange with a dance troupe from Sierra Leone. Ferrone was an only child, born out of wedlock, when such a thing was rare and not at all easy to negotiate. Even without mixed-race parents.

Ferrone got his Italian name from the midwife who helped bring him into the world. "I looked sort of olive colored when I came out," he explains, "so they said, 'We're safe! He looks Italian.' And this midwife had been to see Alfred Hitchcock's *Lifeboat*, where there was a guy at the back of the boat whose name no one could remember. They'd say, 'Mister . . . Mister . . . Ferroni!' The midwife wanted to call me Tony Ferroni. And my mother went along with that." Somewhere along the line, a little tampering added an "e" to his birth certificate, and Ferroni became Ferrone. In an act of maternal solidarity, the mother took the son's name. She became the father in the household, going to work each day, while Ferrone's grandmother assumed the maternal role, cooking and caring for the boy, even heading down the block to confront the man who called Ferrone "a black bastard." If the young Steve Ferrone wasn't thoroughly confused by that time, he was probably going to be okay.

By the time Ferrone met Mike Campbell, the two musicians among those "borrowed," mostly from Eric Clapton's band, for a George Harrison performance at Royal Albert Hall, Ferrone had played in early Stones-era blues bands, studied jazz and learned to read music, joined the Average White Band as a full member, and found a mentor in Arif Mardin, with several stops in between. He was a well-respected session player and a first-call live drummer. Campbell liked the way Ferrone played and mentioned the drummer's name to Petty. It was a year or so later when Ferrone received a call from a booker in Los Angeles, wondering if he'd be interested in doing a "top secret" session. The money was right, and Ferrone was okay with not knowing who he'd be working for. "I walked into Sound City," he says, "and it was Mike and Tom sitting there."

It was more than a background in tap dancing that made Ferrone the right guy for Petty's second solo project. What Petty had been looking to find was in some ways what Ferrone had been training to be. While working with French drummer Christian Vander and his stepfather, Maurice Vander, Ferrone was told to throw away his metronome, to instead practice with James Brown and Ray Charles records playing in the background as he worked with written music. A metronome offered perfect time. Those records offered time *and* feel. Much later, when he got busy as a session musician, Ferrone learned that drummers who wanted to work needed to make peace with the machine. It was the eighties. "I was moaning to Jeff Porcaro," Ferrone says, "about having to play with a click track. Jeff sort of sat there, listened to me, and then said, 'Well, you can play with a click track, right? You don't have a problem doing that?' I said, 'No, it's easy. If you've got time, it's the easiest thing in the world.' Jeff looked at me and said, 'Take the money.' It worked. It changed my attitude completely." During sessions with producer Russ Titelman, Ferrone recorded drum tracks playing each part of his kit separately. One track had the hi-hat, another the kick, another the snare, and so forth, each part of the kit played independently of the others. It was an approach Arif Mardin had arrived at and Titelman had picked up on, allowing maximum control over the sound of the drums. It was not unlike what Jeff Lynne had done on *Full Moon Fever* and *Into the Great Wide Open*. Ferrone's job would be to make it sound like a drummer was sitting at a kit, playing it all at once. And he could do that.

At Sound City, with introductions and pleasantries behind them, Petty and Campbell plugged in and got to experience what it would be like if the Heartbreakers had a drummer with Ferrone's kind of control and feel. In Tom Petty and Rick Rubin's recollections, they auditioned five drummers, maybe more, but started Ferrone on the song "Hard on Me." "He shows up, sets up his drums," says Campbell, "and we count the song off as a practice. And it was the take. We were like, 'Wow. This guy's time is amazing.' How about 'You Wreck Me'? We played it once, and it was done. 'Okay, let's talk business.' "

"The only problem for Steve," explains Campbell, "was that he was coming from a more active type of playing, and he really had to break it down to essentials. No drum fills. We wanted the songs to speak without any business in the drums. He had to get used to that." You can hear what they were after by listening to "You Don't Know How It Feels." "When Tom was in front of Stan," says Bugs Weidel, "there was always this thing in his mind of 'Are we speeding up? Are we slowing down? Are things in control? Should we rein it in?' That was always kind of in the back of his mind. With Ferrone, it's like there's a rhythm machine back there. None of that is even an issue. For the first time in Tom's life it was like, 'Drummer? There's a drummer?'" When Ferrone was asked to do something, he responded like a session man and did it. "To this day, it's never been any of my business what happened with Stan. They made great records with him, I know that," says Ferrone. For Petty, though, it was impossible to see Ferrone except as a point of contrast to Stan Lynch. And he liked the difference. With Ferrone in the studio, the *Wildflowers* sessions began. They'd go on for a few years. It almost seemed that if Petty had his way, the sessions would still be going today.

■

At the same time that Steve Ferrone walked into Sound City, Stan Lynch was already out in the world, sharing his views, voicing his discontent a few decibels louder than he had in the past. *Wildflowers* was another album he claimed not to understand from the outset. He went out of his way to say he didn't like the songs. Everyone loves to hear shit about the top man. Petty picked up the chatter secondhand, got mad about it behind closed doors, and carried on. He felt betrayed when Lynch played the under-dog. As a layer on top of that, what happened between Campbell and Lynch on the Dylan tour had started something that was begging for some kind of culmination. Everyone was surprised at how long Campbell refused to speak to Lynch. No one in the band or on the crew wanted that to be accepted as the way things would be.

During the making of *Wildflowers*, the studio was Petty's bomb shelter in the backyard, and he didn't want Stan Lynch or Jane Petty near it. That it took two years to cut the album is as much a testament to Petty's belief in what he and Rick Rubin were chasing as it was a sign that he was using the studio as an alibi, the place he could hide out to avoid confronting the troubles around him. "There was definitely tension in his life," says Rick Rubin. "I would say that of all the records we worked on together—and we worked on a good amount of stuff—he was the most engaged and put the most time into *Wildflowers*. And I would also say that it seemed he didn't really want to leave the studio. Like he didn't want to do anything else in his life. I think he wanted to take his mind off whatever was going on at home." By Rubin's estimate, they had thirty songs ready to go before they even started recording tracks.

Petty seemed to be putting all of his honesty into the songs. Not in how he lived but in what he wrote and sang about. The music was getting all of him. "That's the divorce album," says Petty. "It just came before I left." Where the Jeff Lynne recordings had the shimmer of pop music built for the radio, *Wildflowers* is the most intimate song cycle Petty had yet created, with tracks that felt largely unadorned, no matter the complexity of what went into them as productions. "Time to Move On," "Hard on Me," "Only a Broken Heart," "To Find a Friend," "Don't Fade on Me"—they were all snapshots in a dark family album. When the Pettys gathered at their beach house in Florida to listen to the finished record, as they always did, Adria Petty says she "knew the marriage was over." She heard it in every track on *Wildflowers*. He was leaving. But before that would happen, band matters came to a head and bought the family some time, for better or for worse.

■

"In the middle of making *Wildflowers*, we had to record a few things for the *Greatest Hits* album," says Rick Rubin. "And Tom was adamant that he didn't want to take anything from what we were doing with *Wildflowers* for that album. He wanted to go into a different studio, with Stan, and do the Heartbreakers separately. I think one of them was 'Mary Jane's Last Dance,' then 'Something in the Air.' But we did some others for the boxed set." Stan Lynch came in from Florida. They worked quickly, cutting live as the band so often had, with Rubin acting as producer and Petty working up an old, unfinished song that needed a chorus, a song that would become, that afternoon, "Mary Jane's Last Dance."

"I was told [by Rick Rubin] that the drums should sound like 'Gimme Shelter,'" says Stan Lynch. "And he only wanted to hear one fill. First off, I'm going, 'Who the fuck are you anyway? You seem like a cool guy. You seem to be successful, and that's great. But I don't really give a shit about you. You're a hired gun. There's five guys here that matter, and you ain't one of them. Fuck you.' So I'm discounting every piece of input, being the total dickwad that I have to be to sign my work." It would be Lynch's last recording session with the band. By all accounts, he certainly wasn't endearing himself to the producer.

"I felt *somewhat* like I had spiked the ball," says Lynch. "They gave me a song cold, as they always did, and expected me to come up with something cool. And I did. Take two. Still, the producer and his pleb are in there, muttering about 'Gimme Shelter' or something. I just put the sticks down. There's no vibe. Nobody high-fives me. Nobody went like, 'Hey! Fuckin' A!' It felt more like, 'Get him the fuck out of here.' So I did that for them. I walked out. And that was that. I flew home." It's another moment of tension between the various accounts of what happened. George Drakoulias remembers cutting *many* more tracks than "Mary Jane's Last Dance," as does Mike Campbell. On the subject of high-fives, there's a general consensus that any such gesture would have been curiously out of place in a Heartbreaker session. They didn't deny themselves the satisfaction that accompanied a good take but, at the same time, they never responded like a sports team, and certainly never named an MVP. They were a band.

■

Petty saw Lynch again when his family went to St. Augustine after the *Wildflowers* recording was completed. It was Petty's last effort to cut through the tension, with the practical matter of planning a tour on his mind. "I went over to see him," recalls Petty, "and said, you know, 'Let's put our difficulties behind us and do this tour.' It was a huge tour we were going to go out on. But all he'd say was, 'Really?' I said, 'Yeah. I'm going to need you. If you want to do it, the offer's there.' 'Really?' he asked again. 'Yes.' And I just never got a confirmation that he'd do it, not then, not later. About a month before *Wildflowers* was coming out, the Heartbreakers were scheduled to play the Bridge School benefit, and I saw him again at that."

Neil Young's Bridge School benefits had been a regular thing for the Heartbreakers. Lynch flew in from Florida to make the Bay Area show. "It was two nights. And the first night was one of the only times I remember just being embarrassed by a performance," says Petty. "We were so bad. Just *bad*. And it was bad because of Stan. He just couldn't, or wouldn't, play the shit. His heart was not in it. His mind was not in it. Then, after a big argument in the van after the show, we had to do it again. And the next night, I was sitting in the dressing room, with the window open next to me, and I hear Stan talking to one of the guys in Crazy Horse. I don't think he remembers this. He was doing his usual bullshit, like, 'What are you guys up to? What are you doing?' And whoever it was said, 'Oh, you know, we're doing this thing with Neil. Then I've got a little time off.' Then he asks Stan what he's up to, and Stan goes, 'Well, this ain't my main gig. I've got some other stuff goin' on, like . . .' I was incensed. Like, 'This ain't your main gig?' Later, I found out he'd been doing auditions that past year. That was it for me."

Bugs Weidel remembers the Bridge School concert as another turning point for the band and crew. "During the course of the weekend," Weidel recalls, "Stan systematically pissed off most of the band, most of the crew, the people in the office. We came back that Monday, and everybody was going, 'That's it.' I think he knew that was the only way it was going to end. Like, he couldn't quit, and he knew that Petty wasn't going to fire him. So I think it was just like, 'Let's force the issue.'" Lynch doesn't necessarily challenge that idea. "Yeah," he says. "Maybe." Regarding what Petty overheard, Lynch says, "I probably did say that. I imagine that was my direct response to 'What do you do when Tom does all these solo records? What do you do when he takes two years off the road?' I must have said something like, 'Well, I have other things I do.' I mean, 'You didn't call me for two years, and you make records without me?' Why the fuck wouldn't I find something else to do?"

At his tree farm outside of Gainesville today, just back from sessions in Nashville, Lynch looks as much the farmer as anything. He hasn't previously talked publicly about the Heartbreakers to any great extent, but he's finally opening up. The conversation goes some eight hours over two days. "We're coming into the final chapter here," he says, suggesting that it's time to talk and time to move on a few steps more. "And we all went through something together." After discussing the Heartbreakers at length, moving between a recognition of just how good it was and an anger at how it went sour, he's asked what he could have done differently over the course of his time as a Heartbreaker. And he takes the question seriously. The twenty years since that Bridge School show have given him time to think it over. But, not surprisingly, the subject is difficult. He moves between anger and regret, wearing himself out after hours of going between the two. If he's moved on, it's not complete. And it probably won't ever be complete. It certainly isn't for Petty.

"When nobody wanted me to do my thing," Lynch says, "that's when I went, 'Shit.' When my thing, whatever it was, wasn't their thing, it went shitty on me. But I could've been calm. I didn't need to be . . .

emotionally, I was shooting flies with a shotgun. I didn't need to be so big, so loud, so fucking noisy. I see that guy in the room now, and I don't like him. If I could talk to that guy, if I was the father of that guy, I would've gone, 'Son, you are a fool. You just don't know it yet. So why don't you keep your fucking mouth shut and let a few things work around you.'"

He regrets how it ended, but he doesn't have an entirely realistic version of how it might have been different. "I would change the exit," he says. "The last act was so bad, was shit. Give me a chance to acknowledge that I'm leaving. I was told by a therapist years ago that I like ceremony. I needed some of that. I had to burn things. I literally burned a drum set, set fire to it. I burned pictures. I tore some up and threw them in the ocean so the tide would take them out. Because I needed the ceremony of, like, 'This is gone now.' I needed closure. I don't like the ending. But I love the book." He suggests that one last tour might have been that closure but also understands that perhaps such a thing would not have been possible, that there was just too much garbage in the soil to do any planting.

As far as the music goes, Lynch vacillates between feeling he didn't get what he deserved as a player, particularly in the studio, and that something had to change, and he was it. "The musical component wore itself out," he says. "Tom wanted to go somewhere that I was incapable of going. It wasn't even a question of whether I *wanted* to. But if Tom had just said, 'Stan, it ain't you. It's the playing.' That would have been the kindest thing." The last part of what Lynch says, however, doesn't ring true. The only thing harder than telling a band member of twenty years that he's not cutting it musically would be *hearing* it from a band leader. There's no sign in Lynch's character that suggests such criticisms would have sat well. Not then and not now. He's human in that way. But, possibly more to the point, he *was* hearing about his drumming. More than he wanted to. Since early on. And he never liked it.

"I think I probably should've faced up to it much earlier on than I did," says Petty. "And I'm not talking about just the drumming. I didn't agree with the way Stan felt about a lot of things, with his take on life. I knew that, behind my back, he was trying to undo me. And that meant undoing the band. I kept this romantic notion in my head that everything would be okay, that everything would right itself. But it didn't right itself. It got worse and worse and worse. I think I should've maybe seen that very early on and done something about it, but I didn't. And when I did, it was really ugly. He had invested twenty years of his life. But I was young, and learning along the way."

Petty went to the other Heartbreakers before the final call was made. "I asked everybody in the band, told them I was thinking about firing Stan," Petty says. "I went, 'What do you think?' And to a man, they said, 'It's got to happen.'" Benmont Tench was in Nashville, writing. "I remember getting the phone call from Tom," Tench says. "Stanley had been really unhappy because we'd been making a record without him. And I can understand why. If everybody's on a record but you? *Into the Great Wide Open* was made with Stan on the whole record, and I played a few piano flourishes. I know how uncomfortable it is. I didn't like having an unhappy Stan in the band. But, more so, I realized that Tom couldn't work with Stan anymore. He couldn't do it. And I didn't want to see the band end. I thought if he tried to work with Stan anymore it's just going to blow up. We're going to destroy a good thing. It broke my heart into a million pieces, but I told Tom, 'You've got to do what you've got to do.'"

Bugs Weidel speaks of a deceit that colored Lynch's dealings with the band, particularly with regard to Petty. "Stan had a devious side. It evolved over the years," he says. "He could create elaborate stories. I mean, I love him, and wouldn't be here without him. But he could engineer situations. That shit was going on all the time with him. So, in the end, the bigger question is: how did Petty put up with that all these years? And the answer is: because Tom wanted the band. Talk about someone who's going to make a commitment and follow it through. For fuck's sake, it would've been easier for him to go, 'Okay, you're outta here. Who am I hiring next?'"

Tony Dimitriades made the call after that. "The first thing out of Stan's mouth," Dimitriades says, "was, 'Am I fired?' And I said, 'You are, Stan.'"

■

"Stan would do these impressions," assistant road manager Mark Carpenter says of Lynch, with Richard Fernandez at his side, smiling in agreement. "He could impersonate anybody. David Lee Roth, Dylan. He could do Tom. Stan was one of the funniest guys I have ever been around. To the point where you're screaming at him, 'Stop! Stop!' He'd keep working your ass, until you couldn't breathe."

"He could have been a Vegas performer," says Petty. "He did it so well. He would find those little mannerisms and phrases, just nail a person's character. He could kill us. We did have a lot of good times together. It was an extraordinary thing we went through. I try to look at it from that side of things. But I can't make myself believe he was really completely on our team. I could never fully believe what Stan was telling me. I know on the stage he was on my side. He wanted that to work. When we made the *Live Anthology*, which, to me, is the most accurate document of what we were and are, the real warts-and-all picture, without studio glorification, I was very impressed with his drumming and how great his singing was. I wanted to write him a note and say, 'I hope you realize how great some of this music was that we made together. I hope you'll listen to it and remember it that way.' But I don't think we've had two conversations since the last one we had. And since he left, it's funny, but there haven't been a lot of arguments in the band. Little ones, sure. But the political side of things vanished. The problems we faced from there on out were generally artistic, not personal. A complicated band became downright simple to operate. So that's that."

Lynch shows his bitterness, his anger, his love, even gratitude—sometimes all in one look out the window. But he also captures some truths about Petty that only an outsider and an old friend can access. Those still on the payroll won't always say everything they're thinking. And Lynch always had that gift, that curse. "The first time I really checked Petty out," Lynch says, "was also the first time I ever took magic mushrooms. I went to this arcade in Gainesville with a friend who had taken them just before me. There were flashing lights, and it's all going crazy. I'm high out of my fucking mind. And I knew who Tom Petty was from Mudcrutch, knew him but didn't know him. But Tom's there, playing this game at the arcade. And every time a game ends, he puts his hand behind him over his shoulder, staring straight ahead the whole time, and whoever was with him puts a quarter in his hand. He never looks away, totally focused. In my mind, this went on for an hour. His hand keeps going back. Takes the quarter, plays another game. Then my friend on mushrooms goes into a seizure. He didn't tell me he was epileptic. But he's having this massive seizure brought on by the flashing lights. He's on the floor, crying, there are people trying to keep him from swallowing his tongue. I mean, it looks like he's dying. You see what's happening here? I took the mushrooms just after him, and I don't know he's epileptic. I'm thinking I'm next! It was a nightmare. The paramedics came, and then I begin to understand from them that he's an epileptic, so I'm taking a deep breath. I'm going to be okay. But Tom, I realize, has been playing this game the whole time. The arcade's gone crazy behind him, and someone's having a seizure, but his hand just kept going back each time he needs a quarter. Stares straight ahead. Never looks back. That's Tom Petty.

"I could see into him," Lynch goes on. "I knew who he was, even when we started out together in the band. I could see that he was fucking scared. I could see that he wanted to be important. I knew what he wanted. He wanted you to hear him. He wanted to be *that boy*. But I also knew, 'This is a frightened guy.' And we're getting into big things. This is big surf. Part of my job was to reassure him. Like, we're going to come out of this fine. These gigs are ours! We're playing big places, but, you know, 'We got this, motherfucker.' He was ambitious and scared, making damn sure you think he's not either one. Tom's cool. That's what he loved. That's what he became. He made that face for so long, it became permanent. But early in life, he had to invent himself."

21

FULL GROWN BOY

Of all the secrets that set him apart, this may in the end be the worst.

—J. M. COETZEE, BOYHOOD

Lenny Waronker talked Petty and Rubin out of making *Wildflowers* a double album, instead pushing them to assemble something that would stand as one of the great releases of its time. It wasn't always obvious what songs should be included. This wasn't a collection of tracks fighting to be singles. It was an outpouring of moods, meditations, rants, rock and roll, poetry. The bigger decisions would come less in what should be included relative to a song's individual strength and more in how those tracks sat against one another. What were the family traits? Which songs had them? Petty was dogged in making as good a *collection* as he could. Even if it meant leaving something off that *might* be a single. "Even his okay songs are great," says George Drakoulias, who worked alongside Rick Rubin at the time. "Poor guy. You know what I mean?" Even decades later, *Wildflowers* tracks would emerge that seemed too good to have been left off. Rod Stewart recorded a version of one of them, "Leave Virginia Alone." Ryan Ulyate, the band's current coproducer, confidant, and musical archivist, played some of the others for Petty and Mike Campbell in 2013. Certain cuts Petty remembered. But he had no memory at all of "Somewhere Under Heaven," a beautiful recording. It came from a time when such things were lying all around the room, piling up one on another.

The Heartbreakers appeared on *Saturday Night Live* to promote the release of *Wildflowers*. Dave Grohl sat behind the drum kit. The Foo Fighters were still only an idea in the back of Grohl's mind, what he hoped would be an outlet for songs he'd written that were otherwise homeless. It made sense to see the Nirvana drummer up there as the Heartbreakers played "You Don't Know How It Feels" and "Honey Bee." Rock and roll had become a smaller club. The very idea of a band, once the fundamental unit for music making, was just another category among many. But if you were raised during the British Invasion or the punk years, a band was everything, a shield and a shelter. That was no longer true for all kids in the late twentieth century. In their ways of thinking, Petty and Grohl belonged to what would soon have to be acknowledged as a passing age. Grohl made his brief stop in the Heartbreakers as a figure of enthusiasm and light, but it was clear enough to Petty that Grohl had something he needed to go do, a band he needed to form. So Petty put in a call to Steve Ferrone.

"I was in Germany, working with Bryan Ferry," the drummer says. "I got a message from my girlfriend, who said that Tom had called, that the album was finished. I thought, 'I wonder what that's about?' So I called him, and he said, 'What are you doing next week? Wanna go on the road with me?' It was exactly what I wanted to do, but I thought he was going out with the Heartbreakers, so I asked, 'What about Stan?' And he said, 'Well, we've been having our differences.' I asked if he'd spoken to Stan about this, because, you know, I've been in a band and know what it's like. He said that, no, he hadn't discussed it with Stan. I said, 'Well, put it this way: I'm really flattered that you called me, and I'd love to do it, but you should talk to Stan first and just see where you are with that stuff. You've been together such a long time.' Two days later, my phone rang, and it was Tom saying, 'You're working next week.'" Ferrone knew nothing of the Bridge School shows, just as he knew nothing of Petty's efforts to enlist Lynch for the *Wildflowers* tour. But there was too much to start trying to explain to Ferrone. It was either a one-minute conversation—"Stan's out; do you want to be in?"—or a three-hour walk into anger, frustration, and what could only be a subjective account of years of hurt feelings and misunderstanding. Fuck it. Ferrone was in. He could hear all the bullshit later.

Elvis Costello and the Attractions, Bob Seger and the Silver Bullet Band, Bruce Springsteen and the E Street Band, Graham Parker and the Rumour, or Billy Joel and the guys who played with him for a long time and left really pissed off: they were a class of artists who came up in the confession and quiet of the early seventies singer-songwriters but got off on the energy punk rock released, guys who wanted both the intimacy of the folksingers and the powerful live shows of early rock and roll. They wanted it both ways but didn't always have an easy time keeping their bands together. If they could carry on without those bands when the burdens of leadership got to be too much, they generally did exactly that. Sometimes a man knows when he just can't see the bass player's face in the hotel lobby one more morning. The problem is: when he lets that bass player go, the troubles are often *out there*, among the fans. The kids who bought the records, the ones who believed from the beginning, they don't want to see Mick Jagger or any other bandleader take up with another group. They've been asked to make an investment in an idea, and they did it. There isn't an off switch for their commitment to that original band. And as it turns out, the fans have more power than they know—as a collective, they have the governing vote. Springsteen released *Human Touch* and *Lucky Town* in 1992, left the E Street Band and recorded and went on the road with new players. But it was clear that his audience didn't approve of this latest fling; they liked to see Springsteen backed by the guys who knew him when. If inadvertently, *Lucky Town* and *Human Touch* were public reminders of what bands meant to the fans who had invested in them, ever since the Beatles transformed and deepened the concept. A band wasn't a group of backing musicians. That was something else, even if it went by the same name.

More than his peers, Petty remained aware of what a band meant, and of the history to which the idea was attached. It was being in a band that had made this world a habitable place for Tom Petty. And he stuck at building one long enough for that rarest thing to transpire: his group found a sound all their own. Even the finest musicians could come together without achieving that result. It typically took years, and even then happened infrequently. The Beatles and the Stones got there. The Heartbreakers did, too. Most of their peers didn't. They lost patience or couldn't manage it. But with the Heartbreakers, there was something in the way Mike Campbell and Petty played together, in the way Benmont Tench and Mike Campbell found melodic spaces without the place getting overcrowded, in the way those three together landed on a Petty original. That was the center. They weren't the sole architects—but they were the sine qua non of the Heartbreaker sound. Whatever went on with Petty's adventures as a solo artist, he'd never stray far from that. The idea of a solo record? Possible. The idea of a solo tour? Never. The *Wildflowers* tour, as with every tour before and after, was a Heartbreakers event.

By the time the band was on the road, it was clear that *Wildflowers* was going to be a big record for Petty. It sold two million copies within just a few months. "When *Wildflowers* came out," says Rick Rubin, "and it did as well as it did—and it did *really* well—I remember being a little surprised. And I think the reason I was surprised has to do with the idea of a grown-up making a good record. There were so few grown-ups making good records that it really stood out, for just that reason. When you think of the great songwriters, they *weren't* making great albums at that point. I can't remember what Paul Simon record or what Paul McCartney record came out around that time. But I'm guessing they just weren't as good. *Wildflowers* had a lot of good songs. I knew there were enough to make a great double album. It didn't have to be. But we had the quality to be able to do it. It's a really special record."

If *Long After Dark* was an album in which Petty looked into the troubled places beyond love's gilded entryway, *Wildflowers* was something else, one man's open journal of love's demise and the dream of more. It was equally direct and fiercely personal but often quieter. "Time to move on, time to get going / What lies ahead I have no way of knowing." There's a stark, distilled poetry to the lyrics and an almost unnerving openness. In "Don't Fade on Me," Petty speaks to someone with whom he could no longer speak: "I remember you so clearly, the first one through the door / And I returned to find you drifting too far from the shore / I remember feeling this way, you can lose it without knowing / You wake up and you don't notice which way the wind is blowing." "To Find a Friend" begins as a more comedic playlet, a character-driven song that steps back from the intimacy of "Don't Fade on Me." But even there, Petty becomes the man in the song, as though he's rehearsing some future moment, trying to see where things will land in his own life, or if they will. "In the middle of his life, left his wife / And went off to be bad, boy, it was sad / He bought a new car, found a new bar / Went under another name, created a whole new game / And the days went by like paper in the wind / Everything changed, then changed again / It's hard to find a friend, hard to find a friend."

It all made for what was possibly the best album of his career. But, for the family at home, it could have been seen as a betrayal. What Petty could do in the songs, he couldn't do in his life. No one called it betrayal, of course. The family had learned to live with it, found a way to see it as something else. They just called it songwriting. But all of his openness was reserved for the art, and it left little if anything for his family. It would have made no difference, anyway. But the discrepancy between the world of songs, where things were talked about, addressed, and explored, and the world at home would wear on Petty. Would break him. And a few of those around him.

■

The firing of Stan Lynch was in some ways the first round, practice in doing the unthinkable. Petty had been with Lynch almost as long as he'd been married to Jane Benyo. And the drummer had been, in Bugs Weidel's words, "so much a part of the vibe and the identity of the Heartbreakers." But when Lynch was let go, the mail still came through the same slot at the same time. Tickets got sold, songs got written, records were made, gossip leaked into the atmosphere but didn't become headlines. Petty's anxieties had exaggerated what Lynch's firing might mean to the stability of his band, to the fans. Lynch went his way, and perhaps not surprisingly the two men had little to say about each other that wasn't underpinned by anger and disappointment. But everyone landed in a room with a soft bed where a window revealed the sun coming up the next morning. It could be done. Somewhere inside, that's what Petty needed to see. He was as ready as he'd ever be.

"In ways, I see those relationships in similar lights," says Petty, "because they both lasted about the same amount of time and through the same years of change, *dramatic* change, that affected all of our lives. We all started as kids, didn't even show up on anyone's radar. Then things got moving so fast I'm not sure anyone was having an easy time keeping up. Everything kept getting bigger around us, but we stayed the same size. You could get a little lost in your new clothes. And we all did, to some degree. One relationship was in a band and one was in a family, which makes them as different as they are similar. But they were both decisions I put off making, that I kick myself for. I knew I was going to make this decision, and I didn't act on it." But when the *Wildflowers* touring came to a close, he did. With Jane, there was some bargaining at the end, prolonging the inevitable. He'd stay through Christmas, that kind of thing. But the theater of the marriage—and that's what it had become—was over. Soon enough the bargaining was over, too.

"I've read that *Echo* is my 'divorce album,'" says Petty, "but *Wildflowers* is the divorce album. That's me getting ready to leave. I don't even know how conscious I was of it when I was writing it. I don't go into this stuff with elaborate plans. But I'm positive that's what *Wildflowers* is. It just took me getting up the guts to leave this huge empire that we had built, to walk out. My kids . . . I knew this was going to be devastating to the whole family. I was leaving them there, without me to balance things out. My kids knew that a nightmare was coming. Adria was already out of the house, but Annakim was just entering her teens. But staying there was finishing me off. I'd become a different person." After Petty's therapist heard the song "Wildflowers," he asked who the singer was addressing. "I told him I wasn't sure," Petty says. "And then he said, 'I know. That song is about you. That's you singing to yourself what you needed to hear.' It kind of knocked me back. But I realized he was right. It was me singing to me."

Petty moved into the house in Pacific Palisades, the "chicken shack." "It was *really* cool," says Rick Rubin. "Like a little log cabin on a lot of land. Going there was like stepping back in time, to a hunting lodge or something. The house was all wood, not modern, with giant trees—redwoods, I think—all around. If Levon Helm walked in, you wouldn't think twice." But Petty didn't know how to set up a home for himself. He went to the supermarket but didn't know how to shop for food, because that hadn't been a part of his adult life. It was as if he didn't have a point of reference for everyday activities. For their part, the band members, back from the *Wildflowers* tour, were off in their own lives. The Heartbreakers weren't holding hands and asking about one another's feelings. That just wasn't the culture that had been established. Bugs Weidel and Scott Thurston may have known more than anyone else about Petty's struggles, but that didn't mean that either man felt like there was a lot he could do beyond listening. This was the boss, and that was his life.

"I went over to the house in Pacific Palisades," says Stevie Nicks. "I could get there quickly because I was fifteen minutes away in Santa Monica. It was a beautiful house. You wouldn't even have imagined it was there. It was almost like a bird sanctuary. He was . . . you know . . . he was *alone*. Jane had been such a huge personality. She was one of those women that, when she was in the room, there was no one else there. And so, all of a sudden, he's in this really nice, beautiful, small house, with all these birds everywhere. But alone." It could have been a place for new beginnings, and surely that was the idea at the outset. But it never became that. It was, instead, a place of endings and isolation, of being lost in one's own creation.

"I left, but then I had this huge realization of what had happened," says Petty. "There was terrible pain and guilt, as I guess comes to anybody who leaves a family. But I didn't foresee the shit storm that was going to come my way when I left. I thought it would be more like, 'Okay, the door has finally been shut. That's the end of it.' But that ain't the way it happens. Annakim didn't know what to do. I took her in, and she stayed for about a month. But it would be like, 'Look, I have to go to the studio. Do you want to come to the studio with me?' She'd say, 'No, I'd rather stay here.' But I had to realize that I couldn't live with this kid and just leave her all alone when I had to do something. Annakim was right in the middle. It was so painful." By the time Petty *wasn't* going to the studio, wasn't even getting out of bed on some days, Annakim was already gone.

"My sister was with my dad for maybe a month," explains Adria Petty. "Then she was with me. And there was a long time when I was really angry with him. I was twenty-one, and Annakim was fourteen or fifteen. I got her into a school in Boston, but she got kicked out and came to live with me in Greenwich Village. I drove her to school every day, took care of her for a long time, which created problems between me and him." But by that time, Petty had fallen into a clinical depression. In Adria's words, "He just couldn't get up." Jane, getting closer to the point at which those around her recognized that her problems went beyond drugs and alcohol, was sliding into a mental illness that had, in fact, held her down for years. No one was getting the help they needed. They were caught behind closed doors.

"The human condition is the same for everyone," says Olivia Harrison. "But once you're isolated, it's even worse. When those big life events happen, you can't see your way out of them. When you're in the world, you have outreach. When you're in a bubble, how do you see outside of that? How do people get in? And then you feel like you really don't *want* people to see what your troubles are, you're so private at that point. It's really easy to not get help." The boundaries Petty had set up with his band and crew, which helped keep the Heartbreakers going as an enterprise, became the walls that kept friends away when he could have used them. And for some people who had been around Tom and Jane for years, it would be hard to adjust to the end of their marriage, no matter how far down it had gone. "I didn't discuss it with anyone," says Petty, "so no one knew."

Even George Harrison didn't know. "I didn't talk to him much about that," says Petty. "And then, when I moved out, he called me up and said, 'Are you sure you know what you're doing here?' I said, 'Yes, I do. You don't know anything about what I've been through here. I have to do this.' He said, 'Well, I've come around to really liking Jane.' After we split up, he went to see her a few times, sent her some letters and stuff. But he didn't know." Tom and Jane had been there long enough that people used them in that way, as something permanent amid the flux. "I didn't realize," says Olivia Harrison, "how difficult it would have been in that marriage. I think that Tom did try to keep his family together and did a good job making it *seem* like it was all working. Had he not been a musician and had his music and his studio and his songwriting, it probably would have fallen apart a lot sooner. You can always go sit down, play a song, and sort of put your head in the sand and express yourself."

"My mother was a really soulful, gregarious, fun person," says Adria Petty, "and she loved him so much and had so much pride in his success. At the same time, she was very insecure, very resentful, very unclear about her place in the world. She also suffered from mental illness. And being married to someone who is mentally ill for a long time is really painful and isn't the kind of thing you can do a sound bite on. It's not neatly tied up with a bow. My mom could be a mean person. She'd been really verbally abusive and cruel to my dad, had disregard for all three of us, way before they were even on the verge of divorce. I think my dad's reticence to admit that there was a problem there was so prolonged and sort of avoided by continued success . . . I think that only when I went to college did it become more obvious that he was in the house with someone who was unwell. I just hated watching what she did to him." Adria and Annakim

Petty were quickly cast into the middle, in a powerful, poisonous stream of anger and resentment. Petty left because things were bad, but then they got worse.

Stevie Nicks tried to get Petty to write with her, an effort to distract him from his pain. "I said, 'Let's just write some songs. I don't write songs with anybody, and, really, neither do you. Let's write some.' He said, 'Well, okay. Maybe.' So I went home, thinking I'm going to go there every day, until six at night, and we're going to write. The next day I arrive with my grocery bags, with like Hershey chocolate syrup, instant coffee, and the kind of milk that I like. He's looking at me like I'm crazy. I say, 'I'm going to be here, so I need my supplies.' He's like, 'Your supplies?' I say, 'Supplies! Like when you go camping.' I'll never forget, just because of the look on his face. It didn't really work out. And really, I knew it wouldn't. So I said, 'Okay, so we're not going to write songs together. But I'll come visit you, and I'll keep in touch.' But also, by that time, Dana had come into the picture."

Petty had seen Dana York at a show in Texas in the early nineties. But that was it. He'd only *seen* her. "But her face . . . I remembered her face," Petty says. "And that night, when I fell asleep, I had a dream, and I saw her, so clearly." The following night, Petty was at the hotel after an Austin show, where there was a party in the lounge. Dana, there with her husband, himself a musician and, like her, a lifelong rock-and-roll fan, came up and introduced herself. "It zapped my brain, like, '*This* is the girl I dreamed about last night.' But there was no real conversation, other than when she said, 'I'm Dana,' and I said, 'Of course you are.'" Petty and York would run into each other on tours, Dana there with her husband. Some in the Heartbreakers camp picked up on the energy. And some of them didn't like it. However many problems Jane had brought into the bandleader's life, they were used to Jane. But this wasn't the band's or the crew's or the kids' decision to make. When Petty saw Dana at a Johnny Cash show in Los Angeles in 1996, she was no longer married. And neither was Petty. "I felt like I'd known him my whole life," recalls Dana Petty.

"I got her number at that Cash show," Petty explains. "And I was calling her, and finally convinced her to come back to LA, on a weekend when she didn't have her son, Dylan. I thought she was the most beautiful, wonderful thing in the world. And we started, you know, we started seeing each other. And really, I was so deep in the trouble because of my family life falling apart . . . she was kind of my release from that. Every few weeks she'd come out. But two things were happening at the time. I was falling apart, and I was falling in love. It can happen like that. But the fact was, Dana didn't know how fucked up I was. I mean, I didn't know." York didn't move to Los Angeles until a year or so after the Cash show, by which time Petty, in therapy more regularly but struggling to keep the darkness at bay, had started doing heroin. He kept it from her. From most everyone.

The people around him didn't know a lot about many things in Petty's life. He was isolated. There was an awareness that Howie Epstein was using heroin, as far back as *Southern Accents*. The drug was around the band. When Petty came up against a deep depression of the sort he'd never known and saw a chance to shut down his feelings altogether, he took it. "I knew that Jane had troubles. She retreated to her bedroom years before I left," Petty says. "And I sometimes thought, 'This is because of me. My extraordinary life, what's happened to me, has had some bad effect on her.' And, really, she wasn't opposed to it when I started thinking like this. It shifted her load onto me. But when I went into therapy, before I got divorced, I started seeing some things differently, learning some things about myself that otherwise might not have dawned on me. It always went back to childhood and what happened there. I mean, I was amazingly resilient, could find things to make me happy, could push the bad stuff down. But there was a nightmare back there. And when I went from that nightmare into a marriage that became as conflicted as my childhood had been, I went from the frying pan into the fire. And I just kept pushing it all down inside, like I always had. When it all came up, it was more than I could handle. Years of it just flooded me."

Dana York couldn't have known that the rock-and-roll star she was dating was dealing with scenes that went back to a two-bedroom ranch house in Gainesville. And she didn't immediately know what Petty was using as anesthesia to soothe the shame, guilt, and anger. When York would visit, Petty would be lifted; "life would turn good," as Petty says. But when he was alone, there was nothing holding the darkness at bay. He was all the way in both directions. "I was used to living in hell," says Petty. "My parents' marriage was hell, and I lived through that. I lived through being terribly abused as a kid, and then I found myself in an abusive marriage. But I managed to be somewhat optimistic, to see something ahead. I sometimes wonder if my career would have been more or less productive if it hadn't all gone that way, you know? Songs were a safe place to be. And I needed a safe place. So I went there a lot."

Stevie Nicks cautioned Petty to watch what he was getting himself into with Dana York—not because of anything on York's side but because of everything on Petty's side. "I told him, 'Well, don't sleep with her!'" says Nicks with a laugh. "'Right now, you're trying to heal what happened between you and Jane. You're still fighting that. You gotta fix yourself from this last thing.'" But when Nicks realized that Petty was doing heroin, she felt a door closing between herself and an old friend. "I would never imagine, not in a million years," she says, "that Tom Petty would start using heroin. I mean, we used to sit around and drink, and we did coke and smoked pot—and that was hard enough on us. But if you'd have said to me that Tom Petty was doing that, I wouldn't have believed you for a second." No matter what Nicks felt coming between herself and Petty, when Dana did finally move to LA, it was Nicks who offered her a place to stay in Santa Monica.

"That's how close we were," says Petty of his long friendship with Nicks. "That was someone I would talk to about my more private thoughts. Stevie would visit me at the house, and she'd go, 'You're moving too fast [with Dana]. You've just gotten out of this other thing. I don't think you should dive into this.' But I told her that I was only seeing Dana every two weeks, and that there was no one else I was interested in, that I'd been mad for this girl all my life. That's when she offered Dana a place to live. Then, by sheer coincidence, some gossip magazine, *The Star* or something, published a picture of me and Stevie, saying we were a couple, and Dana saw it on the plane coming to see me one weekend. So Dana thought I was full of shit, just using her while I was dating Stevie Nicks. Dana wasn't from this world of ours. Trying to take someone who's not from show business and convince them that this bullshit goes on all the time, that it's not real? It takes a minute. Dana felt weird about it all and ended up renting a tiny little apartment. I mean, she kept that apartment for a long time. We were married five years before she let it go. But in the beginning, I didn't want her living at the chicken shack. We'd fallen in love, but I was broken. And I was using. I did not want her to know about that. I kept that from her for a long time."

It was beginnings and endings overlapping, tangling. A lot of the time, Petty felt like he wasn't out of his marriage, that it had followed him. Jane would call regularly, obsessively, and threaten suicide if he said he was hanging up. After she got Dana on the phone, he finally had to change the number at the Palisades house. Petty refused to engage with Jane through Adria and Annakim, who were hearing a lot from their mother. Jane told them that Petty left the marriage because of Dana, but Petty trusted that the girls knew better and waited it out.

Amid it all, Dana York's young son, Dylan, saw a side of Petty that stood in stark contrast to what Petty's daughters were hearing about their father. Dylan, three and four at the time, saw his mother in love and got to know Petty as a friend. "Tommy was great with Dylan," Dana says. "They'd rollerblade on the tennis courts. He'd write songs with Dylan's name in them. He taught him to dance like James Brown and set him up with a guitar and a fuzz pedal with a whammy bar. I'd stepped onto a fast-moving train, but we were having moments of tremendous happiness. Chaos and darkness, and all this happiness at the same time."

It was the first time Petty had taken an extended break of this kind, but that didn't mean that the office closed. Pulling from the pile of *Wildflowers* outtakes, Petty and Rick Rubin put together a soundtrack for Ed Burns's *She's the One*, which starred Jennifer Aniston and Cameron Diaz. In the end, it seemed like this was an easy way to get a release out when Petty, forty-six at the time, was mostly isolated, not working at full strength, at far more than an arm's length from his team.

"I was approached about putting together a soundtrack for the movie," says Petty. "I liked what I'd seen of Ed Burns's work. But when I took the job, I didn't think it through. I wound up in a situation where they wanted different artists for a soundtrack. They had a few but said they wanted me to call more artists. I made a couple calls, and I felt terrible. I went, 'Oh my God, I'm one of those guys.' I called Tony and said, 'I just can't do this.' That's when Jimmy [Iovine] called and said, 'You should do it, but like Paul Simon did for *The Graduate*. Hey, bang it out. It'll be easy. You don't have to go to all these artists asking favors.' Somehow, he talked me into it. I blame him. I shouldn't, but I wouldn't have done this on my own. After that it was matter of having a deadline, hurriedly doing some overdubs and mixing. I was completely off my game. I was doing something that went against my grain. Some people thought I was following up *Wildflowers*. Then, with everything being done at such an incredible rate of speed so that the record could come out with the film—with me making my deadline—they held the film back six months. My record came out with no movie. I was so depressed—that just made me more depressed."

The *New York Daily News* captured the general feeling of things after the album's release: "His last album, the soundtrack to *She's the One*, sold only 490,000 copies, the sole commercial disappointment in his career." In an interview with the publication, Petty played down the album's importance to his catalogue: "It was marketed as a soundtrack and put in [those kinds of] bins," he says. "And I didn't promote it. I think it's a good record, but I don't look at it as one of our normal albums." It went gold, but without Petty's spirit behind it.

There was no hint in the article that anything was out of place in Petty's life. But he was getting into deeper troubles. "I probably spent a month not getting out of bed, just waking up and going, 'Oh, fuck.' Lying there," he says. "The only thing that stopped the pain was drugs. But it was stupid. I'd never come up against anything that was bigger than me, something that I couldn't control. But it starts running your life. It went for a while before Dana and my family got involved. And *Echo* came in the middle of that mess. I'm lucky I came through. Not everyone does. My therapist said something to me that, in that moment, cut through all the clutter: 'People with your level of depression don't live. They kill themselves or someone else.' I said, 'You're kidding.' 'No,' he tells me, 'with this level of depression, people *can't* live.' Maybe that was when I realized that in fact I *wasn't* living, that I was heading in the other direction."

Petty says he knew he wasn't doing his job when he went in to make *Echo*. For Mike Campbell, it was a period of time—and a project—that became something to get through. The man Campbell had worked with for so many years was only half there. By that time, Campbell was well established as Petty's partner. He'd cowritten some of the best-loved Heartbreakers songs, and he was a guitar player who never used a song as an excuse to show what he could do *as* a guitar player. Most of what he was capable of, he left out—unless a song asked for it, he didn't play it. Mike Campbell wasn't there to give the light man something to do at shows. His interest was in songs and records. In the musician community, Campbell was viewed as the quiet presence who was Petty's equal in sheer consistency. With *Echo*, however, he had more to do than he had in the past. Petty was belowdecks for much of the storm.

During *Wildflowers*, Petty and Rubin had worked through an abundance of material, picking the best. They'd meditate in the control room before sessions. All that was over. *Echo* didn't stimulate Rubin in the same way. He liked working closely with artists, and this artist was under a few layers that couldn't be unwrapped. Which meant that Rubin, too, wasn't as present. Campbell was the one who remained accountable. There was tension, and no one—true to Heartbreakers style—was addressing it directly.

There were efforts to change the mood. Rubin went to Barnes and Noble and purchased several magnetic poetry sets, the boxes of words intended for building phrases on refrigerators. "I went through them all," explains Rubin, "and took out all the little words, 'the' and 'to' and 'for,' and then put the rest of them on a music stand. You know the metal music stands? Then, when Tom had songs without words, just chord changes and melodies, he'd randomly look at words and make up sentences. I could show you specific lines he wrote that were words from the poetry set. It was remarkable and beautiful. He could draw on this pool of information to create the stories. His mind works *very* fast. But there were often sour feelings. I remember that there was a while where Tom was walking with a cane. It got bad."

"You do the best you can in whatever condition you're in," says Mike Campbell. "We always strive for greatness. Sometimes we fall short. It was a hard record. That one, definitely, I don't put on. There were good moments, times we had fun. Doing 'Free Girl Now' was fun, here at my house. Tom was singing great, and we put a surveillance camera on his mic. A fisheye thing on Tom's face, and we had a monitor up to see it. He looked all warped out. The energy on that was good. I don't know how that album holds up against others. Probably not that well."

No matter his own condition, Petty was angry that Rubin left *Echo* before it was mixed, moving on to a Red Hot Chili Peppers project. "We got up to do the mix on that record," Petty says, "and Rick left, *right* when we were going to mix. That infuriated me. So I mixed the record with Richard

Dodd and Mike. And I changed the production credits to 'Produced by Tom Petty and Mike Campbell *with* Rick Rubin.' Which pissed Rick off. But I thought, 'If you don't mix the record, you're not the producer.'" It was the last time they'd work with Rick Rubin.

In addition to *Wildflowers* and *She's the One*, Rubin and Petty had worked together on *Unchained*, the second Johnny Cash album for Rubin's American Recordings. It was a brighter experience than *Echo*, coming on the heels of *Wildflowers* and before Petty started losing his way. Petty had been there when Rubin courted Cash and vehemently supported the idea of a collaboration. The experience of making *Unchained* affected not just Petty but the other Heartbreakers, who came in as the band. Cash's paternal character, spiritual side, humor, and, of course, music came at a time when the whole band needed a shot of something real from another side of life. Here was a man who'd seen a few things and who had turned what he'd seen into a kind of wisdom he could pass along, if those around him were interested. And they were all interested. Petty felt genuine pride as the agile Heartbreakers settled in as Cash's backing group. *Unchained* went on to win the Grammy for Country Album of the Year, without any support from country radio. Years after Cash's death, standing in the living room of his Malibu home, Petty pulls out a postcard Cash had written. It says on the back, "Tom, you're a good man to ride the river with." It's another one of a few treasures Petty has kept from the past few decades. But for all Rubin and Petty had been through together, whether with Cash or as creative people in recording studios, sentiment wasn't going to keep them together.

"*Echo* was the only time," Rubin says, "that I saw anything like ego-y behavior in Tom. I feel like there was a frustration but also a sense of acceptance that this was out of our control. You know? I didn't confront him, but, like I said, he was less present for conversation. He was in his head more, less open, wearing shades all the time. Just, like, *separate*. Different from the *Wildflowers* sessions, where we worked long hours. He wasn't wanting to work much. We'd come in, work for a few hours, and he'd be like, 'Let's just pick it up tomorrow. You can take off.' Short hours."

The miracle of *Echo* may be just how good it is. Dana Petty, years later, made her husband listen back, just so she could show him *how* good. But Petty had been writing songs since he was a young man. He didn't have much of anything outside of that. When, years later, he showed an interest in basketball, taking Jack Nicholson's Lakers tickets on nights the actor couldn't use them, it was big news around the Heartbreakers' management office. *Tom has a hobby.* Until then, it was all songs and records and the pains he went through to make them great and get as many people as possible to hear them. Likely that's the reason Petty's writing on *Echo* has the strength it does. The years of almost obsessive creative work, of focus and intention, meant the factory on the inside just kept turning out product, even as the head engineer dozed off. "Counting on You," "Free Girl Now," "Room at the Top," "Swingin'"—these were songs written by a man fumbling for his keys in the darkness of unmanageable loss. If Petty and Mike Campbell have a hard time listening to the record, it's likely because they're seeing that man. And another: Howie Epstein.

■

"That was such a dark time," says Campbell. "It represents Tom being really sick and my friend dying. I don't know . . . for some reason I don't want to go there, psychically. It was an unpleasant period." The fact was, Petty's drug use was partially obscured by Howie Epstein's more dramatic decline. By *Echo*, the heroin was fully in charge of Epstein's life. No one was counting on him for anything. He might show up, and he might not. When it came time to do a shoot for the cover of *Echo*, Epstein promised to be there. When, after hours of waiting, he wasn't, Petty made the decision to carry on without him. He's not on the cover of his band's record. It had gotten to that point. A second photo shoot was planned. "Out in Malibu, yeah," recalls Campbell. "It was just too sad. He showed up real late, went to the bathroom, and when I went in there after, there was blood in the sink. I thought, 'Oh fuck, man. If this guy's doing it this often . . .'"

Though Petty had cleaned up by the *Echo* tour, refusing to let his drug use overlap with a Heartbreakers tour, for Epstein things were coming to a head. It was different from earlier road work. Petty, because of the album's association with his own world of shadows, didn't want to play songs from the record that they were supposed to be supporting. And across the stage, Epstein was half there, though the band members, who would see the bass player only at show time, didn't know the full extent of the damage. Epstein's beloved German shepherd, Dingo, was his closest companion on the road, sitting by his bass amp during shows. The crew had to keep it all together, working to prevent Epstein from going into withdrawal. "The band and all of us on the crew, we knew," explains Richard Fernandez. "And Howie knew that we knew. It was one of those. But during the last two months of the tour, he was waking me up every night. I'd be getting calls at three or four in the morning and have to go over. But he promised that this was it. We had it all set up for Howie to go into another rehab, and he promised he'd go. We'd had enough conversations during all of this, had been told he'd get help. So when the tour ended in Indianapolis, there were two planes. One was going to the Bahamas, where the rehab was. The other was going to Van Nuys. We spent an hour trying to get Howie to go to the Bahamas. He went to Van Nuys. And when he did, I knew it wasn't going to be good. But I couldn't do it anymore. I didn't want to have anything to do with his situation." It wasn't the first time they'd set up a rehab for Epstein.

Mike Campbell and Mark Carpenter are listening to Fernandez share his account, the three of them in a hotel room in Texas. "I think the truth is," says Campbell, "and I'm talking about myself here, I didn't know anything about hard-core addiction. I was insensitive to it, didn't understand it. I get it now, because I've been through some things with people I know. So now I understand better where Howie was at, but at the time, I was just pissed off at him. Because I didn't know better. I wasn't educated. From what I know now, though, and what I know about where Howie was at, I don't think counseling would have done it." After the *Echo* tour, Howie Epstein would no longer be working as a Heartbreaker. "We were told we were being enablers," Petty says, "and we were advised by these drug counselors to let him go. It was a brutal decision. I'd tried to tell him he could do it, that I had and he could. But we had to send a message about the seriousness of this. We hoped he'd come back clean, but there weren't a lot of signs that it was going that way."

■

It was in the midst of making *Echo* that Petty started to fathom the trouble he was in himself. That was also when Dana York found out what was going on and started working to convince Petty he could be helped. "It was a lot of me and Tommy, just us, talking," she remembers. "I couldn't lose him. He needed to know that things would get better." The songwriting process Rubin described, with Petty playing with random, magnetic

words on a music stand, almost like the automatic writing of the Surreal-
ists, helps one to understand how Petty might have managed to put songs
together at the time of his struggles, and how the songs themselves might
have pulled up a few blinds. "Put down your things and rest a while / You
know we've both nowhere to go / Yeah, daddy had to crash / Was always
halfway there, you know." Using someone else's words allowed him a little
distance from an experience that was, in truth, pushing him up against
the wall. It was an approach that allowed him to write, very directly,
about the only thing he *could* write about at that moment. Maybe he
needed to feel like they were someone else's words because his had too
much pain in them. "The end of any marriage is tough, but that was a
really long marriage," says Benmont Tench. "And you look at *Echo*, and
you see a very sad record. The talk goes around about Howie being at a
low point, but Tom was at his own kind of low point. Those were beautiful sessions. But they were dark. I have very vivid memories of them. A lot
of really beautiful music got made. But there was some kind of dark
energy going on."

It would be hard to know what would have happened if Dana York had
not been there, as some kind of reminder of all that was worth sticking
around for. She was the only one close to Petty at the time who had no
connection to the past. No matter that those around Petty, the Heartbreakers family, didn't yet trust her. Maybe the shared borders between the end
of his marriage, his relationship with York, and the growing drug use made
them doubt the whole scene. That York didn't know about the heroin for
some time was lost on them. As a couple, they moved slowly, waiting a few
years before moving in together. They never lived together at the Palisades
house. In the earliest period of the relationship, she would come to Los
Angeles every other weekend, sometimes with Dylan, sometimes alone.
Petty's drug use was a secret he kept from her as long as he could. "A lot of
them were really hard on Dana," says Petty. "Someone else might have been
driven away by the pressure of being with me. And by the situation I'd created for myself. There are all sorts of little jealousies and insecurities that
come up, people worrying about her influence on me. Everyone gets para-
noid. 'What's this about? What's this girl want?' And she didn't want anything. But she had to prove that."

"I think maybe she saved him," says Olivia Harrison. But that was a hard thing to see amid the mess. In the months before *Echo* was finished, he was still a man with kids he couldn't help. Still a man with tremendous wreckage in his personal life, a man divorcing his longtime wife, a woman who was struggling with delusional thoughts and a mind that was turning on her. He was still a man playing at the edge of death. It might have been hard for insiders to welcome York as a guiding light. Petty was in too much trouble for anyone to believe he was moving toward a better place. But he was. "She did save me," Petty says. "I know that."

"He just went off with Dana," says Adria, "and I think that's something he was very ashamed of. It complicates the guilt. He couldn't just stand up and deal with my sister, with this out-of-control teenager who really needed him. But he was in a massive depression and struggling with drugs, struggling with all sorts of stuff, and he just couldn't stand up and do it. I felt happy that he was changing his life. And I felt like taking on the responsibility of my sister, at least I could do that while he was trying to get his life going. I don't know if I could have been in his shoes. My mother, who had loved him for such a long time, had started to abuse him. But I think he felt responsible for the failure of the family, and it kept him from leaving, for far too long. By the time he did leave, he didn't have enough left in him to handle it. He was up against something that took precedence over parenting. But I don't think it ever took precedence over the amount of love he has for us."

At the Palisades house, alone with Dana one night, Petty saw his wife, Jane, in silhouette. By that time the divorcing couple had been through a few years of negotiations. It was late, and Jane was in a limo at the end of his driveway. She was yelling toward the house, trying to get the driver to ram the gate. Petty and York could hear their names, even York's son's, Dylan's. It startled the neighbors, who called the police. Standing partway down his driveway, hidden in the dark, Petty saw Jane's profile in the flashing blue lights. It would be the last time he saw her.

22

HALF OF ME IS OCEAN,
HALF OF ME IS SKY

Grief turns out to be a place none of us know until we reach it.
—JOAN DIDION

Earl Petty died in 1999. The losses were piling up. Though Tom Petty had not attended his mother's funeral, he did fly to Gainesville to see his father off. "I went back there," Petty says. "Bugs was with me. He drove me over to the funeral home. It was either a funeral home or a church. I can't remember. I met my brother there. We went in, saw Earl there in the box, checked him out. He looked peaceful. We'd picked some music for them to play, some music that Earl liked. We didn't stay long. Gainesville could be tricky to navigate." But the scene wasn't one of quiet remembrance and unencumbered farewells.

"After things had gone well enough, and we were getting ready to leave," Petty says, "Earl's twin sister, Pearl, shows up. And she just lets out this huge scream, like, 'Nobody told me *you* were going to be here! Come here, come here!' And I was like, 'No, we're leaving right now.' And she's grabbing my arm, insisting, 'No, you can't leave—I got stuff ya'll gotta sign!' I mean, I'm walking away from my dad's coffin. It's a hundred feet away from us, right? I'm thinking, 'He's your brother, for Christ's sake, and you're looking for autographs at his funeral?' I'm just shaking my head. So we get in the car kind of as quick as we can, and we start to back out, and she's at the window, banging on the window. And she gets her hand on the door handle of the car, trying to open the door. I just said, 'Bugs, go.' And we took off, with this screaming woman in the background. That was my father's funeral." The swamp had sent its ambassador.

Some weeks earlier, however, Petty had talked with Earl. His father had extended a hand. It may have been too little too late, a meager feeding of paternal recognition, but it was something. "He called me one night," Petty remembers, "and it was the last conversation I would have with him there at the end of his life, right before he died. He said, 'I'm calling because I don't think I've got a lot of time left, and there are issues to work out with the will.' I said, 'Look, I don't want anything. Give it all to my brother. Thanks for speaking to me about it, but I don't want anything.' Then he went on and said, 'I just had to tell you, I'm really proud of the way things have gone for you.' He goes, 'It always just sounded . . . I couldn't hear anything in what you were doing. It always just sounded really out there to me. But you must have done it really good, because you've done so well.' He said, 'I remember you telling me when you were a teenager that if I'd just leave you alone, you'd be a millionaire before you were thirty. Damn if you weren't.' Then he said, 'So it kind of proves that you were right and I was wrong. And I love you. I just wanted to say that.'"

It was the only time Petty could recall his father saying those words. They were tacked on, hanging there a little awkwardly at the end of the conversation, a burp of emotion. Petty describes it as "kind of a touching moment." But he had to wonder why it couldn't have come sooner. Forgiveness would come in time. But right then, he felt the waste. And when he felt himself judging his father, it brought his own failings to the surface. Self-recrimination was just one thought away from any judgment of Earl. But both were easier than grieving. And by that time, Petty didn't have the heroin to help him hide from the grief. He'd gotten clean. Struggled to get there. The *Echo* tour found him uncomfortable in the strange world he'd built but no longer willing to abandon the place through drugs.

■

Petty hasn't talked about his heroin use, not during that time and not after. He worried what kind of message he'd be putting out there—another rock star with tales of excess to clog up the minds of young people? Who needs that. He discussed it during the interviews for Peter Bogdanovich's *Runnin'*

Down a Dream documentary, which chronicled the Heartbreakers' first three decades. But then he insisted that the section be cut.

"I wasn't a guy that grooved on being a junkie. I was a more clandestine drug addict," he says. "But people picked up on it. I know Rick [Rubin] was worried about me. But he finally dealt with it by going behind my back and telling my kids. I was so mad at him. I was pissed off for a long time. Because I just thought, 'That's none of your business. Why are you doing that?' I think his take was, 'Well, we had to do something to shock you.' But I was like, 'No.' I felt like I knew what was going on, and I knew I had to get out of it. And right as I'm getting out of it, he busted me to my kids? Maybe he had the best intentions. I don't know."

It's difficult to hear Petty talk about it and not understand Rubin's side. Petty was in trouble and *needed* that shock. "I was feeling so lost," Petty says. "I remember waking up one day and just thinking, 'Why even wake up?' Dana wasn't around right then. I had to get some food, and I went into town and bought myself a sandwich. I went back home with the sandwich and just sat there, watching it get dark. The phone's not ringing. Everybody has their own lives they're busy with and I've got no life. I'm just sitting there. I'm still better than where I was. But I'm between that and wherever I'm going. And I'm really starting to wonder if I'm going *anywhere*."

The drugs played what Petty calls their "dirty trick" on him, initially relieving his depression and then compounding it. "You start losing your soul," he says, obviously troubled by the memory and ashamed to have found himself there. "You realize one day, 'Shit, I've lost myself. I'm hanging out with people I wouldn't be seen with in a million years and I have to get out of this.' I wanted to quit. Using heroin went against my grain. I didn't want to be enslaved to anything. So I was always trying to figure out how to do less, and then that wouldn't work. Tried to go cold turkey, and that wouldn't work. It's an ugly fucking thing. Really ugly. I fear that if I talk about it, people will think, 'Well, I could do it and get off.' But you can't. Very few people do. Very few."

By the time Dana York realized what was happening, she grasped more completely just how sensitive and emotionally spent Petty was. She was no stranger to addiction. Her own father had struggled with it most of his life. When she moved out to Los Angeles, to be with the man she'd fallen in love with, his drug use was no longer something he could easily conceal.

Maybe he wanted to be seen, to be helped. "When he was using," she recalls, "he was alone. He was alone with his thoughts and pain. I have tremendous empathy for anyone who is in so much pain that they turn to drugs. Addiction is often misunderstood. I wanted to protect Tommy from the drugs *and* from the misunderstandings about them. He was suffering from a real depression. He needed help."

"I was worried," says Mike Campbell. "I remember going over to that house. I always kind of felt like, 'He's having a hard time, but I didn't know what to do other than to be a friend.' I kind of thought, 'He's strong. He's got a core, something that will get him through this.' With Howie, I didn't think, at least by that time, that there was a core." As Petty tells it, however, his core was being dismantled quickly enough as he entered into the last months of using.

"I was in therapy," he says. "And I finally said to the doctor, 'Look, I've become a drug addict. I don't want to be one. But I am. What do I do?' And that's when it began, the first steps in turning this thing around. I'd tried to kick it so many times, but that's just the worst thing that you can dream of. I couldn't do it. So they put me in this hospital, and I did this detox thing, where they put you to sleep. And they shoot this drug into you that literally drives the heroin out, and your body goes into spasms. It forces the detox process. When I woke up from that, I felt different. And I said to the nurse, 'So, it went okay?' She says, 'Yeah, it went okay.' I said, 'How long have I been asleep?' She says, 'Two days.' "

After that, a doctor would arrive every day at Petty's Palisades house, administering a medication that would block the effects of an opiate. He'd hold a flashlight up, making sure the pills went down. "They made me eat them every day, for months and months and months. And I started to feel alive again." When he did begin to return to himself, Dana York was still there, hadn't gone anywhere. She'd talked him through it, talked him back to himself. She was the reminder.

"Tom built something really good with Dana," says Benmont Tench, "out of a period that was really unhappy, really hard. And I think it was a fight to build it. But against a lot of bad odds, they created something really, really beautiful." By the time the Heartbreakers headed out to tour behind *Echo*, with Petty clean, Dana was there with him. More than once, people who worked with the band thanked her for what she'd done. "It confused me," she says. "They'd tell me, 'Tommy's so happy. He's so different.' I just thought, 'Really? What was he like before? Did he never talk to anyone?' The man I knew was the only one I've *ever* known."

■

"Reborn" is how Petty once described the change. But somehow that's too neat. It obscures more than it reveals. He moved, this time with Dana, to Malibu, just across the street from where Denny Cordell had once lived, though Petty only realized that later. Within a few years they married. Twice. Once in a private ceremony in Las Vegas and a second time at the new place, with Little Richard officiating and fifty friends and family in attendance. There was enough there to make some onlookers think that "reborn" was a fitting description. And it is a good story, the best one to tell if you want to divide a life into discrete parts and get on with things. But Petty wasn't reborn. Rebuilt, maybe. But from parts left over from a wreck. He wouldn't be the same man again. No one goes that low without carrying traces of where he's been. There remains a frailty in Petty that wasn't there before. And it wasn't just the effects of drug use. It was a long trail that went back to that small house in Florida. It may be that a lifelong depression, masked by years of activity, found its moment to come toward the surface and came. Some days you can see the seams where the break happened. It's a relationship with the pain of the past that doesn't preclude joy. But Petty's history seems to be there in everything, even the joy. He's like some of the men he always admired. Men like Johnny Cash. The ones who had seen a lot and survived a lot but were still there, playing shows, writing songs, telling their stories, passing something along. Because that's what they knew how to do. He'd become one of them. And there was a beauty in it.

"It was a rocky moment near *Echo*," Adria Petty says. "I think that record says a lot. It tells you everything that was going on in his head. I always laugh, because he'll say, 'Oh, I divine these songs. They're not really about anyone or anything.' He'll try to deflect the sentiment that's right there in the albums. But they're very autobiographical. You can really tell, on beautiful albums, like *Into the Great Wide Open* and 'Two Gunslingers' or 'King's Highway,' that he's struggling, constantly fighting, just to find a peaceful place."

■

While Petty was down, and through the time he spent, with Dana at his side, getting himself back, he lost some things he cherished. Some he could get back, like his connection to his daughters. Others he couldn't. George Harrison was one of the latter. Harrison went public about his throat cancer around 1998. He fought it with positive results, after which he and Olivia had traveled widely, what she describes as a "couple of great years." But in 1999, Harrison was brutally stabbed by an intruder at Friar Park, their home in Oxfordshire, England. It weakened him. When he died, Harrison was in Los Angeles. He saw very few people in his last days. "When we came, in 2001, to Malibu," says Olivia Harrison, "George was really ill and going through some treatment. We didn't see Tom then. I saw Tom and Dana shortly after George died. He came to the *Concert for George* and he was amazing. Eric Clapton reached out to him, and Tom flew his whole band over. He was all over it, the rehearsals, the show. Then I saw him again, back here in LA. Both Tom and Dana. They were so kind. They sat in a room with me, put their arms around me. We all cried. And Tom said, 'Don't worry. We're not leaving you.' And he meant that not just for that moment but *for life*. I have a special fondness for him. It makes you feel a little bit safer to know that someone like Tom is there for you. It's a good umbrella to be standing under."

What Petty could do for Olivia he may not have been able to do for George. He wonders. "I don't know if I could have handled it, seeing George then," says Petty of Harrison's last days. "But I don't struggle with my decision. Everyone has their own way. I often feel George around me. Still." His father, his mother, his marriage, what might have been his closest friend: for a man in the middle of his life, Petty seemed to be making a business of loss. The past had too many representatives milling about in his mind. After taking more than the usual amount of time off from work to settle into his new life in Malibu, Petty was ready to get busy. The best thing he could do for his family, for his new marriage, for his band and the people who worked alongside them, was to force his gaze toward something that lay ahead, whatever that might be. He was prepared to write his way there. That's how it had to start. Songs. He needed songs.

Producer George Drakoulias had been in the background throughout the years when Rick Rubin was working with Petty. Sometimes what Drakoulias was doing caught the attention of the band. He was the kind of guy who might crack the code on a song they were trying to cut, just as much as he might be the guy who figured out how to reach up into the vending machine for Sour Patch Kids. Drakoulias had a lightness, an enthusiasm, and an irreverence about him that suited the Heartbreakers. He'd been at Rubin's side since NYU, when records got shipped from a dorm room and hip-hop was making its way to the center of American life. But he'd also been a freak for the Heartbreakers since his high school band covered "Refugee."

Petty was looking to effect a kind of return. It had been more than three years since *Echo*'s release. But like some modern-day, Malibu-based Rip Van Winkle, Petty had come out of his slumbers to find that the music industry in which he'd been living since he was a young man was in a state of accelerated change. And he didn't like what he saw. So he started writing songs about it. "I went by his house," Drakoulias says, "and I was asking him how they made those Jeff Lynne records. He and Mike ended up showing me the way they'd layer acoustics, switching guitars after each take so the sounds and feels could blend. Pretty soon we were recording. It wasn't like there was a master plan. It just happened. 'The Last DJ' was one of the first songs that came."

More than any album since *Southern Accents*, this one was emerging as a concept album. The corporate influence on twenty-first-century pop music was addressed and redressed in a number of the songs. By the end of 2001, the biggest acts that could be thought of as rock and roll were bands like Train and Matchbox Twenty, not exactly beacons in the night for rock and rollers raised on Jerry Lee Lewis and James Brown. There was good stuff happening closer to the margins, but Petty had lived for so long on the charts that he didn't look to the periphery to understand the moment—he looked at the mainstream, and it appeared that the end-times were coming. He wasn't alone in seeing that.

The sound of the record had some of the lean strength of *Echo* but also the shimmer and tight production of *Full Moon Fever*. Benmont Tench suggested bringing in Jon Brion to write some string arrangements. Brion had been making records with Aimee Mann and Rufus Wainwright, which was proof that good things were happening in the world of pop music. Tench knew that Brion was a bit like the Heartbreakers themselves, a guy who played in bands and liked songs that sounded best when bands played them. His arrangement for "Money Becomes King" quickly showed him to be a sympathetic collaborator. The hole left by Howie Epstein was filled by Petty and Campbell, who switched off on bass, except for the two tracks played by Ron Blair.

Blair had stayed in touch with Mike Campbell. "I played a little bit over those years," Blair explains. "With some kind of songwriter guys, a few gigs at the Palomino Club. We opened for the Ventures." He was obviously not a man working with publicists and managers to craft a return to the business. "When I had the surf shop," Blair says, describing the period immediately after leaving the Heartbreakers in 1982, "I had a burglary at my house, and a lot of stuff was stolen. After that I sold everything that was left, kind of felt disgusted. For fifteen years there, I think all I had was an acoustic guitar. I hardly played, mostly withdrew." Mike Campbell was his one link. "Mike kept me on some kind of thin tether, kept me from drifting off into a black hole. He'd invite me over to his house, show me the latest thing, MIDI keyboards or something. He'd be working with Patti Scialfa or on a Stevie Nicks track. I remember being at his house and saying to him, after ten or twelve years, 'Mike, I think I'm living the wrong life.'"

Campbell had been holding what Blair calls "workshops" at his house, bringing in musicians to record songs, sometimes in batches of ten or more—Steve Ferrone, Jim Keltner, Charley Drayton—the group's makeup would shift, but Blair was a part of it. When one of the recordings from a workshop was being recut for the new Heartbreakers' album, Campbell suggested to Petty that they bring down the guy who played the bass on the demo. "I went down to the studio," Blair describes, "and it went pretty good. I worked a couple of nights, and I was thinking, 'Wow, this is interesting.' There was a kind of tension in the air, like a *nice* kind of tension, right? There I was, after so many years. By the end of the second night, Tom asked me, 'So, what are you doing this summer?' 'Nothing, brother,' I tell him. 'Nothing I couldn't get out of.'"

The reuniting of an original Heartbreaker with the band was more meaningful to Petty than anyone likely knew. Petty didn't want to run auditions. "Mike had suggested bringing Ron in. And he played so well," says

Petty, "that I suggested we bring him back the next day. I knew we had to come up with a bass player for the tour that was being planned. I was standing with Ron on the back steps at Ocean Way studio, and I just said, 'What would you think about coming back and playing on the tour?' I hadn't talked to Ben or Mike about how I was feeling, but the idea of bringing in someone new, someone we didn't really know, no matter how good a player, would have been just . . . too many missing people. I need to be a member of a band. Or not. Ron was an answer to my concerns. Had he not appeared, I think I would have put an end to the band. I couldn't have done it with a hired gun. His appearance was almost mystical to me. And, then, the band just got better, gelled in a really good way. And I think that's when we all became friends again." Drakoulias believes the reunion brought a kind of heightened sensitivity to the group in the studio. "Everyone wanted to bring the best parts of themselves," he says. "Ron's return leveled things out in some way. There wasn't anyone saying, 'What kind of fucking sandwich is this? I know this is what I ordered, but this is not what I wanted.' Everyone brought in their best behavior."

Adria Petty served as art director for *The Last DJ*, coming up with one of the most memorable among the Heartbreakers album packages. In the years since her parents split, she'd managed to maintain a strong connection to her father. Dana Petty's patience and care for the family had helped everyone. Adria finished her undergraduate studies at Sarah Lawrence, attended film school at NYU, and would soon enough be directing major music video and commercial projects. But in her father's world, she was already among his closest advisers. "There was a lifetime of healing to be done," says Dana Petty. "You could say there are few things more difficult than dating a man with teenage daughters, but Adria and Annakim had been through so much, had been denied so much. I always felt their pain. But, finally, our world began revolving around family as much as music." With the making of *The Last DJ*, Petty felt he'd really come through something.

When the Heartbreakers headed out to support the record, however, they already sensed that not everyone wanted to hear what Tom Petty had to say about the state of the music industry. *The Last DJ* suggested that the business was a mess caused by greed, much altered from its glory days, and that everyone knew it. But the hitch was this: that didn't mean everyone wanted to listen to songs about it, particularly from a well-compensated career artist who had likely paid off his mortgage with ease, if he even knew what a mortgage was. A *Rolling Stone* review set the tone for the album's reception, evenhanded but tough in a way that signaled trouble:

> On *The Last DJ,* Tom Petty sounds like the crankiest middle-aged punk this side of Neil Young. "Well, you can't turn him into a company man /You can't turn him into a whore," Petty declares on the title track that ushers in his thirteenth studio album in twenty-six years, a loosely constructed concept piece about how much the music industry sucks.

"Dreamville" stands out as a song that perhaps reveals more about where Petty's mind and heart really were than does "Joe." As Rick Rubin had remarked, Petty had always written from the place he was in, whether as a young man, a grown-up, or as a guy blown down in midlife. The songs followed him. He didn't chase them backward in time. Coming up on fifty, Petty was looking around, considering where he came from, what was left of that place. "What I think about with Tom," says Jackson Browne, "is, 'How did he become that writer? How does he know what he knows?' He's so good I have to ask these questions, like he's that kind of a figure to me. The songs are so compelling. There is such an intimacy to them. But, thinking of *The Last DJ,* when this same artist, who for so long has delivered emotional truths, suddenly goes after *historical* truths, the audience has a hard time swallowing it. *The Last DJ* was a fucking great record that nonetheless suffered that fate. But then, in the middle of it, there's 'Dreamville,' and this image of like, Tom Petty, this skinny little white kid, shivering by the pool with blue lips, whose mom took him places. It's masterful. And it's that emotional truth, full on." Petty thinks of it as among his best songs and recordings. "Sometimes," he says, "they just come out like you hear them in your head. That's one of those."

"Dreamville" was the clue hinting at what was coming in the next decade of Petty's artistic life. He would be going back, sorting through some boxes, questioning old friends to see what they knew, calling old numbers to see who picked up. Those who saw only nostalgia in "Dreamville" were going to miss the subtlety of it all. If "nostalgia" is an empty effort to recover some idealized past, an escape from the present, then, no, this isn't what Petty was engaged in. Before the release of *The Last DJ* and Ron Blair's official return, in 2002 the Heartbreakers would accept induction into the Rock and Roll Hall of Fame. Then, starting in 2005, Petty would work with director Peter Bogdanovich to capture the story of his band in a four-hour documentary. Petty would collect a few awards, create a few anthologies. But he didn't approach it all as an archivist. One got the sense that he was going back because he'd left something there and needed to go find it. When he rummaged back there, it was as much about his future as it was his past.

■

"We were standing in some hallway," says Tom Petty, "waiting to be inducted. But we couldn't hear what was going on out there. We're just kind of looking at each other. I know Stan said something like, 'You know what this means, right?' Like he really appreciated the meaning of it all. I was kind of touched by that." Tony Dimitriades had called Jakob Dylan, Bob Dylan's son and the leader of the Wallflowers, to let Jakob know that Petty would like him to induct the band into the Rock and Roll Hall of Fame. "He asked me that," recalls Dylan, "said my name had come up. And, honestly, I was kind of taken aback. To go to a room like that and induct someone into the Rock and Roll Hall of Fame? I was concerned that maybe I wasn't the right person." As a teenager, Dylan was sidestage watching the Heartbreakers when they backed his father. "I used to sit with Bugs," he says. "By the amplifiers. Soaking it up, learning as much as I could. I couldn't have asked for much more at sixteen years old than to watch those guys play every night." Still, Jakob Dylan didn't feel like he was the one for this job.

"I asked Tony who else they had in mind," he says. "Like, if I decide I'm not the right guy for it, who are they thinking of? He tells me, 'You're the only choice.' He wasn't going to let me off the hook. Then he said, 'You know, Jakob, if you want to be one of those guys, like the ones you really admire, these are the kinds of things you've got to do.' He was right. I belonged up there and deserved to be there if Tom was asking me to do this. I knew their career so well. It began to make sense to me. I hung up the phone thinking, 'Hell, yeah, you're going to do that. Are you kidding?' I was younger then."

The Heartbreakers rehearsed in Los Angeles. Stan Lynch flew in from Florida. Howie Epstein and Ron Blair were both there. "I drove Tom to rehearsals that day," says Mark Carpenter. "I certainly wondered what it was going to be like. But Tom walked in, saw Stan, broke into a grin, and they had a genuine hug. It just broke the tension. My instinct had been that Tom wouldn't want to go back there again. But the rehearsals were great." No doubt it was harder to walk into that rehearsal space for the guys who were no longer Heartbreakers. They'd be in their old band for one more evening in New York City. But that was it. "I felt at the Hall of Fame," says Lynch, "that I had no connection to anybody in the room. They didn't even let me travel with them to the event. I thought, 'They don't want to relive this.'" That Lynch hadn't asked anyone if he could travel with the band has to be noted. Petty gives a quizzical look after hearing Lynch's remark: "Didn't he go back to Florida, then on to New York? As God is my witness, he would have been with us if he'd asked for that." After rehearsals in Los Angeles, the band's equipment went by truck to New York, and everyone scattered for the days prior to departure. Lynch, apparently still in Los Angeles, was on his own. As was everyone else.

Jakob Dylan had among the best lines of the evening, describing from the podium a moment during the early dates his father did with the Heartbreakers. "On that tour," he said, "[Tom] had his two daughters there. And I remember sitting with his daughters, I remember thinking, 'Jesus, your dad is *Tom Petty*.'" Once they were at the front of the room, the Heartbreakers took turns sharing a few words. They thanked one another, thanked girlfriends, wives, children. But Petty delivered the message. "I'm very proud that we're being inducted as a group, as Tom Petty and the Heartbreakers, 'cause they're the best fucking band in America."

Campbell was in a purple suit; Howie Epstein looked very sick; Stan Lynch seemed, somehow, larger than ever; Benmont Tench was professorial; Ron Blair looked like Ron Blair. If their appearance as a group could have been captured in music, it would have been dissonant. But they got up and played "American Girl" and "Mary Jane's Last Dance" under imperfect conditions, and it was the Heartbreakers. They sounded like that band.

In the men's room, Stan Lynch found himself at the urinal next to Steve Ferrone. "We're both pissing," says Lynch. "Two drummers trying not to look at their dicks. Looking at each other and looking at the wall. I wished someone could have taken a picture of this. I said, 'Steve, thanks for lending me the band.' Then I poured myself a couple martinis and danced on the table while Isaac Hayes did 'Shaft.'"

Going to New York, Lynch was on a flight with one of the Ramones and a few other guys who had once been in bands. The Heartbreakers were, of course, on their private plane. After the event, he sent Petty a letter. "It was a very nice note," says Petty, "and it hinted at the idea that we'd be seeing more of each other. But I never saw him or heard from him again. I'm sure if we ran into each other he'd be very pleasant, and I would, too. But there's a lot that went on there. We grew up together, for Christ's sake. I feel like that was when I grew from being a boy to being a man. In that band. We confronted the real world, changed, saw a hell of lot, and went through an experience you couldn't really explain to anybody who wasn't there. But I'm glad he was there. I'm glad they were all there. To have been alone would have been a nightmare. But there's a difference now: I'm still in that band, and Stan isn't. Hasn't been for a while. I need to take care of the band I'm in."

2006

It was a couple weeks of the unexpected for me. First came a call from Diana Ross, with whom I'd had no previous contact. She left a message on my voice mail. That wasn't something major pop stars do. Most work through handlers. She said she'd picked up my small book *Dusty in Memphis* in a London airport and wondered if I would be willing to sit down with her and talk about writing projects.

We met a few days later at her floor-through apartment at the Pierre, across from the Plaza Hotel. I wasn't aware of any assistant. Lobby security checked my driver's license, after which I took an elevator that opened directly onto Miss Ross's apartment. She met me there, wearing jeans, her hair down, and we sat in the living room. Within ten minutes of conversation, she was crying, sharing her feeling that no book had really shown her for who she is. It was a two-hour visit. I wanted to help, we made plans, but she never returned any of my calls after that.

One week later, I got an e-mail from Tom Petty's management, saying that Tom wanted to meet up in Los Angeles, that he'd read *Dusty in Memphis* and wanted to talk about it. I knew that the book was in a few shops, that it had gotten a handful of reviews, but I also knew that it was an indie affair. This Diana Ross and Tom Petty stuff was strange business. I still thought of myself as an academic. I'd gotten my PhD and stayed out of the music business for more than a decade, had only one foot in at that point. Petty and I hadn't had any contact for fifteen years.

Mary Klauzer from Petty's management set up a dinner in Malibu. The restaurant was off the Pacific Coast Highway, and I waited just outside, by the valet parking. Petty was a little late, so I kept an eye out for his car, standing close to a maître d', who seemed to enjoy watching me wait, though I didn't understand what prompted his amusement, until he said, "Good evening," looking toward the road. Petty stepped through some bushes, wearing an army jacket. I couldn't tell if he'd been dropped off, run across the PCH, or what. But obviously this had happened before. The maître d' didn't care *how* the celebrities got to his restaurant, as long as they got there.

Petty had just finished up or almost finished up a new record, *Highway Companion*, his third solo album. He'd gone back to work with Jeff Lynne but under very different conditions from those of either *Full Moon Fever* or *Into the Great Wide Open*. Time had passed. Del Shannon was dead, a suicide. George Harrison had been gone for five years at that point, Roy Orbison almost eighteen. Johnny Cash had died three years before, Howie Epstein the same year. Several of the people who first watched Lynne and Petty collaborate weren't around to see that the friendship had lasted and music was still being made.

We sat by the ocean, talking as we ate. It wasn't the first mealtime I'd shared with Petty. The first was in Encino in the mid-eighties. My brother and I had gone out to the Petty house on a Sunday and stuck around long enough that our hosts offered dinner. Still a little unsure how to behave at a rock star's home, we welcomed the invitation. Jane Petty was apologetic, letting us know she wasn't entirely sure what they had for food. We went into the kitchen, all of us, including Adria and Annakim, watching as Jane opened cupboards. She found some spaghetti and a jar of sauce but looked uncertain about what to do with it. This was something my brother and I could handle, and it felt good to have a little authority. It was only when we'd finished cooking the food that my brother and I realized the family had no intention of eating with us. They watched as we ate very large plates of spaghetti. We asked Petty questions, and he told us stories. The kids took it all in. Jane offered commentary. We drove out of the gates later that evening, thinking, "The guy who wrote 'Even the Losers' just watched us eat spaghetti."

Sitting there in Malibu so many years later, Petty told me he'd written a song after reading *Dusty in Memphis*, and that he wanted me to hear it. After dinner, we went back to his house. I gave him a ride in my rental car. *Highway Companion* sounded different from the other Jeff Lynne recordings. It had a spare quality, showing off more space. It made room for the voice of what seemed to me a detached observer, in some cases a narrator-voyeur, floating above it all. "I'm passing over cities, country homes and ranches / watching life between the branches below," he sang on the first track, "Saving Grace." It established a position he'd take throughout much of the album, set up the proceedings. "Square One," the second cut, seemed like the centerpiece, a survivor account. At that time, I didn't know what Petty's life had been like since I'd seen him last. I only knew that he was different by a shade. A melancholy was coming through, like a couple layers of anger had been peeled off, and that's what was left.

"Down South," the recording he wanted me to hear, went to a southern landscape as much mythic as it was based on Petty's background. I could tell that as a songwriter he cared as much as he ever had about the craft and its powers. These were songs finely tooled, but breathing life. We listened through the whole album, drinking Cokes, talking between cuts, and I left. But everything I ever thought about the man, while listening to the records that raised me, was confirmed. Again. And Petty was himself happy with *Highway Companion*. As I came to see over the next several years, that's how it's been for Petty: he makes an album, and it buys him a number of months in which he can almost enjoy the beauty of it all. Then either he gets to work on the next thing or trouble shows up at his back gate.

23

EVERYTHING CHANGED, THEN CHANGED AGAIN

We've got to start thinking beyond our guns. Those days
are closin' fast.

—*THE WILD BUNCH*

Everyone at the Hall of Fame inductions was shocked at Howie Epstein's condition.
He looked like a different person—thin, smaller, his face changed. Heroin
had stolen the boyishness for which he'd always been known. It was the
last time most of them would see their old bandmate, if they were seeing him
even then. At a show in New Mexico, he would appear one last time, asking
to see Dana Petty. "By that time," says Tom Petty, "most people in the Heartbreakers camp knew that talking to Dana was like talking to all of us." Assistant road manager Mark Carpenter didn't bring Epstein's message to her,
though. He made the decision not to, knowing he was protecting her from
something that would break her heart. Epstein wasn't himself anymore.

Benmont Tench and Stan Lynch attended Howie Epstein's funeral in
Milwaukee. Petty and Campbell didn't, and some judged them for it. As late
as 2011, a *Milwaukee Magazine* writer, in a piece about Epstein, charged Petty
with a "career cold-bloodedness that has allowed [him] to stay at the top of
his game for almost 40 years." Stan Lynch, interviewed for the story, helps
the writer along: "I'm really pissed that Howie was allowed to die while in
the employ of a multimillion-dollar corporation." In the same article, however, the writer describes Epstein's arrest, two days before his last tour with
the Heartbreakers. Epstein and Carlene Carter were found with 2.9 grams of
black tar heroin, considerable amounts of drug paraphernalia, driving a

stolen car. Things had gotten way out of control. It was no casual matter when the Heartbreakers stopped working with Epstein. And the fact that
they had stopped working with him certainly didn't mean his death didn't
affect them. With little to no basis, the *Milwaukee Magazine* writer, and Lynch,
suggested otherwise. In some ways, Lynch is still at work on that angle.

"I never forgave Tom for not being at his funeral," says Stan Lynch. "I
can't. I wish I could. You know, 'If I could fly to Milwaukee in the winter,
why couldn't you?' I'll never forgive him. It doesn't mean I don't love him,
and maybe I even understand why. But, no, Howie was buried in Milwaukee
in the snow, on a cold fucking winter day, and it sucked." Lynch put a pair
of drumsticks in with the casket. When he did, the rabbi asked him who
he was to Howie Epstein. Hearing that Lynch and Epstein were bandmates,
the rabbi asked Lynch how he could have let this happen. There are those
who don't understand addiction. Maybe the rabbi was one such person.
Neither he nor Stan Lynch knew what the Heartbreakers had done to try
to help their friend.

"I didn't go to Howie's funeral in Milwaukee. Everyone has their own
way of processing death," says Mike Campbell. "I don't have any guilt about
that. We had our own memorial. And it felt like a proper way of saying
good-bye. I don't see how my choice has anything to do with my love for
him." The band's memorial was held at McCabe's Guitar Shop in Santa
Monica. "It was full of people," Campbell continues. "It was friends, the
band, everyone. It was spiritual. I felt better afterward, taking the time to
remember, to say good-bye. I don't usually speak in public, but I felt moved
to get up and speak. It was bittersweet. Was Stan at that?"

"Everybody loved Howie," says Benmont Tench. "Everyone was devas-
tated when he died. The memorial that Tom organized here was really,
really beautiful. Respectful. Worthy of Howie. Tom wouldn't have done
that if he was practicing avoidance or if he didn't care."

"I heard people insinuate that Howie died for the Tom Petty machine,"
Petty says. "Stan did some of that. Suggestive stuff. It hinges on the idea
that we didn't love Howie. That's absolute bullshit. I don't think Stan knows
what we went through with Howie. Nobody does. I owe Howie more than
to tell those tales. But I will say that I miss him all the time. I hear his voice
on records, and it just kills me. I miss that voice. Just like I miss Stan's.
We were a powerful vocal group. I feel awful about Howie's death. And I

know what Stan meant to the Heartbreakers. None of this was ever taken lightly. But if you're going to run a rock-and-roll band for forty years, there will be some casualties. I don't know of anyone in my spot who has gotten away without having to face some."

Whether or not it was because of that Heartbreakers reunion in New York or because of Howie Epstein's death shortly thereafter, around that time Petty became a little more reflective about the band. He'd always seen himself as a member of a group. He worked to put one together, and fought to keep it. His words at the Hall of Fame podium made his respect clear. But Petty was beginning to put ever more thought into just what that band meant, what allowed it to survive. Why he needed one so much in the first place, what it gave to him. You could hold a band together through power, through fear, through money, through anger. You could hold a band together through love. Most bands were bound by some combination of those things. Just like families. And Petty had watched his family fall apart. So what, he had to ask, held his band together?

■

There's something about the way Dana Petty came into the Heartbreakers' world that made even the tougher critics bend a bit. "She knew," says her husband, "that you don't walk right into the Heartbreakers' dressing room. There are girls that will do that. But to this day, Dana won't go in. It's a hard circle to break into, but she put in the miles with these guys. She was respectful, never said to anyone, 'Hey, carry my bag.'" Even now, when she's on the road, Dana Petty watches every show, standing by the monitor board. "Dana has my back and knows what matters in my life," says Petty. On tours, it was Dana who went to every show, something even managers rarely do. She became part of the fabric of the touring organization, always out there, always offering a hand where she could. She earned the respect of the crew, not something that's offered up to the undeserving.

Dana became the one who could say what the others couldn't. She stood up to Petty's rage when she saw it. "Where it comes from is hard to know," Petty says. "But in that moment, I snap, and some of it comes out. It *really* comes out, in a scary way. Tony got the worst of it. And when I was younger, it happened too much. It could come without me expecting it. And it's not how you want people to see you. But I didn't even realize until I was with

Dana what shouting was. I was used to people talking that way. But she would say, 'Stop yelling at me.' She insisted on some change. But I already knew that it had to go. That's not how you want your band or your family to think of you. There were some things I no longer wanted to get away with."

Playing in Washington, DC, during Ron Blair's first year back, Petty was having problems with his amp. Yelling at Bugs Weidel onstage, Petty got frustrated, started to tell himself the band wasn't trying. "I thought the Heartbreakers sounded like shit," he says. "I kept getting into it with Bugs. I thought the band was just phoning it in. It might have all been in my head. I got in this bad space. In the middle of the show, I just started playing 'High Heel Sneakers.' They were all looking back and forth at each other, but they went along with it. I was so uptight, I went across the stage and played what must be the worst solo in the history of rock. I think I shocked people. Then I got mad at myself, was yelling more at Bugs. When we came off stage before the encore, I just lost my shit on the band. I'm yelling at everybody. I was even screaming at Richard [Fernandez], putting him in the Tony position. I think Mike tried to calm me down. Like, 'Hey, it's okay. It's just a show. Everything's fine.' No matter how bad we were playing, my behavior wasn't called for. I knew it. When we got to the plane, I told Richard, 'I'm really sorry for yelling.' I admitted that it was a problem. But Richard didn't really give it up. He looked at me and kind of nodded but no words of, you know, 'That's okay.' He let me know in his own way that I was out of line. And I never did that again. But it showed me that it's still in there. I have to be careful."

Knowing Tony Dimitriades had gotten more of it than anyone, Dana Petty talked to Tom. "She said to me, 'That guy loves you,'" Petty recalls. "'He's dedicated his life to you. And you're not thinking that you're hurting him, but you are.' She looked at me and said, 'Do you ever tell Tony you love him? *I* know you love him. But he should hear it. He's not just your manager; he's one of your best friends.' I thought about it for a few minutes, and then I just picked up the phone and called Tony. I called him and I apologized to him. And I said, 'I really love you, and I really value our friendship. And I may never say it again, but I wanted you to know it.' It felt good to say it. After Dana, Tony's my most trusted friend. He doesn't get the credit he deserves. But he's a perfect manager. He never makes it about himself. He's a smart guy. And he stuck with me all the fucking way."

In the studio, it was Campbell who was most consistently at Petty's side. But Campbell, it seems, never got the call that Dimitriades did. Nor did he make it. Petty will tell a third party that he loves Mike Campbell, and Campbell will tell a third party that he loves Tom Petty. But that's as close as it gets.

"I love Mike," says Petty. "His opinion means the world to me. We have a natural working relationship. I give Mike and Ben a song, and they return it to me better than I pictured it in the first place. They make me better. I honestly don't think I would have made the mark I made in music without them." For those band members who have believed or worried that Petty sits atop the Heartbreakers power structure, casually considering his next move, waiting to see what comes his way: they've misunderstood their band leader. As much as anyone, Petty has tied his identity to this band.

"The solo records," says Petty, "made me realize how good the band is. But the solo records were also important to the *life* of the band. I always came back different. Things need to breathe. The marriage metaphor doesn't always work. I wasn't out cheating, even if some people need to see it that way. Just recently, I was doing some album promotion, and this guy is asking me questions, going, 'Do you think you're a tough guy?' I say, 'Tough guy?' 'Like rugged,' he says. 'I don't know. I guess,' I tell him. 'Have you ever been brutal? Do you think you're brutal?' he asks. I thought for a second and went, 'Yeah.' He gave me the dirtiest fucking look, like he despised me. And I thought, 'Brother, I've had to be brutal, and it's not fucking fun. You misunderstand brutal.' There are times when it fell on me to do something, and I had to do it to save this thing that's become bigger than all five of us, all six of us. It's a much more important thing than any one of us now. And if it were to go away, none of us would want to be the guy that ended it."

■

Around the time of *Highway Companion*, the core relationship in the Heartbreakers was quietly tested, when the balance between Petty and Campbell got thrown off-kilter. For so many years they had worked together closely, fusing their individual strengths. "I've always written music," explains Campbell. "And I also made a lot of it that Tom just couldn't process. He'd pick what he thought were the best tracks, and sometimes I felt like he overlooked some pretty good ones." Campbell had given a lot of material to Petty over the years, far more than the Heartbreakers could have used, and that pile of tracks started to weigh on him. "I just wanted to write words to this stuff," says Campbell, "to sing it myself, see what it sounds like. I wish I'd done it earlier in my life, but I never felt the driving ambition. I wanted to see what my voice sounds like, if I could write words that are any good. Just for myself." But who really does that just for himself? Campbell was leaning into Petty's area. If the Heartbreakers were Tom Petty and some backing musicians, it wouldn't have mattered. But they're a group, their identities bound up with one another's, and the delicacy of the dynamic revealed itself. Particularly when Campbell put a band together and made himself the front man. But also because Campbell's vocals sounded like, well, Tom Petty's.

When Howie Epstein was in rehab, he called Mike Campbell to talk about the band. "We'd talked for a while," Campbell says, "and I asked him what was bugging him. He goes, 'Part of it is, you know, in the band you and Tom dictate the bass. Sometimes you play it, and I'm not allowed to play as much as I'd like to.' And I said, 'Well, you know, Howie, I'm not allowed to write all the songs I'd like to write either, but I accept my role. Why can't you just accept your role?'"

Now Campbell was questioning that role. He handed Petty a demo, as had happened so many times before, but this one included complete lyrics and lead vocals. "I had no idea," Petty says, "that there was any part of his personality that wanted that. I had *no* idea that he had even the slightest dream of fronting a band." Petty called Bugs Weidel, who had moved up to Santa Maria. "I got this call from Tom," Weidel explains. "He goes, 'Can you come over?' 'Um, yeah,' I tell him, 'but you know I don't live there anymore. I live a long way away.' He goes, 'How soon can you get here?' I drove down, just thinking, 'What's going on now?' I get there, and he says, 'I had to share this with somebody.' He puts on this cassette. And like, after all these years, Mike had made an album." For someone on the outside, it might have seemed that Petty was out to limit what his band members were doing. And in some ways, he was. The harder thing to consider was why. Was he protecting his own ego or protecting the band as it had been built?

The truth of the Heartbreakers' operation is in their sound. The way Campbell and Tench move in and out on a Petty song. The way Petty's and

Campbell's guitars sit against each other. The way Ferrone plays to Petty's vocal. When one man moves, the next man feels it and responds accordingly. That was how they arrived at a definable, defining aesthetic. Now Campbell had abruptly stepped out of his position. A few bodies fell over when they went to lean on him. This wasn't Keith Richards taking a song on a Rolling Stones album. There was no tradition here. Apart from one song on *Echo*, Campbell didn't play the role of singer and lyricist.

This wasn't like Howie Epstein's earlier work with John Prine or Benmont's session work, or even Campbell's cowriting or outside production with other artists. This wasn't Campbell's surf band. All of that had gone on for years, with Petty supporting it. This was Campbell as a front man, on a project that sounded kind of like the Heartbreakers. "It was just close enough," says Petty, "to fuck with my head." As the one responsible for guiding the band, Petty had to address the issue. "We had a long conversation," says Petty, "the only time we talked about this. We were on the phone a couple hours. I was completely honest with him about what I thought. I said, 'Look, you know I'm going to be pissed if you make a record that people think is us.' I'm going to protect, desperately, the quality and character of what goes out in our name. If somebody doesn't play this role, the whole thing will run off the rails. We created something that needs to be respected and cared for."

"I didn't realize that I sounded like Tom until he said something," Campbell says. "I wasn't hearing it that way. I said, 'Well, that's good that it sounds like you. That means it's good, right?' It perplexed me for a while. I started to hear a little of it in there, tried to filter it out. I told him that I didn't know I was doing it. He said, 'I know you don't mean to do it, but it's there. We grew up in the same neighborhoods, spoke the same slang. But that's not how you want to present yourself.' It was great advice. But I could tell it made him uncomfortable. When I step out of my box, it throws him off his game. That was never our dynamic in the beginning, so he doesn't know what to do with it. And I understand that." When Benmont Tench made a solo recording several years later, it was music that lived at a distance from the Heartbreakers' sound. "He had the best players," says Petty. "He went out, took on the front man role with ease. You would have thought he'd been doing it his whole life. He could talk to the crowd, lead the show. It was fantastic. And it wasn't too close to what we do." Petty had invited Campbell, more than anyone, into the center of his creative life. But there was a trade-off. It would limit Campbell's freedoms elsewhere. He wasn't a sideman. He was a partner.

■

Highway Companion may well be the last Tom Petty solo recording. Petty came out of it thinking more about the Heartbreakers, about the preciousness and precariousness of what he has. *Highway Companion* didn't necessarily cause that, but it's where he landed when the album and the roadwork supporting it were completed. Something shifted, and whether because of therapy or aging Petty was doing more than ever before to understand his close relationships, his mind, his past. "I had this discussion the other day with Tony," Petty says. "We were talking about getting old, and out of the blue, he said, 'Do you find yourself thinking about the past more than you do the future?' I said, 'Actually, I think about the present most of the time.' I'm not necessarily a nostalgic person. You know, I look back, but I don't stare." The music business, however, had gotten nostalgic. Nostalgia made cash registers ring. By the turn of the millennium, the major artists of the sixties and seventies had to think about legacy projects, about the archive, as much as they did their new recordings. Often more. Neil Young, Bob Dylan, the Rolling Stones—they were putting out their classic records, remastered with new bonus tracks, releasing "official" live albums from earlier periods, making documentaries that picked through their careers.

After the airing of Martin Scorsese's Dylan documentary, *No Direction Home*, the legacy culture of the music business seemed to gather more momentum still, at least among those artists with meaningful back catalogues and paying audiences. Being in that mind-set personally, Petty was in sync with the business when he went into the more than two-year process of making *Runnin' Down a Dream*. The Peter Bogdanovich documentary came out as a four-hour film but was cut down from something closer to eight. Bogdanovich's *The Last Picture Show* is perhaps the most obvious clue that the director has a sympathy for the American landscape from which the Heartbreakers emerged, but George Drakoulias says the inspiration for their directorial choice was less that and more about some tapes he'd given Petty. The tapes, recordings of conversations between Bogdanovich and Orson Welles, revealed Bogdanovich to be almost as much of a character as Welles, full of opinions, a history of film in his head. Petty dug into Bogdanovich's writings on John Ford, Hitchcock, American screwball comedy. He liked the director's mind.

Warner Bros. had already approached Tony Dimitriades about the possibility of a thirtieth-anniversary film. A meeting between Petty and Bogdanovich, much of which revolved around a discussion of films such as Howard Hawks's *Red River* and John Ford's *The Searchers*, proved that the most important question—would Petty and Bogdanovich make a connection?—could be answered in the affirmative. The secondary question—does Peter Bogdanovich know anything about Tom Petty and the Heartbreakers?—was merely that, secondary. He didn't. Not a thing.

"In some ways," Drakoulias insists, "it's better that way. He's learning, rather than coming in with preconceived notions. The process started with me and Peter meeting in a hotel room here in LA. We watched—I'm not kidding—hundreds of hours of footage. We'd meet at noon, have a sandwich, and screen every piece of footage that existed. Pretty soon we were labeling stuff, separating it into years. By the end, and this is almost three years later, I'm not sure Peter wanted it to end. I remember we were out on the road at one point, and he's on the side of the stage. He's looking out at the audience. He asks me, 'Are all those people waiting for Tom? Who are those girls? Do you think those girls want to sleep with him?' I go, 'I really don't think that's where Tom is at.' Peter just says, 'I chose the wrong path.'"

The first Petty interview session was done at the Heartbreakers' clubhouse, a warehouse in the valley where the band stores their gear, rehearses, and, these days, makes their records. The racks of Fenders, Gibsons, Rickenbackers, Martins, oddball Silvertones, and other guitars dwarfed the film crew's equipment. Bogdanovich was there, wearing a cravat. He was also suffering from acute back pain. On and off the couch, he conducted interviews, with Drakoulias standing behind him whispering band history, suggesting follow-ups.

As the film slowly came together, Petty was obliged to think about it all, from childhood on. But Mudcrutch was the thing that, for some reason, stuck in his mind. He began hatching the idea of trying, as a kind of experiment, to put that band back together, to see if his gut feeling was accurate. "I just thought," Petty explains, "that maybe there was some music back there. Mudcrutch never really got to be a band and make records. But we were good. It was a different thing than the Heartbreakers. But it really was a good little band." Petty initially thought to run the idea past Mike Campbell first. But when he approached Campbell, the guitar player was distracted, so Petty waited. In the interim, though only in passing, he mentioned the idea to Bogdanovich, who thought it sounded like a whim, a one-off at best.

"My brother Bernie, and also my brother Mark," recalls Tom Leadon, "had left me some messages saying that Tom's manager, Tony, was trying to get ahold of me, that it might be important. So I called the number I'd been given. It might have been Mary [Klauzer] that I talked to first. She asked if I'd be willing to be in the movie. Of course, I said I'd be glad to. We set it up for Peter Bogdanovich and the film crew to come to the music school where I teach. When Peter showed up, we were looking around for a space to shoot. I showed him the room I teach in, but it wasn't big enough. I didn't realize they'd have lights and sound. But we found a spot, and while they were setting up, Peter asked if I had any old photos of Mudcrutch. I showed him what I had. As he's looking at them, he says, kind of offhand-edly, 'Yeah, Tom's thinking of having a reunion of Mudcrutch.' And his words, just him saying that, shot through me like a bolt of lightning. Some-how, I could almost see the whole thing in that instant, that this band could be really good . . . like the whole thing. I could see it. I was trying to act like I hadn't been hit with 186,000 volts. Then Peter said he'd asked Tom why he'd do that. You know, 'Why have a reunion?' I was thinking to myself, 'No, don't ask him that. *Don't* say that. Please don't question that.'"

Petty had responded to Bogdanovich by saying only, "Well, I just want to do it." To Leadon, that seemed promising. "I heard that," says Leadon, "and thought, 'That's just what Tom would say if he really did want to do it.'" But Petty was wrapped up in finishing the film and the thirtieth-anniversary tour. With opening acts that included Pearl Jam, the Allman Brothers, the Black Crowes, and a few others, and with Stevie Nicks join-ing for several shows, the tour was a complicated production, demand-ing all of Petty's time. When the film came out, it quickly got a lot of attention. In the *New York Times*, David Carr described the film as "a vivid reminder that Mr. Petty remains one of the coolest guys out of the South since William Faulkner." A double platinum success, the film was the event that caught the attention of the Super Bowl's production team, and not long after that the Heartbreakers were on a football field, playing to television cameras that brought them into homes across the world. It led to the biggest spike in sales of any Super Bowl act to date. The Heartbreakers didn't engage in a lot of theatrics; they let the songs do the work. "American Girl," "I Won't Back Down," "Free Fallin'," "Runnin' Down a Dream." You could hear a stadium on background vocals.

Some six months after the film was finished, however, Leadon, working as a guitar teacher in the Nashville area, got a call. "I'd been at the supermarket," he says, "and was on my way home with my groceries. My cell phone rang, I answered it, and the voice said, 'This is Tom Petty.' I didn't believe it was really him. I thought maybe it was one of my friends pulling a prank. I wasn't going to fall for it. He had to convince me it was him. We hadn't talked on the phone for thirty years. The last time I remember talking to him on the phone was 1977."

No one's experience was going to be as high as Leadon's. "The anticipation was just amazing," he says. "I remember getting my gear together for the trip. I had a case I converted into a flight case for my Gibson 335. I remember being on the plane, like it was some kind of dream I was flying into."

The Heartbreakers' clubhouse was made into a studio for the Mudcrutch sessions. With Ryan Ulyate engineering and coproducing alongside Petty and Mike Campbell, the crew set it up so that the band could play without headphones, everyone hearing one another through their own monitor mixes, as if they were back in Gainesville playing a club show. It meant that separation would be impossible, that one instrument would bleed into the next man's microphone. To get a usable take was possible only if each individual performance was good top to bottom. There wasn't a lot of room for error. It was closer to how records were made when the Beatles walked into George Martin's world, which might have been fine for a band that had been playing together for some time. But this was a group that had *dis*banded thirty years earlier. It was a calculated gamble on Petty's part. If it wasn't going to work, they'd know about a minute into the first song. "I think," Leadon recalls, "it was 'Swinging Doors,' the Merle Haggard song." Petty thinks the Haggard track could have been the warmup song but knows his original "A Special Place" was the first thing they recorded. "It was good," Petty recalls. "But then we cut 'Crystal River.' It was one take. When we listened back we saw no reason to do it again. It was one of the greatest nights of my life. I went home and started writing more songs while the other guys slept. That's always a good sign."

You didn't see Billy Joel re-forming the Hassles or Bruce Springsteen re-forming Steel Mill. Probably for very legitimate reasons. It was a career move that could stop a manager's heart. But Dimitriades knew Petty. And Petty didn't always think in terms of what made sense; it was all about the songs that he thought "might be back there." He didn't re-form the band as a bit of theater meant to prod the aching hearts of a rock-and-roll audience grown older. They didn't know Mudcrutch anyway. Warner Bros. certainly hadn't asked for this. "To see Tommy with them," Dana Petty says, "was so different from seeing him with the Heartbreakers. He's not the main guy in the same way. I think a lot of stress was taken off. And there he was, back with Tom Leadon, who he'd known since he was seventeen and Tom [Leadon] was fifteen, and Randall Marsh. It was just beautiful to watch how much fun they were having."

Once the reunion was under way, Petty paid attention to the details. He wanted it to be true to what the band had been. When Mudcrutch was active, Petty wasn't the only songwriter. The band members didn't have vast collections of guitars, just the one or two that got them through the gig. Petty played on bass. So Benmont Tench brought in a few songs and sang them, as did Tom Leadon. And Campbell stuck to his B-Bender Telecaster. Petty stayed on bass, and, of course, Randall Marsh was on drums. In some ways, they may as well have been playing at Dub's Steer Room. Except that it became a top-ten album.

"I didn't do it to share the spoils," Petty says. "I didn't think of that. It wasn't me trying to be generous. I did it because I love those guys. We're all getting older. And one of the luxuries of this great success is we can pick and choose our projects. When you pick something that's fun, you usually get good art."

24

SOMEWHERE UNDER HEAVEN

When I was young, before MTV and before I was going out to gigs, I didn't have any sense of music being attached to fan hysteria or anything like that. I just thought of music as a place you could kind of enter. And my dad was very conscious of taking me there. He was like, "Hey, do you want to check out this beautiful place where I go a lot?" Music was so important to me growing up, because of that. So even though my dad was very private about his writing, he'd bring me in.

—ADRIA PETTY

Mudcrutch released their record, and the band did a short tour on the West Coast, playing the Troubadour in Los Angeles and the Fillmore in San Francisco, among a handful of other stops. It did for Petty just what he hoped: got him some songs and inspired him to go after more. It also gave him a vision for how he wanted to make the next Heartbreakers recording. No studio rentals, no producers. Petty wanted his band to meet where they stored their gear and make something that captured the sound he heard when no one was around but the six of them.

During that same time, Ryan Ulyate was digging through the Heartbreakers' vaults, attempting to make order of the vast collection of live recordings the band amassed over three-plus decades. Over a period of several months, Ulyate pulled what he felt were strong recordings from across their career, hundreds of cuts for Petty and Campbell to review. What they put together from all of that could have been many different kinds of collections, depending on the emphasis, the sequence, the years from which they culled recordings. But by the end of the process, Petty felt that *The Live Anthology* was a testimonial in forty-seven tracks. He was struck by what Ulyate had found. For thirty-five years, Petty had been too busy to look at last night because he was preparing for tonight. There was a lot to forget along the way, covers he didn't remember doing, originals he didn't recall having ever performed. And there was his rock-and-roll band: the most consistently great American band to have come out of the seventies and found their way into the new century. "It's the most accurate record," Petty says, "of just who we are."

The sequencing on the collection isn't chronological. It's intuitive. "Nightwatchman" opens the first disc, a clue that this isn't going to be a straight road through town. "I didn't want it to be the greatest hits, played slightly faster," Petty remarked. "And I wanted the view from inside the house. It's a good place to take it all in from." The recordings are a reminder of just how much Stan Lynch brought to the band's musical identity during his time as a Heartbreaker. Howie Epstein's high tenor is as beautiful against Petty's lead as any voice ever would be. Benmont Tench and Mike Campbell, good enough to take a song anywhere but always knowing where it was meant to be. Steve Ferrone, Ron Blair, and Scott Thurston, giving the Heartbreakers a second life and sound. For all of the hard choices Petty had made in order to keep his band together, here was a collection that told him it had been worth it.

■

The tours through that period were intermittent, mostly summer affairs, with sets built around the big songs. From the time Dana Petty first came into Tom's world, the longer outings were kept to the warmer months, when school was out, so that Dylan wouldn't miss classes. It was a reflection of changing priorities. Petty wasn't the man he'd been at twenty-six. But even by the time he was coming into his early sixties, he still struggled with stage fright—if "stage fright" is even the right term for what sometimes took him by the throat. Its appearance was irregular but powerful when it came, and the irregularity left Petty not knowing when he needed to be on his guard. By the early nineties, he'd stopped doing sound checks because of it. "I was extremely neurotic about them," he says. "I'd get to the sound check and become incredibly nervous, and this would make me neurotic, driving the monitor people crazy, driving everyone on stage crazy." Even before that, however, Petty had started avoiding guests before and after the shows, streamlining the entire performance process. He stuck to the job and left the social part of it to others. "TCFP," Stan Lynch called it. *Too cool for pussy.* "No, that's not quite it," says Petty. "My adrenaline would go so high during a show I wouldn't come down for hours. I'm kind of delicate mentally. People would be talking to me backstage, and I couldn't take in much of anything they're saying to me. You start to feel hypocritical. I'd be in such a different place than the folks coming back to see me. But, on another level, imagine if I rolled into some guy's office, sat down next to his desk, and said, 'Let's get drunk! Let's smoke one, whaddya say? I got some people I want you to meet!' Right? When I'm playing a show, *I'm* at the office."

Were it not for the fans and the records that needed support, the touring might have ended already. But the records never stopped mattering to Petty. In 2010, after taking the Heartbreakers into the band's clubhouse to make a record in the same manner as Mudcrutch's debut, Petty had an album on his hands, *Mojo*, which he loved, and loved enough to know he had to tour behind it. Everyone in the band wanted to get out there. So did Petty, with reservations. He knew that the stage anxieties would be there waiting for him. And if they hadn't gotten worse, they had certainly become more of a burden to deal with.

Mojo was introduced as the Heartbreakers' blues album, but in some ways the description fails the project. There was more to *Mojo*. It wasn't blues in the sense that most people thought of the blues, through no fault of their own. When the Heartbreakers played the blues, they tended to do it in the way that Slim Harpo had, in the way that Jimmy Reed had, as *songs*, two-and-half- and three-minute things. "Jefferson Jericho Blues," "Candy," "U.S. 41"—those *Mojo* cuts fit the Heartbreakers' version of the blues. It wasn't guys making contorted faces while they bent strings for long periods of time. But *Mojo* also had songs like "First Flash of Freedom," "Don't Pull Me Over," "No Reason to Cry," material only tangentially related to a strict blues tradition. Regardless of the misdirection of the "blues" tag, it was a Heartbreakers project, and a lot of people had been waiting for it. The Heartbreakers were more like the great country acts of the past, getting better as they logged miles and years. New territories were still opening up.

On the tour, opening acts included My Morning Jacket, Joe Cocker, Drive-By Truckers, and Crosby, Stills, and Nash. The Heartbreakers brought on performers, young and old, whom they respected. In the case of Cocker and CSN, Petty had his heroes opening shows. "When we first played with Crosby, Stills, and Nash opening," Petty says, "we'd been on tour for a while by that time, with no real problems of me being nervous or anything. We were in Atlanta when they joined us. Stephen [Stills] especially was a big hero of mine. But all these guys, really. Buffalo Springfield, Byrds, Hollies, this is heavy for me. I walked out and watched for a little from the side of the stage, and they were really good that night, really hitting it, and the place was going crazy. I got nervous, thinking to myself, 'God, I can't follow that. I can't possibly follow that.' So I go to my dressing room to pull myself together. Then the door opens and it's Stephen, and he wants to rap. And that just makes me more nervous."

Though the Heartbreakers didn't notice, and the arena of fans didn't notice, Petty got lost somewhere in his head. By the time he was onstage, aware that Crosby, Stills, and Nash were at the side, watching him, Petty was slipping. "I felt like I couldn't sustain a note," he says. "My voice started to kind of quiver. It was driving me mad. I was thinking, 'I have to pull this together. I can't sing in vibrato through the whole show. This is bad news.' It took me like three or four songs, but I got to where I could sustain notes without vibrato. On the plane that night, I asked the band, 'Did you notice that I sang the first quarter of the show in vibrato?' They said, 'No, you didn't.' I said, 'Yeah, I did.' Scott said, 'No, I would have heard that. I have your voice right in my ear.' I thought, 'Did I imagine that I sang in vibrato?' And then the next day, it was all fine. We played two more weeks with them. Nothing."

On their first trip to Japan, in 1980, Petty had buckled over with stomach pains in the hours before a show and was rushed through the streets to a doctor, who pronounced Petty "nervous." During the *Into the Great Wide Open* tour, with Petty down to 140 pounds and struggling with stomach issues, George Harrison sent his friend to an acupuncturist, who put needles into the singer, burned herbs around his stomach, and finally concluded that Petty was "nervous." "I'm enough of a pro to calm myself down, to relax and do the gig," he explains. "I can do that, and no one will notice. But inside, when it happens, I'm dying. Sometimes years have gone past without any trouble. And then it comes back. Sometimes I just need to be told that I'm nervous, and things improve. But it's always back there as a possibility, even when those years go past." Playing the Super Bowl, headlining

Bonnaroo, the possibility was there with him, something he lived with. It was a private affair but robbed him of some joy, made it harder to let spontaneity guide an evening onstage. The structure of a set list was something to lean on.

"Oh, you have no idea," says Adria Petty. "It was always there. I think some people think that he's kind of antisocial or just doesn't like people. Really, he's just terrified. I remember my dad met a Formula One driver with George [Harrison], and my dad asked him what he did to avoid being nervous. The driver told my dad that he ran the whole track in his mind, did the race mentally, visualized winning. And I think that helped. But I don't know where it comes from. Was there a moment when he just wasn't prepared? I don't know. He's *so* prepared now. His discipline is extraordinary." The 2012 European tour found Petty hitting a new level of comfort, as if something had come off his back. Without acupuncture and the burning of herbs, there was a shift. It was a quieter, more comfortable time on the road. Not quick to trust any such change, Petty nonetheless entered a period in his life when he felt the years of anxiety lift a little. The tours that followed confirmed it. It helped that Dana Petty was out there with him, letting him know he was nervous, when that's what he needed to know.

In 2013, Petty took the band into the Beacon in New York City and the Fonda in Los Angeles for residencies, bringing to those cities what the Heartbreakers had done at the Fillmore in San Francisco some years earlier. The smaller rooms gave the band more room to run. The set lists went into album tracks and a few unexpected covers, and you could see Petty enjoying himself. It didn't hurt that by that time he had another recording nearly finished, *Hypnotic Eye*, cut in much the way they recorded *Mojo. Hypnotic Eye* reminded him anew just how good the band had gotten. Life had changed enough that the group members would go months without seeing one another. But when they came back together, Petty couldn't help but be struck by the way they dropped into new material. Were they actually getting better? It made him more interested than ever in making records.

"I've come full circle," Petty says. "When I make a record now, I know what I want to do. I don't need that spark of an outside producer. I spark myself. I don't want anybody's advice. And I could not possibly put up with any kind of struggle with a producer, about how to do something. I've worked with great, great producers and learned a lot. And I'm sure there's something I could gain by working with another one. But it would also take things away. At this point in my life, I'm just happy doing it myself. I've got a good team, with Ryan and Mike to bounce things off." After the tour that included the Fonda and Beacon shows, Petty went in to finish *Hypnotic Eye*, with a second Mudcrutch album already in the back of his mind. Even if the record business had changed, and recordings just didn't sell like they used to, it was too late to make Petty into a different man. He'd been in the album cycle since he was a kid, and he was going to stay there as long as he could. There was no reason to do otherwise. He didn't have any other tricks.

The songs that emerged as the Heartbreakers started making *Hypnotic Eye* looked outward as much as they did inward. Perhaps still affected by the backlash that met *The Last DJ*, Petty was careful not to make his view of contemporary life and its sad contradictions overly explicit—but it was clear enough from the record that the world he would be leaving behind for his children and their children isn't one that leaves him feeling he's done them right. But if that message is there, it's embedded in a rock-and-roll record that doesn't let up. With only enough time between tracks to take a gulp of air, he keeps it moving, limiting the recording to eleven tracks. One journalist started a *Hypnotic Eye* interview by asking Petty, "Did you know you didn't have to make the album this good?" He'd done enough by that time that he could rest on reputation, if he wasn't still busy trying to top himself. Like *Mojo*, it was nominated for a Grammy. And it entered at number one on the album charts. His first number one record, after decades of getting close. Even now, with Petty in his midsixties, his fans knew that the next Tom Petty and the Heartbreakers record might be the best of the lot. That's always been the deal. That's the brand.

"I hadn't seen him in, I guess, six months," says George Drakoulias. "But I wanted to talk to him, just to say, 'Well, you did it!' I called Dana, and she gave me his number. What I didn't know was that he'd just gotten his first cell phone, his own number. I mean, *just* gotten this thing. So it rings, and he figures out how to answer it. And I realize that he's like, 'So, now this thing works? And it's going to ring?' Instant regret. But I was just happy for him, having the number one record in the country, and wanted to say it. Past due. Well deserved. He made another great record. *Another* great record. There's just no one like this guy."

With a new record out there, people wanted more of the "work" out of him. The interviews, appearances, the tweets he hadn't fully accepted as a part of his life. "It's like Tom Waits said," Petty remarks. "'I'm an artist, but I'm still in show business.' At this point, though, the show business part of it is what I'm trying to keep to a minimum. With all of the social media and Internet outlets, promoting a record these days is almost like being punished for making it. I remember doing a European press tour for *Wildflowers*, that far back, and I was doing press all day, from morning through dinner, realizing after four or five days that it had gotten to be too much. I said, 'Either you show me that this has really got some huge return to it, or I'm not gonna do it, because you're using me to throw darts at the wall in hopes that something sticks.' I started taking a different approach." His first inclination with *Hypnotic Eye* was to avoid touring and simply do the bare minimum press and promotion. He wanted to start on a new Mudcrutch recording, just stay in the studio. But the thought that fewer people would hear *Hypnotic Eye* if he didn't tour behind it made him reach for his luggage. He wonders some days how long he'll have to keep doing this. On others he worries that he'll have to stop.

■

The music business has taken different forms since Tom Petty first entered a recording studio. There are now more people who have left the industry than stayed to watch its dissolution. Boom times these are not. Music isn't going anywhere, of course. It's in more spaces, public and private, than at any previous time in history. But the means of distribution, the processes through which artists and songwriters will be compensated, the strategies for promotion, the role of the record company: all will likely change a few times before the future of the music business reveals itself. It's a good time for charlatans and bullshitters, or, at least, an even *better* time than usual. Anyone who can convincingly say they know what's coming next, or even how to handle the present, can have a lot of influence and make a lot of money. For a few minutes.

The music business toward which Tom Petty turned a critical eye in *The Last DJ* is now a thing of the past, almost quaint when compared with what's followed. But Petty has grown less interested in attempting to understand the industry's careening path, its next developments and disintegrations. He leaves that for others. His mind is elsewhere. Even as he continues to make records, as inspired as he's ever been, he's more detached from what has become the sometimes desperate search for a way to get music out there. "There are records that make their way through the sheer force of the music," Petty says. "Good recordings seem to find their way into the world. Gram Parsons never had a hit record. But his stuff came through, people found it. Ann Peebles, one of my all-time favorites, was teaching in a preschool or something when I first heard one of her records. Now I play her music all the time on my radio show. What these people created got to me—and not through anyone's marketing plan. I have to go on this. I have to let that mean something to me. *Things happen with good records.* Maybe not right when they come out, maybe not for millions of listeners. But good records seem to get to the people who need them the most. I guess I have to believe that the best marketing tool is still a good song. And that it's probably better that I put my time into writing one of those than learning how to do social media properly."

Petty's songs do keep finding the people who need them. And they've gotten their own celebrations over the past few years. In New York, San Francisco, Los Angeles, Austin, Seattle, and Nashville, with more cities coming, musicians have been gathering to play material from Petty's catalogue. It was nothing he saw coming, nothing he knew about until it was already happening. They call them "Pettyfests." Jakob Dylan is among the many who have shown up to play a song. "You just can't find a Petty song that's not worth singing," Dylan says. "And at those shows, the songs just fill the room with joy. I don't know how you write songs that are that good that consistently." To watch one of the Pettyfests from the back of the hall is to be reminded of what Tom Petty shares with songwriters like Buddy Holly and Hank Williams, artists who created songs that are easy to get into and hard to forget. But as it is with Holly and Williams, once you're in a Petty song, another world is unlocked, a place of story, emotion, characters you feel you know, longing, some sense of freedom. And when a group of people gathers to play those songs through, it is as Dylan says: a joy comes into the room. Song after song. In their own way, those shows are one more reminder that Petty belongs to a tradition of American songwriting that includes only a handful of masters.

But Petty won't be remembered as a great songwriter who grabbed pickup bands in whatever town he was in. Chuck Berry's problems were never Petty's. Petty remains a band member, a band *leader*, and that will be as much a part of his legacy as the songs themselves. "He could have been a solo artist," says Mike Campbell. "But a band is cool. If it's a *real* band. And he's a good leader. I think I know him pretty well. I know how I look at the band, and I think I know how he looks at the band. I think of Tom as a best friend. I didn't bellyache, and when he'd turn to me and say, 'What should we do here?' I'd say what I thought. If it was a good idea, he'd respect me for it. What can I say? He treated me good." The life of Petty's songs was made longer and richer because the guys who first played them kept playing them.

"I don't know how you keep a group of musicians together that long," Jakob Dylan says. "But I think this is the goal. And ninety-nine percent of us probably fail at keeping *anything* together half as long as Tom Petty's kept his band together. But their example makes you believe that you can come up with these people, at a young age, and make that bond, musically. But, let's face it, it's an opportunity that comes when you're really young, when all anybody needs is a little food and rent. You don't make really great groups in your thirties. Petty did it at the right time, and then, incredibly, he kept it together. I'm lucky that I got to watch a few guys do it, whether it's the Rolling Stones or Tom Petty and the Heartbreakers. They've done it for so long that I get to learn from them. I don't think those bands had anyone to watch in that way. Tom has said that he had no idea he'd get to do this his whole life, year after year. But I know you can—because I got to watch *him* do it."

Benmont Tench, sitting quietly for a moment after a few hours of talk, most of it about band politics and the changes that came as the Heartbreakers struggled to stay together, breaks his silence as though he's caught himself. "I've got massive respect for Tom and massive love for Tom," he says. "I can tell you all about the things that went on, how crazy it might have gotten at times, but being a part of this band has been so important to me. I would never want to be the one who brought this to an end." Earlier in that conversation, he'd inadvertently given what might have been the best description of the Heartbreakers. "It's Tom's band," he said. "It's Tom and Mike's band. But it's Tom's band. It's our band, all of us. But it's Tom's band. You know?" And that's about as simple as anyone was going to be able to make it.

■

Tom Petty hasn't ever made it his business to explain himself, to tell you the story of who he is, to construct a master narrative that positions him in some larger framework of American artists. He's let the songs do the bulk of that work, going home when the show is over. His social life has been quiet, the friendships limited. The major artists who have worked with him have either come upon Petty by chance or actively sought him out, many of them sticking around to provide the most formative friendships of Petty's life.

Of those in the band and on the crew, it's Bugs Weidel who saw Petty up close more than anyone, who more than the others got to look in through what Jeff Jourard called Petty's "tinted windows." The two of them were side by side in Weidel's pickup truck, for decades, stuck in traffic half the time, just like any other Angelenos. The two of them, talking. Sitting for the only interview he's ever done, Weidel doesn't even think to say his boss is a perfect man. But, like most everyone who's made a life in and around music, Weidel isn't much interested in perfect men.

Petty has a mind that pulls toward the darkness. It still moves in on him sometimes. Who knows how much of that is born of what he went through as a child, or what he repeated from that childhood in his first marriage. But there's little question that songwriting has been the thing that has made it all more livable. The songs have been his safe house. In them you can hear a man wanting a little more freedom and a little more peace. It's something people can connect with. "As an artist, as a husband, as a father, as a friend," Bugs Weidel says, "this guy has spent his life trying to improve. In every single way. That's what I've seen." Weidel knew Earl Petty, heard some things about the world Tom Petty came from, even saw parts of it firsthand. He knows the distance Petty has come.

But the trouble Petty's walked away from is something he talks about less these days. He speaks more about his children, Adria, Annakim, and Dylan, about his granddaughter, Everly, about Dana. He reschedules an interview session because Everly is missing her pacifier. He and Dana drive to Venice from Malibu to deliver the one that was left at their house. "One of the great moments of my life," he says, "was seeing Everly when she realized I was coming in with that pacifier. We stayed for hours, didn't care how late it was." He talks about his daughters, how much it means to him to watch them as artists. Tells me Dylan is writing songs with someone and happy with what he's getting. Describes the Christmas season, when his brother comes to Malibu with all of the cousins, with his own grandchildren and in-laws. "We were poor kids," Petty says, "and there's still enough of that inside of us that it means something when we say, 'Okay, it's Christmas, and we're gonna live like kings. We're gonna watch Westerns, go to Lakers games, hire a chef.'"

Surrounded by his family, he's got a little more quiet around him. But sometimes, when the house is dark and the others are sleeping, he goes out to the studio, turns on some lights, and looks to see what might come. And a few songs have been coming lately. He's not sure if they're for Mudcrutch or the Heartbreakers. He can figure that out later.

2015

I was trying to explain Tom Petty and the Heartbreakers to my sons. They've known the music all their lives. Petty's stuff was playing when they came out. But they listen with no reference to history, like it's all from one big album called *Tom Petty*. "Even the Losers," "King's Highway," "Wildflowers," "Nightwatchman," "Walls," "Forgotten Man," "The Wild One, Forever." These are some they love. They're ten and twelve. I was eleven when I first heard "Breakdown."

Imagine, I said, having someone make a record that goes straight into that place where the important records go, and then he keeps making them. Every few years, a new one, following you through your life. He's there when you get your first girlfriend. He's there when you form your first band. He's there when you go back to school, when you get married, when you have kids, when you get divorced. My sons weren't sure what I was getting at. It doesn't matter anyway, because it won't be an option for them. They don't have a Tom Petty. They're borrowing mine.

Petty's life and career cover an era that is, in some ways, over. Whatever comes next is going to be so different that comparisons won't make sense. The long careers, and the handful of artists who have had them, will be a story that gets told. Petty came out of the golden age of bands, I say to my sons. I remind them that there's still something to carry forward, no matter how much the world has changed since 1976. If they want it. But at that point I'm just saying what parents say, without considering whether I actually believe it. But I hope some voice will come out of the American wilderness and take hold of them. And show them things.

ACKNOWLEDGMENTS

Help arrived when it was needed.

I've bothered Peter Guralnick about many things. And he's been an unfailing resource. From parenting to assholes at work to writing in the first person, he's generally had a point of view. And when he didn't have one, he told me so. My first conversations about this book were with Peter, and they weren't our last on the topic. Thank you, Peter, for your generosity.

Sloan Harris figured me out straightaway. Without putting me in a category, such as *the-type-who-needs-a-babysitter,* Sloan found a way to work with me. He didn't climb up my shirt and hit me on the back of the head until I finished writing a book. But he did make sure I was working, and in the right direction. For a while there, it was just the two of us.

Gillian Blake at Holt started our first conversation by referencing a cover song Petty and his band recorded, John Sebastian's "Stories We Could Tell." She understood its imagery, the beauty of Petty's version, the backbone in craft that made the song work. I needed someone with a mind-and-heart connection to the subject, someone who had fallen in love with this stuff. Gillian brought all that as well as consistently good ideas.

Tony Dimitriades has been a great help to this project, sharing his own stories, making introductions, the gentleman at the door of the

Heartbreakers' world. In his office, Mary Klauzer has been a singular help, for a long time. If she knew me back then, a kid in the opening band, she didn't hold that against me. She welcomed me as an adult. In the East End Management office there has been a collective humor and intelligence that is certainly not industry standard. Laurence Freedman, Tiffany Goble, and Evan Bright have been in there with the others and helped me on numerous occasions.

I'm not quite sure how to thank the Heartbreakers, where to begin. After Tom Petty, Benmont Tench has been my longest, steadiest connection to the band. He came to me through Alison Reynolds, and in the years when I had all but left the music business, I still spoke with Ben on occasion. He expressed an interest in my unlikely academic pursuits and that meant more than he probably knew.

I was struck when Mike Campbell looked at me and said, "This is some deep shit you're getting into here." His point, as I took it, wasn't that I should get off his property. He opened himself to what was happening, which no one had to do, and he expressed himself with a dignity that made my work more comfortable and effective. Stan Lynch did the same, eventually. It took a while to secure an interview, but in time we had one on the schedule. And, frankly, I don't want to imagine what this book would have been without Stan's participation. We met at his tree farm outside Gainesville, and at the start of the second day he said, "Do you mind if I lie on the couch while we do this?"

I was sure Ron Blair was avoiding me. As the guy who had left the band and then returned twenty years later, perhaps he was more interested in keeping his job than in digging through the emotional rubble. Once cornered, however, he quickly and graciously gave himself to the interviews. Scott Thurston was every bit the Heartbreaker in his humor and storytelling. He sat in a few hotel lobbies and let me poke around. If a somewhat marginal figure in this volume, there's another book in which Scott is the protagonist. Steve Ferrone, too. Follow Ferrone's life, and you get a good picture of popular music in the second half of the twentieth century. As a man, he's a bit of a pied piper. After a few interviews with Ferrone while on the road in Texas, I found myself a part of his crowd, waking early for breakfasts that were often forget-to-eat-your-food hilarious. He was among the most welcoming in a group that has been generous, warm, and thoughtful.

Adria and Dana Petty: they both made this process possible, if in very different ways. They are the inner circle. Adria was a girl when we first met. And she was beyond her years then, as she is now. Her insights were crucial as I put together an account of her father's life. Dana Petty came in at an important moment, opening herself to the process and bringing the kind, generous spirit for which she is known. Her mother, Nancy, often welcomed me at the house, getting me a cup of the remarkable coffee that comes out of the Petty kitchen. Tom's brother, Bruce, was unguarded in his interview. Without ever parading it or profiting from it, he's been an emotional buoy to his brother. There's a longer story in that relationship, but Bruce let me look into it. I needed that. To know the man, one needs to know the family. And they have been a lovely, funny, smart bunch throughout this process.

Bugs Weidel had never done an interview. I am very grateful that he stepped up for this. He let it all hang out. As I hope this book makes clear, Bugs was right there the whole time. I came away with a great admiration for him. He loves this band. Richard Fernandez and Mark Turner sat, with Mike Campbell, for an interview that could have been its own television show. The Heartbreakers' world is often very, very funny. They have a shorthand with one another that comes only from decades of practice. They have all been helpful in so many ways, but just getting to be near that band culture was enormously valuable to me. You may not see them when you go to a Tom Petty and the Heartbreakers show, but they're back there—or the band wouldn't be up there. There are people among the crew not mentioned here. But I extend a collective thank-you to that bunch as a whole.

Tom Leadon is like no other. He invited me to meet his family, talked whenever I needed him, and has a relationship with the past that is lucid and respectful and fully alive. Alison Reynolds was an important early connection to Tom Petty, a friend and an ally. Maia Pilot, Kane Balser, and Chris Steffen helped transcribe interviews, often with very little turnaround time and always for less pay than they deserved. Sean Weber-Small and his family put me up in Los Angeles during a number of my interview visits. Ken and Anna Zankel put me up, in the most perfect place and in the most perfect way, when I needed it and the project needed it. Chuck Prophet, driven by the force of his own opinions, was always ready to talk Petty. He understands the importance of the subject. My conversations with Steven Van Zandt have shaped my thinking about rock and roll in the wide, anthropological sense. Mad for the stuff and ready to fight for it: this is a man who believes. His encouragement has meant as much as my conversations with him.

There are others who have helped, sometimes without knowing it: Stanley Booth, John Biguenet, Dan Zanes, Julia Zanes, Hope Zanes, Paula Greif, Harry Butterworth, Anna Zanes, Isak Saaf, Olaf Saaf, Trigger Cook, Brad Jones, Daniel Tashian, Bill Flanagan, Angelo, Don Fleming, Michael Azzerad, David Barker, Joe Pernice, Terry Stewart, Bruce Warren, Anisia Lapina-Yang, Peter Bogdanovich, Jeff Dupre, Morgan Neville, Gil Friesen, Scott Robinson, Jed Hilly, Weil-Vincequerra-Dobo-Mesek, David Newgarden, Geoff Edgers, Mary Davis, Parker Quillen, Phil Galdston, Jackson Browne, Brian Henson, Ryan Ulyate, Margaret Bodde, Evan Cutler, the Shelters, Jann Wenner, and Aimee Mann. At Henry Holt: Stephen Rubin, Patricia Eisemann, Maggie Richards, Leslie Brandon, Meryl Levavi, Eleanor Embry, Chris O'Connell, Emily Kobel, and Jason Liebman. At ICM: Heather Karpas, Liz Farrell, Kevin Keyes, and Henry Reisch.

I thank all of the folks who talked to me about Petty and his history. They provided the fabric of the book. Many are mentioned above, but there are others who helped significantly: Jimmy Iovine, Stevie Nicks, Jim Lenahan, Elliot Roberts, Ricky Rucker, Dickie Underwood, Don Felder, David Mason, Marty Jourard, Jeff Jourard, Danny Roberts, Rick Rubin, Jeff Lynne, Olivia Harrison, Jakob Dylan, Charles Ramirez, William Crawford, George Drakoulias, Charlie Souza, Mike Lembo, Chris Blackwell, Al Hospers, Peter Holsapple, William Crawford, Mike Lembo, and Harvey Kubernik.

This book is born of interviews. The many days spent with Tom Petty, sitting down at his house in Malibu, sorting through the past and talking about a life making records, will remain among my favorite possessions. Mostly, we were at work. We'd sometimes break for a meal after a few hours. The table would always be set in advance of our arrival, with a vegetarian dish awaiting us. If only occasionally, I sometimes spoke of whatever was going on with me. The day I mentioned that I was getting divorced, Tom got out his stationary, with a still from Méliès's *Trip to the Moon* on the front, and wrote notes to my sons. He thanked them for loaning their father, told them they should come out for a visit, wished them luck in their new house, finally drawing a caricature of himself for their immense pleasure. Those notes still hang on the walls of my sons' bedrooms. Petty's been like that for me, ever since I first met him.

There were times I knew I was writing things that would be hard for Tom to see in print. But he always insisted that this was my book, and he wasn't there to say what went in and what didn't. He was there to work with me, but he didn't want it to be a whitewashed account. Sometimes I worried that the friendship we'd come into might not survive the process. That thought, however, I had to set aside. The job required that I think not about him but about the people who want to know more about him. He's never been much of a self-promoter, never constructed his own mythology, never hinted that he'd like to lead the people through the streets. He has put the songs out there, then waited to see what happened. And the songs, and the records made of them, have been so good that plenty has happened. But as someone raised on that music, I believed there were people who wanted more. All that was required was that he let me in. And he did. I thank him for the style with which he did that. He's still the coolest man in rock and roll. And I've learned a tremendous amount from him during the time we've spent together.

And, of course, my sons, Lucian and Piero. You brought humor, ideas, a love for good songs, and a patience for life's sometimes wonderful, sometimes strange happenings. Thank you for being in this with me. I can't always get you what you need, want, or deserve, but you seem to get all of that for me. You are my treasure.

Lastly, Svetlana Lapina. I was too busy celebrating your arrival to ask how you got here. What timing! Whose plan was this? You helped me so much. You brought the motion and belief back into my life. The blood started circulating again, to the brain as to the heart. You made a good save, Svetlana Lapina. Thank you.

INDEX

ABOUT THE AUTHOR

WARREN ZANES has been on the faculty at several American universities and is currently teaching at New York University. He was a member of the Del Fuegos from 1983 to 1989 and is set to release his fourth solo recording. His writing has appeared in the *Oxford American*, the *Los Angeles Times*, *Rolling Stone*, the *Cleveland Plain Dealer*, and more. He has written books about the history of Warner Bros. Records and Dusty Springfield's *Dusty in Memphis* and coedited a collection of writings on Jimmie Rodgers. He was a consulting producer on Morgan Neville's Oscar-winning documentary *20 Feet from Stardom* and conducted interviews for Martin Scorsese's *George Harrison: Living in the Material World*. A former vice president of education and programs at the Rock and Roll Hall of Fame and Museum, he is currently the executive director of Steven Van Zandt's Rock and Roll Forever Foundation.

① Ant stuff
: dropcloths
-

Ⓐ
— Pepe. Grace
  Basid Mgt
— Remax Central.
  403 710 7979
  Sun 8pm 34
  edenstone way N

Ⓑ
— Irene Hollett — Dhalias.
  Grace — 1143 edgeut. Rd.
            N.W
  403 239 7534.
  10am tomorrow
  — 2 garden beds
  $ perennial
  she can do the plants